DEDICATION

"This book really belongs to the long-suffering Nigerian people, those who are subjected to the daily scandal of mis-governance, to those who deserve better healthcare, to the child who has a right to decent education and also the family who simply want to live in security."

FOREWORD

At a time when the act of reading books as a recreative pursuit is increasingly becoming a dying art amongst the Nigerian public, a much regrettable occurrence, which is matched and exacerbated in its worrisomeness by the fact that the act of writing books too, is fast becoming a diminishing art amongst Nigerians. So it is against this discouraging background that this literary offering 'I Found My Voice' by Dr Olu Ojedokun is a welcome addition to the lean corpus of books authored by Nigerians in recent times.

'I Found My Voice' portrays as well as paints a portrait of a complex protagonist who at different times is passionate, provocative, pro-active, precocious, presumptuous, paranoid, pensive, pedantic, persuasive, punctilious, puritanical, plucky, pugnacious, persistent, principled, populist, politically minded, power-driven and possessed of a seemingly unquenchable desire to immerse himself in student political activity in order to achieve political relevance and agitate for improvements in the lot of the student constituencies he represents at the different educational institutions he attends. In pursuing such objectives, he comes into conflict with different authority figures, who he sees, through his youthful eyes as forces of conservatism resistant to reform and interested only in maintaining and sustaining the status quo. In his not too infrequent brushes with these figures he succeeds in provoking their chagrin causing them much irritation and discomfort.

But as conflictual and controversial as some of his causes are, he is almost always careful to ensure that the ground, upon which he stands and fights his various battles, is always firm. He never raises his head above the parapet without first of all ensuring that his actions and pronouncements accord with the letter and spirit of the documentary instruments from which he derives his legitimacy to agitate for change. This masterful ploy, which he often employs and deploys to wrong foot his antagonists, who, on account of his youth are minded to underestimate the depth of his acuity and his state of preparedness.   This fact alone, serves to rescue him on the occasions, when he is thought by these authority figures to have overreached himself.

In acting as he does, he reveals an intrepid side to his personality which not only endears him to those on whose behalf he agitates, but also ensures his enduring popularity in their collective estimation. Such that, every so often, he feels confident enough to approach them with new political propositions which require their endorsement, and which he often obtains.

As admirable as the numerous causes and agitations he pursues and undertakes are, it is not immediately evident from the narrative, what it is, in his personality or psychological make-up that propels, impels and even compels him to set upon the path of seeming restlessness in pursuit of what he considers to be right. Could the reason(s) lie in his proximity, at a young age, to radical individuals within the University of Lagos

Students' Union? Or could it be due to the abrupt and cruel transformation in his family's fortunes, at a tender age, which saw his family displaced from their comfortable lodgings and surroundings to much less salubrious environs? Or could it be his conversion to Christianity in 1979? My guess is that the answer lies in a combination of all these factors, which coalesced within him to produce the young socio-politico and religious agitator and reformer we read about on the pages of this book.

In contemplating the varied patchwork into which he weaves the threads of his numerous and often hilarious experiences, it is the stitch of one thread that stands out above all others in this interesting tapestry of a narrative. His love for, and seemingly irresistible attraction to politics, political expression and political office. Right from the days of his mock election as the 'child president' of Sadiku Lane, Lagos to his sophisticated and strategically run political campaigns at King's College, Lagos and the University of Ife, he comes across as one utterly consumed by politics; a full bloodied political animal, equipped with all the necessary instincts to survive and thrive in a political jungle.

But as apparent as this may seem to anyone who reads the book, one cannot help but deduce an underlying tension between his political activism and his Christian ideals. This tension is never fully or satisfactorily resolved. In fact, it seems to wittingly or unwittingly circumscribe the protagonist's ability to function simultaneously with efficacy in both realms. Thus, the impression is conveyed, perhaps unintentionally, that the ideal of Christianity and idea of politics are somewhat mutually exclusive and cannot be practiced effectively in tandem. Active participation in one somehow dilutes or precludes the spirited participation in the other.

Should this, however, be so? I think not. In my view, this tension should merely create and present, a dialectical conundrum and nothing more. One, which with proper contemplation and reflection should give rise to a satisfactory synthesis, which encompasses the nobler aspects of these seemingly discordant material and metaphysical (spiritual) ideologies. Such a synthesis would naturally foster a fusion of ideas, potent enough, to dispel the kind of political confusion so prevalent, at present, in Nigeria. I expect that such a fusion of ideas would not be too dissimilar in output and effect, say, to the Liberation Theologies formulated by Christian philosophical thinkers to advance the cause of social justice in parts of the Americas. In truth, however, I suspect that our protagonist at some level – subconscious or conscious - is only too aware of this tension, and rather cleverly, walks this tightrope using his philosophy of 'Panafism' as a balancing rod to traverse the space between both ends without explicitly saying, or appearing to do, so.

It is often said that school days are the best days of one's life. And nowhere is the truth of this sentiment more evident than on the pages of this book. The author regales the reader with anecdote after anecdote of his numerous adventures, encounters, and brushes with authorities within King's College. If ever the term 'Alma Mater' conveyed the true import of its Latin meaning (i.e. a nourishing mother) it is never truer, than in the instance of the protagonist in this book. This institution seems to have enriched his life and thinking and actions more than any other.

It is, therefore, no real surprise when he reveals in his narrative, that he spent more time than he should have at King's College. Always preoccupied it seems, with more interesting and rewarding extra-curricular activities, than with his primary academic objectives. To the extent, that when the opportunity presents itself to him to sever links with King's College, he wrestles with himself, contemplating whether to take a place in the lower sixth form or proceed to University to read for a degree. In the event, however, the presence of his younger brother, who at this time had joined King's College and the academic progress made by his beloved twin at the University of Ife, spur him to unlatch himself from his Alma Mater's teat and head off to the University of Ife.

Once at the University of Ife, almost without pause, he immerses himself into the thick of student political activity. But unlike the 'paddling pool', that was King's College student politics, he quickly discovers that at Ife, he is now swimming in a much deeper and wider political sea. One which is awash with skillful, calculating, conniving and populist ideologues, all adept at swimming with, and against, the tide. At this point, one is forced to ask some questions of the protagonist. Is his attraction to politics driven by a call to service or a desire to fill political office? Or is it a bit of both? Can he serve without leading or does he need to lead in order to feel able to serve? In partial respect, he is brutally honest in this regard, and confesses that on certain occasions his motivation for office is driven by a desire for power, in and of itself. Such candid self-awareness is commendable.

In any event, at the University of Ife, he enjoys more electoral successes. And even succeeds in carving out a memorable political persona for himself. One based on his unique stylistic dress sense, his moral probity and the effectiveness with which he discharges the duties of his different elective offices. Ironically, this memorable persona unwittingly robs him of the most prized position in campus student politics; presidency of the union. It turns out that many of his supporters identify him by his political persona alone and not his real name; thus on polling day they are unable to identify him on the ballot in the crucial presidential election. So rather paradoxically, he fails to win because of the success of his political branding.

One seeming contradiction, which bears pointing out from the book, has to do with the issue of power and his approach to it. On the one hand, he appears to be most comfortable and at his most effective when confronting and speaking truth to power. But on the other hand, rather quizzically, he appears to be at ease in the company of the powerful, many with whom he forms and enjoys collaborative and productive friendships. This seems somewhat baffling. But then, when one remembers that our protagonist is a product and beneficiary of elitist schools and, therefore, himself, an elite of Nigerian society. It is perhaps only to be expected that he would naturally feel comfortable in such company. Perhaps, the real surprise then, is that given his elitist background, the protagonist is possessed of a social conscience at all. And one that he not only listens to, but on whose leadings and leanings he frequently acts.

In all, this is an immensely enjoyable book with many funny anecdotes, two of which, bear brief mention here. When faced with the prospect of joining either the rigorous King's College Army Cadet Unit or the less demanding Boy Scouts Movement, our protagonist elects to join the latter and conveys the impression to readers that his choice is a virtuous one! And only he, it seems, could have secreted himself at night at a secluded scene, in order to prevent an act of sexual congress from taking place between two hormonally charged consenting students of the opposite sex. He punctures their passion by shouting out anti-fornication admonitions; pricking their conscience, deflating their desire, dissipating their lust and spoiling the mood! And as no good deed goes unpunished, he earns himself, in short order, a thorough thrashing from his sexually frustrated and disappointed hormonal schoolmate, whose best laid plans he thwarts through his religious zealotry.

Having read this wonderful autobiographical account of this high minded, yet mischievous youngster, who sets about changing his immediate world through socio-political and religious fervour; it is easy to look upon the protagonist as the undoubted hero of the book. But in reviewing this telling retelling of memories of youth past, the real hero to me is not the protagonist, but his mother. She flits in and out of the narrative at different points, displaying quiet strength, discipline and resourcefulness, as she strives with industry, diligence and dignity to provide for her children, as she deals stoically with the difficult hand that fate has dealt her. She does so admirably and shines brightly in the background of this narrative.

Dr. Olu Ojedokun has written a thoroughly riveting book. It is my hope that its finds its place on the bookshelves of homes, and school libraries across Nigeria as well as on portable electronic tablet devices. This book has something for everyone, but in particular it will inspire and entertain the young and the middle aged. Young Nigerians can take away from it the fact that it is never too early to engage in the practice of principled political activity in order to effect positive change in their immediate environment. And for the middle aged, it is a beautiful reminder of those halcyon days of – spent and misspent – youth, now long gone. I highly recommend 'I Found My Voice' to a general readership.

- *Sheyi Oriade Esq.*, London, United Kingdom

BOOK REVIEWS

'It took me all morning and into the night but I read it in one day! That's because I couldn't put the book down, I had to know what Olu got up to next! Olu's story, wow! I could almost smell the place, feel it, imagine it!' — **The Revd. Rachel Thompson**

'I have read Dr. Olu Ojedokun's latest book titled 'I found my voice' and I must say that it offers a gripping account of a young boy's rise from the depth of despair to a level of self assuredness. Dr. Ojedokun's writing though seductively easy to understand, transports as it were the reader to the scene of events so vividly and graphically described. His recollection of events from childhood through adolescence and now adulthood is undeniably sharp and mind blowing!

Beyond story telling, however, 'I found my voice' offers hope for anyone going through depressing moments. In fact, a common thread throughout the writer's account is the ability to rise above circumstances and challenges through a combination of determination, hard work, fortuitous circumstances, and above all the unseen hand of God who guided him and his family through.

To be sure, this is a manual for daily living. The book offers hope for the despondent, guidance for the confused, and faith in an omnipotent God. A must read!'
-Kolawole Onifade, Esq.

'I am privileged to have known the author of this book, and to be part of some of the narrative. Olu is an exceptionally talented writer and story teller, with a remarkable memory, and "I found my voice" is a powerful and brilliantly written book, that will inspire you, and keep you on the edge of your seat, making you anticipate what would happen next! In "I found my voice", Olu ingeniously captures his personal difficulties growing up both in England and in Nigeria, and how he overcame adversity to become the man he is today. He also speaks to the Nigerian elite, contributing powerfully to the debate of what to do with the conundrum that is present-day Nigeria. Every reader (including non Nigerians) will have the sense of being taken on a personal journey. At each step, the writer's disarming graciousness and charm makes the journey a pleasurable experience! This is a must read!!'
— Revd. Pedro Okoro, Esq

'A well written and pulsating story; a must read !!!' — **Akinbola Fatoye**

Published by Amazon KDP, USA August 2023

https://www.amazon.com/dp/B0CF4FN9YD

INTRODUCTION:

"To the memory of my twin, Folashade, her soul, I know, will never die and to the present silence of her voice that speaks to us so clearly from the past."

This book was first published in 2014 and achieved the success of a nomination for 'Best Christian Author' in Nigeria. Also, some corrections have been made and an additional three chapters added to update the story. The book flows from a journey of deep introspection, leading through a daring and tortuous path, into a vortex of self-discovery. It was certainly not my ambition to write this book, however, the opportunity presented itself out of bewilderment I continue to feel for the state of Nigeria, interlocked with the enduring grief of twin loss that sentenced me to a period of self-imprisonment. A prolonged hiatus in my creative process produced a convergence and even a conspiracy of events. The hiatus prodded me out of frustrations acquired, introducing a layer of complexity brought about by my inability to understand the reasons for the recurring failure of Nigeria. In the midst of much frustration, I found myself at crossroads and arrived at the idea of telling my story. The process began with my stumbling blindly in dark alleyways, it is then *'I found something'*. That discovery nibbled at the edge of my mind for a while until it crystalised into the idea of writing, leading to the ordering my thoughts and the cataloguing of the early influences in my life. It was at this stage that I was confronted with the words of Martin Luther King Junior stating:

"Our lives begin to end the day we become silent about things that matter."

It is within all these and the fleeting encounters swirling around the space of Facebook with some of my friends that suddenly out of my anguish *'I found my voice'*. My voice created a framework, which led me into a reconstruction of memories from an era when I freely indulged in schoolboy antics and politics. Harshada Rajani, a stroke survivour suggests it is our ability to talk to each other that makes us so human and I agree with this. This book seeks to speak, to talk to others, myself and indeed to

'power', because of my belief in our basic humanity and the strength to effect change.[1]
In paraphrasing the words of Patrice Lumumba, I suggest my modest ambition is for
the day to come when this book will speak out and Nigerians will write their own
history, one full of glory and dignity.

In many parts of this book, I have sought to impart fresh life into some of the places
and characters that many Nigerian readers are familiar. I begin with my time at
secondary school and chart a way forward through the memories drenched by my
experiences. I have recalled events that shaped me through my university years and
in my subconscious offered a narrative, which refers to milestones, signposts and
personalities that I encountered as I trod the path bringing me into the present day.

Throughout the construction of my narrative, my experiences as a student of *'privilege'*
at King's College, Lagos features with prominence. The more time I spent
reconstructing and recovering my memories the more I have become convinced that
a framework can be established linking my setbacks, my successes and redemption to
that of Nigeria. I confess that before *'I found my voice'* the complexities of Nigeria had
overwhelmed me; I have spent endless hours, several discussions with others including
my old university friend and *'political collaborator'* Hillary Okoronkwo. I confess that
the hours spent searching for a way forward have met with several layers of steel.
However, something profound happened when I found my voice soaring with the
rhythm of our times but yet remained pregnant with questions. It was the decision to
move beyond the stage of reconstruction that led me into a voyage of discovery and
the transformation of my personal story into various chapters, which now forms this
book.

The initial process of writing has come from a series of five-minute drafts posted on
Facebook. Through the passage of time I laboured on so many other drafts and
indulged in constructive engagements over emails with my friend, classmate from
King's College, Lagos days and *'Great Ife'* colleague Muhtar Bakare and with Mr.

---

[1] Rijani, Harshada (2012) *'I Found My Voice in a Hopeless Place'* (Accessed on 22nd March 2013 from
http://www.huffingtonpost.com/harshada-rajani/i-found-my-voice-in-a-hop_b_2264756.html)

'Gboyega Banjo an old friend of my father's, former General Manager of Spectrum Books and a former Director of Library and Documentation Services at the Nigerian Institute of International Affairs. However, It was my learned friend and ex-Great Ife colleague, Sheyi Oriade that challenged me to lift my ambitions to another level, encouraging me to be more incisive and to enrich my story with so much more detail. While these engagements are not unexpected in the process of grappling with a book of this nature, in this instance they have enabled me to develop greater clarity as I have sought to crystalise my thoughts on the meaning of Nigeria and the restoration of sanity into our public life. It has also awoken me from my slumbering complacency and brought me to a stuttering realisation that I might not be gifted enough to pull this off. However, with stoic stubbornness, I have relinquished any self-doubt I initially possessed and found the determination to draw upon my creative reserves and painted what I hope is an engaging picture from my cluttered memories. After a few months of writing, I can now reflect back with some contentment, the belief that I have succeeded in articulating a compelling narrative for my country Nigeria. Though the questions still remain about Nigeria's unfulfilled potential!

This book begins by constructing a bridge for its readers and invites them to embark on a journey, which ferries them to a dwelling place, the world of several personal stories. The invitation is an attempt to give voice to my personal story, relating it in simple terms to that of a country once destined for greatness, losing it's footing but is now able to reclaim it because of a generation that dares to believe. The object of chronicling in this book is to produce a narrative or even a roadmap, that does not simply rest on the shelves of libraries but one that sings, flies and slithers into the consciousness of every reader. The hope is that everyone who picks it up or stumbles across it is presented with an unforgettable encounter where every page leaps out, shaping their thoughts and perception of the world and inspiring them with a compelling rapaciousness to confront in confidence the task of *'Speaking Truth to Power'*.

However, we have had too many great writers lament and bemoan our fate as a country, I am not convinced that ending this book in such perpetual lament is the path

I ought to tread. Surely, it must be valid to explore whether *'Speaking Truth to Power'* in Nigeria is enough to provide hope that wrestles it from its descent into an unending maelstrom.

However, what became manifestly clear as I hit the keyboard of my laptop computer at home and on the train back from my regular ministry forays across the United Kingdom, is that I would have to start from within myself and be honest about my limitations, my impetuousness and the impatience that have formed a constant part of my life. That I would confront my inadequacies by staring them in the eye, record distant memories flashing across my mind.

It would seem the choice of this confrontation with my past has always loomed large on the horizon and tackling it was unavoidable whilst contemplating a book of this ambition. This is because it occurred to me that I would have to banish any attempt at self-pretension in telling my story for *'a lie cannot use truth to sustain itself'*. In this book, I have resisted every basic instinct to protect myself from scrutiny. I have rendered an account of my personal, internal journey – the search of a little boy for his father's memories, and through that, a search for the meaning of what the country Nigeria can become. The more I have written, the more my carefully hidden memories have awoken and the more my identity has become subject to scrutiny and a less complex narrative emerges.

This book is unquestionably autobiographical but does not seek to sum up or celebrate my existence, but it questions it in a way I hope evokes answers. I recognise also the danger that my attempt at openness presents, that no matter how honest I might seem a narrative may emerge in such a way that dresses me up in better light or fills the elided parts with half-truths and an incomplete story. In short there is the danger of presenting an incomplete story and I agree with the suggestion of Professor 'Wole Soyinka in his book 'Ibadan', that:

"Any testament after the 'age of innocence' is a lie, or half-truth, doctored truth, selective

truth or annotated truth…….. - a confection of sorts.[2]"

This process has been full of twists and turns, as I indicated earlier, what started as a series of posts on my Facebook page has gone through several re-writes in order to bring out my latent talent for the written word. There are many who have worked with me evincing pains to address my limitations and to bring into fruition my hopes for crafting this into a book that provides an irresistible and essential roadmap to the Nigerian political discourse. A book laced with seriousness of purpose but allowing the reader to experience a great deal of delight. It is the willingness of many to be open about the limits of my writing abilities that has brought me this far.

In providing a voice to my story, I recall my mother plow a lonely furrow with me, through my seven years of secondary education at King's College, Lagos. Even when I experienced a few setbacks and my potential to achieve was under question, she never surrendered the hope she placed in me. Today Nigeria needs those who can be single minded enough to plow the lonely furrow in the face of its confounding problems and maybe with a simple story just like mine it might overcome.

In conclusion, I return to the body of doctoral research I undertook on the South African Truth and Reconciliation Commission, which took me through a journey of *'Speaking Truth to Power'*; is it a model upon which Nigeria can build a new future or an unnecessary luxury, which it cannot afford? Is this sufficient to allow my fading generation to fulfill its duty and find its voice? Is it simply adequate?

"To speak truth to power, not to hide our knowledge in obscurely erudite terminology, nor lose ourselves in scholastic word games, nor speak truth in secret only to each other."

Finally, the question arises whether *'Speaking Truth to Power'* can act as a necessary

---

[2] Soyinka, Wole (1994): *Ibadan; The Penkelemes Years; A Memoir 1946 – 65*; Methuen Publishing Limited, London, p. xii

corrective to the confounding problems we face?

The gratitude for what I hope becomes a seminal work, and to the meshes of solacing words dancing to the beats of memories on every page can be attributed to my family - my wonderful wife, Olajumoke who is my ever present and to my lovely daughters Moyondafoluwa and Oluseyitan who represent my glorious future (as captured by my grand daughter Mofeyinfoluwa born 2015), to my mother, Mrs. Janet Olufunmilayo Ojedokun, without her careful nurture and firm hand of discipline I would not be who I am today. Adebowale, my brother who has shared so much enduring grief with me and ultimately, I must acknowledge Almighty God, who continues to navigate a clear path for me even as I may stumble around blindly in the dark alleyways of the night because afterwards emerges a hope for my country and I which produces joy and the glorious light.

'IN MY MOTHER'S WOMB'

She kicked me again with a forceful thrust! I had grown rather frustrated with this other little person with whom I was sharing the tiny corralled space. I was wearisome from her constant-mini tantrums. It seemed there was not enough room for both of us. It was no great surprise that true to her character trait when the *'call was sounded'* she heard and responded first, bawling her eyes out in delight, scampering out, taking the first opportunity to exit the womb, grabbing a gush of fresh oxygen and leaving me to spend the next eleven minutes trying to follow in her wake. After a fitful struggle, I bit my way through my mother's canal and I joined my twin sister in the outside world. The snatched recollection of this improbable memory was to define our relationship for more than forty-three eventful years.

This is how deep in my subconscious I recall my first encounter with my twin sister. She was always there, a familiar presence, one that occupied my every thought. Now I confirm that since she transitioned into the heavenlies, leaving me to carry on the 'good work' my memories have been accentuated and my power of recall exaggerated. However, deep down I believe in the authenticity of the experiences recounted here. What is indisputable is that as a twin I had and still have a unique relationship, which non-twins may never fully comprehend. When presented with the knowledge of my twin's transition, a common question from some about the nature of our relationship is *'Where you close?'* I suggest this sums up the limitations of their understanding.

Our relationship as twins was a complicated and intense one and sometimes as we were growing up it ranged from over-identification and excessive closeness to profound estrangement and conflict. We had to deal with the significant emotional pain of separation in adolescence but as we matured as adults and got married, we came to love each other more and admire each other more as individuals.

We were born in a South Clapham Hospital, London which used to occupy an imposing but now dilapidated Victorian building opposite the Clapham South tube station in early 1966, and from there we moved with our parents to their home in Wandsworth, a suburb of London. Both of us were very chubby and big babies, however, my twin sister took upon my father's resemblance from the darker skin

13

tones to his looks, his lips and his smile, and this accounts for her second name, 'Feyisara', *'we used this one as a covering'* and I was mostly blessed with my mother's fairer looks.

"Snow, snow, Mummy why is it so white?"

I was only three years old in 1969 but my inquisitive nature had the better of me, I needed my mother to spell out to us why the white powdery stuff falling from above was so freezing cold. My twin the more resilient and reserved stared at me wondering what was the matter with all these questions. We trod carefully along the slushy path on the way through Clapham Commons with my mother pushing the enormous pram, which contained my younger brother's bounteous frame. He, 'Debo had big rosy cheeks, its tenderness invited a stroke from many onlookers, he was quite a handful and large for his age, some portend to the six feet three inches in height he later attained.

In 1968 my father had returned to Nigeria on the successful completion of his doctorate in International Relations which focused on Nigeria's economic relationship with Britain so it was now just the three of us and we were coping as best as we could. We continued staying with Mrs. Cox our nanny in Maidstone, Kent to allow my mother time and the space to work. The arrangement was we were dropped off with Mrs. Cox during the week while my parents went about their business of study and work. Years later after we returned to Nigeria she dutifully kept in touch by sending toys, comics and books to us. When my father was around he was on a full Commonwealth scholarship so he did less of 'working' and more of studying, it was my mother who supplemented our income with a series of part time jobs. I imagine one of the conversations my mother had with the prospective white employers to have started like this:

"You are not Janet Noble are you?"

The burly Caucasian man who was in charge of the office my mother had gone to seek work said with barely disguised disdain. He had sent my mother an interview letter on the assumption that she was white, and he had no intention of employing an African or any black person. My mother's maiden surname was Noble and hence the reference from the gentleman but she did not let her frustrations show. She went on to enroll in Pitman's College training as a secretary and busied herself with a few catering classes to improve her job prospects.

Our temporary sojourn in the United Kingdom had to end, by 1970, the Nigerian Civil War was over and my father who was settled in his job as a lecturer at the University of Lagos, living a bachelor existence with his younger brother Ayoku in the Igbobi College area, now wanted us around him. The affordable option of travel was by the sea, through the stormy Atlantic Ocean. It was fully paid for by the very eager University of Lagos. All our earthly possessions were neatly arranged in trunk boxes and crated up. We sailed on the Elder Dempster, a passenger and cargo ship. We boarded in Southampton and it took a journey of over two weeks to reach the ports of Lagos in Apapa. I remember we constantly fell seasick, also the nursery I attended with my twin sister on the ship's deck.   We arrived at the staff quarters of the University of Lagos at CT36 where my father had managed to secure. It was a comfortable grey encrusted terraced house within a row of five; it all seemed different but rather idyllic. On arrival we were welcomed by Uncles Ayoku and 'Lawale into the realities of Lagos life.

'JAJA HALL'

From the late 1973, burrowed deep in my memories are the frantic clearing of the thick and lush green bushes that concealed the swamps in close proximity to the University of Lagos Staff School. In quick succession diggers, tractors and various kinds of construction equipment and materials appeared at the site. The vibrations from long piles constantly pounded into the swampy grounds became a regular feature of the day. As a seven year old, I found it easier to drift away into a world of vivid imaginations, an escape valve from the prolonged grief following the loss of my father in May1972.

Simply put my imaginations were modest and nothing tortuous, above all they encapsulated an enduring fantasy that always included my father. I sought to recreate that which was impossible. It therefore was not too difficult for me to dream up the illusion that the new construction might be an extension to our school. My mind also filled with curiosity, engaging in some mental excursion, deciding whether the area cleared might reveal snakes and all sorts of wild creatures. At that time in school we had become aware of rumors in circulation relating to one of my classmates, Ayodele Onafeko about the alleged 'snake bite' he had suffered. This seemed to confirm that my imaginations were at least rooted in some reality.

We were privileged to attend the University of Lagos Staff School because of our parents' employment; my father was a History lecturer and mother worked in the University Library and later on in the Bursary Department. The children of University staff attended the school but in some cases, a few privileged ones with tenuous connections received admission. At school I formed a close bond with 'Gbenga Orimoloye who drew sketches with a flourish and was certainly influenced by him. His specialty at the time was sketching airplanes with the 'PANAM' (Pan America) logo. I desperately tried to emulate him but achieved limited success. In time, Omeresan Dediere and Pele Ugboajah gave him stiffer competition and opened up new vistas in the realms of drawing and sketching. It is remarkable how they sketched with near exactness characters from the American Marvel comics. They went beyond inanimate objects to life forms and making it truly life like.

However, it was the friendship of Akin Odulate that enthralled me, he took me under his wings and always offered me choice snacks bought from his holidays abroad; his love of storytelling fascinated me. Akin could weave a simple narrative into one packed, with jokes, laughter and anticipation. In our fourth year, in 1975, 'Segun Alawaiye was very friendly with 'Tunde Kasunmu, his father, a Professor of Law, and because we both regularly arrived early before school started, he would always persuade me to venture with him to the Kasumus' residence in the staff quarters. We would then all walk back down to school before its commencement having fun pretending to be residents of the quarters. I remember 'Kunle Akinbola was always enthusiastic about the football league results; he would regale us every Monday morning with various accounts of football matches that had occurred over the weekend.

It was in 1971 that I first came across a fair complexioned moustache spotting middle-aged man who bore a green army uniform with a glistering Sam Browne belt supported by a narrower strap passing diagonally over his right shoulder, strapped across and around his very trim waistline. On his feet, he wore carefully polished pair of brown army shoes and on his head he was crowned with a peak cap with a red band around it. On top of the cap, in front, bore a single golden coloured line around the Nigerian coat of arms. This man was the Colonel Olufemi Olutoye who later became a Major General, the father of my primary and later secondary and University classmate Dr. Oluyinka Olutoye. He bestrode the corridors of the rows of wooden constructed classrooms purposefully. He marched on with a knowing familiarity of the school as he moved towards Mrs. Karunwi, the headmistress' office. Unknown to me at that time he was also a member of the University of Lagos Governing Council. He was also married to a lecturer in the Arts Faculty, my classmate's mother who would later become a Professor. The General himself was the 2nd graduate to join the Nigerian Army and held a Master's degree from Cambridge. He eventually ascended the exalted throne of Alani in Ido-Ani as his royal majesty the King.

The Head of State, General Murtala Muhammed, later appointed him the Federal Commissioner for Sports and Social Development. In very murky circumstances he was retired by General Muhammed's successor, the then Lt. General Olusegun Obasanjo in 1977. Apparently General Olutoye had confronted Obasanjo about what he described as 'Obasanjo's bending backwards to placate and satisfy Northern interests. The Head of State's response was to summon his deputy the then Brigadier Sheu Musa Yar' Adua and request the General to repeat what he had told him earlier in the day, something that he duly did without fear or compunction.

The price for standing on the principle of what he believed, Major General Olutoye paid dearly with a summary retirement before the day expired. In what seemed a remarkably similar parallel to my story, the Olutoyes had to leave their Ikoyi official residence on Bedwell junction and abruptly relocate to Mushin, a densely populated part of Lagos and a largely a congested residential area with inadequate sanitation and low-quality housing. The General, a man who speaks with clear diction, betraying no hint of his Yoruba origins, remains one of the few commissioners of his generation never besmirched with scandal and sought to serve for its own sake. During his recent award of Doctor of Science by the Adekunle Ajasin University, he was content to boast that given the opportunity to make so much illicit money, he made none!

At staff school, I had quite a bevy of favourite teachers, Mrs. Fatoye, Mrs. Davies, Mrs. Fawehinmi, Mrs. Ogunbanjo, Mrs. Omilani, Mrs. Duncan and of course Mrs. Meshe who shared the fairer complexion with my mother. The teachers indicated in my termly green coloured report cards, that I was prone to bouts of gloominess and sullenness. It was as if I walked around with a gloomy atmosphere as a constant companion and no amount of cheering up from my mother could snap me out of my world. My usual tactic was to feign illness, as I simply preferred the solitude of my own company. At the time, I was facing immense and unremitting grief and that was the only response that helped me cope. However, there were other characters who made my life more bearable and often provided a brief respite from my grief. There was Agboola Abiola whose father Chief M.K.O. Abiola was a rich tycoon, full of life who always provided us much light relief. At the time Chief Abiola was already the Vice President, Africa and Middle East of the entire ITT corporation, which was headquartered in the United States. His wealth was already very evident even though he remained for a while in his Sofidiya residence at Suru-Lere, Lagos. Incidentally, his next-door neighbour was my father's cousin, Mrs. Fagbure, the wife of Mr. Gab Fagbure, a veteran journalist. Abiola's wife Simbiat was a regular visitor to our school and was usually seen holding court with our class teacher, these visits always imposed all manner of restraints upon Agboola, taming him to compliance. Chief M.K.O. Abiola went on to play a prominent role in the second republic of Nigeria and later contested and won the Presidential elections in 1993 but died in 1997 in controversial circumstances in pursuit of his denied mandate.

A harvest of slaps and carefully connecting kicks caught me off guard! I had at the urgings of a few, imitated other boys in teasing 'Ranti' as she was then called but her unpredictable response was swift, vicious and sustained. The tall, slender girl with spindly legs was determined to make an example of me and take me out. Tugging and pulling at her green and white coloured uniform, I attempted to respond in kind. I tepidly grabbed her dress, offering some feeble counterattack before the boys saved me from a potential mauling. Olatokunbo Olayinka Tuyo as she is now called reminded me of that incident more than three decades later when we were reunited in the United Kingdom in 2009.

By 1977, Ibironke Odetoyinbo, now Mrs. Oluwa was our classroom monitor in Class Four (Primary 6) Adenugba; she assumed maturity quite beyond her years and brooked no nonsense from the errant boys in the class. A natural charisma followed her but many also feared and respected her. It was with minimal effort she imposed and maintained order amongst her peers and I attribute her dexterity in this respect to the fact she had three older brothers at home.

The University of Lagos's accommodation at Mariere Hall aka *'Baluba Kingdom, the bottle breakers'* the only male hostel on the main campus was already bursting at its seams. The residents of 'Baluba Kingdom' always took pride in their notoriety for bottle breaking. Usually under the guise of darkness caused by the incessant power cuts a few students would sneak up to the third floor flat roof and begin hauling bottles at unsuspecting passers by below causing mayhem and scrambles for safety. In my view, it was mindless and senseless vandalism brought about by sheer youthful exuberance. The buttery owner, Mrs. Oyediran, a colleague of my mother's did not find these antics funny and was always complaining about the incalculable damage this penchant for bottle breaking was causing her business.

It was at the nick of time that in 1974 a *'futuristic'* student's hall of residence emerged from the cleared bushes and reclaimed swamps. It was three-storeys' high had four blocks linked together it was a very functional building with large louvered windows extending right through the length of each of its 400 rooms. It was named after King Jaja of Opobo an early fighter against British imperialism but it was simply called 'Jaja Hall'. The hall's bricks were coated in light yellow paint and enclosed all around it were linked verandahs, which allowed easy access to each room. It also had a few choice rooms concealed away from the verandahs, which were in much demand by students. While it was being built, my mother had given us some hint that she would take on the tenancy of the buttery but we did not understand the implication of how it would transform our lives.

At last, the hall was declared open and it initially served as a mixed sex hostel while Moremi Hall further down the road was being extended. Mrs. Jacks was the Hall's first Matron and she happened to be the mother of one of my primary school classmates, Amaso. I discovered with time that my mother's tenancy at the buttery attracted some benefits; it was opposite our school so we had easy access to a variety of freshly made snacks and drinks. However, it also had what we considered a disadvantage, for we were required to put in some hours of work. This usually involved collecting and recycling used drink bottles from all the three floors of the hall.

In Nigeria, the empty bottles of beverages technically belonged to the bottling companies and to obtain new supplies you were required to return the empty bottles. It was this recycling that necessitated our chores. It was hard work, collecting empty bottles from each room and then struggling with it in a carton box placed upon my head and proceed nimbly down the flight of staircase to the buttery on the ground floor for sorting. It was a time I spent daydreaming and would usually prolong the task while I chatted to the resident students. However, there was always the reward of a meat pie made from potatoes mixed with minced beef and some fizzy drink at the end of the chore. I would hallucinate about an iced cold Schweppes Bitter Lemon drink awaiting me while wrestling with the weight of the carton of bottles I endured atop my head.

Once or twice disaster struck, the carton spilt from the bottom and the bottles tumbled out, rolling, crashing and splintering into numerous pieces as it bounced off the hard floor surface, inadvertently transforming me into a 'bottle breaker'. Sometimes we had to assist the workers, our relatives, Brothers 'Niyi and Olaiya in serving customers and in later years, I covered the buttery during the long vacation holidays. During those times I filled in the mundane routine by playing and appreciating the record (vinyl) collection of Brother 'Niyi usually the music of *'Bob Marley and The Wailers.'* Those songs usually sent me into my private dream world from where I derived some inspiration.

My mother was very enterprising and took the opportunity of the liberalisation of student's feeding and removal of the government subsidies in the 1980s to transform the buttery into a restaurant/canteen where delicacies of various kinds were cooked and served. The beginning of the removal of subsidies came at a heavy price to the government, the resistance of the students under NUNS led by 'Segun Okeowo led to the *'Ali Must Go'* riots, the death of a student Akintunde Ojo and the dismissal of the well-respected historian, Prof. J. F. Ade Ajayi from his position as Vice-Chancellor of University of Lagos. The effect of the crises continued to reverberate around the University with two prominent factions emerging, the pro-Ajayi and pro-Adadevoh. This eventually led to the resignation of the new Vice Chancellor Professor Babatunde Kwaku Adadevoh and the purported dismissal of the Registrar Mr. 'Femi Eperokun with some other professors, Ekundayo, Olawoye, Ogunye (my friends' fathers), Olaniyan, Oragun and Durojaiye. The case ended six years later after the courts reinstated them following a declaration that their dismissals were null and void and ultra vires and of no effect.

My mother was especially renowned for the plates of beans and plantains and deliciously sauced selections of fried meats prettied with onions, which she regularly prepared. Many students also visited from far and wide in search of her famed freshly baked meat pies and cookies. The verandah at our home was filled with sacks of potatoes one of the vital ingredients for preparing the pies. At Jaja Hall the porters were very friendly, treated us kindly, and once or twice gave me a lift on their motorcycles, I loved the instant recognition being the son of the buttery owner conferred on me.

It was from my childhood friend, Ayowale Ogunye that I discovered that the buttery's tenancy was given to my mother by the University of Lagos Students' Union leadership in recognition of my father's past support and commitment to their cause. It is obvious that my father left a mark on the Students' Union and in death they attempted to repay his wife. My recent visit to Jaja Hall revealed it was a shadow of its glorious self; the decay that has afflicted Nigeria has not escaped it.

'ABULE – OJA'

Abule-Oja remains a small rustic settlement on the outskirts of Lagos in Yaba, besieged by some of the swamps and canals flowing through and around the area. It is a short distance from the University of Lagos in Akoka. In 1973, its narrow roads were untarred, caked in clay, very uneven and littered with potholes of varying depths. The roads gave rise to clouds of dust, stifling one's breathing. The residents were from a variety of tribes, the Yorubas, the Efiks, the Igbos and the Esans who had settled there in the 1950s, it had its early origins as a market settlement. I am told that the earlier settlers were from the Ijesha stock in Yorubaland. Another version suggests that the Eletu Odibo Chieftaincy family owned most of the land in the area. Abule-Oja had one main artery of untarred road feeding though the 'village' and filtering off it into smaller alleyways and paths, some too narrow for vehicular traffic to access. When we were much younger, and living on the University campus, we gathered from all kinds of myths that suggested Abule-Oja was very rough, unruly and a place you visited at your own peril. Now we had moved to live there and had to learn to grapple with many of these myths and with time to separate them from reality.

> *"Breadi, breadi…. oni breadi re ooooo, se ra breadi?" ("Bread, bread…this is the seller of bread, will you buy some bread?)*

The words fluttered through my fitful sleep as the sound of her soulful voice, seeking to embroider the quality of her wares penetrated and travelled through the room as my siblings and I slept. I woke up with my heart pounding, thinking it was another dream linked to my father, but no this time it was real. It was a hawker advertising her wares early in the morning just strolling down the cul-de-sac where we lived, called Sadiku Lane. This marked my first morning in Abule-Oja where we had moved to from Ebute-Metta. In 1974 such sounds, drenched in poetic rhythm became a familiar feature while we lived at Abule-Oja. In time my mother also deployed her entrepreneurial skills by employing Aunty Musili and Aunty 'Bola to hawk around the streets and sell some of her freshly prepared *'puff-puff'*, a kind of oil fried pastry.

With Adebowale, Folashade and mother we lived at Number three Sadiku Lane, on a narrow untarred cul-de-sac. The lane began with a bungalow built from bricks made from mud clay of the *'face me I face you'* kind, followed by our own flat which was located within a two storey uncompleted building which sat behind a lowly wall in front and higher walls to the sides and back, and then a block of four flats belonging to the Abiagoms and an uncompleted house owned by a serving Deputy Commissioner of Police, Chief David Adekunle Adeniji, followed. The African Church Bethel, a traditional African church patterned after the Anglican Church was situated at the end of the lane, providing a cover from the swamps beyond. A long wall separated our houses from Mosuro Street, which backed on to us. The only link to our street was through Okoko's house back entrance. Our own walls bordered Ebun Street. The building where our flat was located remained uncompleted for many years. When we heard the whisperings of rain, we knew that some how it would manage to seep in through the ceilings. Over a period, this caused mould to form on the ceilings and the paint to peel off and tarnish it. A set of stairs was the only access to the flat roof, on top of our flat and it later became the top storey flat.

The gangly and brooding staircase leading up was very dangerous because it offered no protection and the flat roof had no barriers at all. I never quite understood why anyone would leave a staircase in that state. It remains something of the miraculous that no one ever had an accident trying to gain access to it. We were warned never to go up there, but once or twice curiosity got the better of me and I ventured there. I was amazed how little everything seemed from above, like ants and I still experience shivers down my spine each time I recall looking down over the edge. The compound of the building was fenced with a wall and the grounds concreted all around. There was more than adequate space for car parking. One of the downsides of our flat was water rarely came through the taps, so we got used to fetching water from the tap down the stairs at the back of the yard, for washing and cooking. Later on we were joined in the flat by my mother's sisters Mama Taiye and then much later Mama 'Femi with their children, Taiye, Folly, 'Dele, Sunday, 'Bunmi and 'Femi. The house became very crowded and lively with its own fair share of dramas.

I can remember my twin engaging Mama Taiye in a few fisticuffs! Occasionally during holidays Mufu Obiyenwa our cousin from Ede, whose mother was an Ojedele would visit us and spend some time with us. He had a silky 'Oyo' Yoruba accent, which I found quite hilarious. In earlier years at various times my father's Brothers 'Lawale, 'Kola and Ayoku stayed with us and for one thing our home was never empty.

The appearance of serenity presented by Sadiku Lane to unsuspecting visitors was deceptive for it concealed a big secret! The bungalow bordering us was a den of iniquity and criminality where a man called Henshaw lived and marketed Cannabis. Henshaw was a man who possessed a small frame, always wore a pair of dark glasses and spotted a chin full of beard. I suspected he disguised his blood shot eyes gained from his regular indulgence in smoking Cannabis, behind the dark glasses. On most days we were treated to the pungent smell of Cannabis, wafting through the air into our flat and my younger brother suffered headaches from the after effects. He had customers who came from far and wide and it was not unusual to find 'Fela Anikulapo-Kuti, the Afrobeat star and social critic's vehicles parked there while his drivers went in to purchase some smoke. There were sporadic raids by the police, but the man simply had Teflon qualities and always seemed to disappear before each raid. However, it will be inaccurate to suggest that this criminality defined our existence on the lane, for most times we simply ignored Henshaw and got on with our lives. I did observe that we were never victims of armed robbery raids on the lane, so prevalent in the 1970s because of the presence of Henshaw.

We got used to our flat and with time I became close to Nnanna Ehiribe, now of blessed memory, the young boy who lived on the ground floor flat underneath us, he was of the Igbo heritage and fun to be with, he had two brothers, two sisters one of which was called Obichi. In later years, my twin and I were reunited with Nnanna at the Law Faculty in Ile-Ife where he became the Director of Socials of the Law Students Association under the Presidency of Ibrahim Pam. Ibrahim had been my senior at King's College. He was the son of Lieutenant Colonel James Pam, the assassinated Nigerian Army's Adjutant General. The Colonel was the first military officer from Benue-Plateau (Berom) and indeed the entire middle belt of Nigeria and the first Nigerian Artillery officer. He received Queen's commission in July 1955. (The royal military academy England), he was killed on 15th January 1966 during the first Nigerian military coup. Ibrahim had a fearsome older brother Yusufu at King's College whom I usually made sure to avoid but once or twice our paths crossed with unpleasant results, leaving me with recurring nightmares even years afterwards.

25

Across the walls of our compound, we had the Okogbenins, Callistus, Sylvannus, Antonia, Angela and with time two more siblings Emmanuel and Jude joined the family. I always wondered why their mother was extremely fair complexioned and they all seemed to retain such complexion. It was so natural and never induced by bleaching from creams, a beauty regimen so common amongst high society ladies in Lagos at the time. It was only more recently that one of her daughters revealed there was some European blood in their ancestry; one of their mother's parents was white. They were from Ubiaja in the then Bendel State and spoke Ishan a language closely related to Edo spoken by the Benin people. As a seven-year-old boy, in my ignorance I sometimes described them, as *'Igbos'* and they always responded firmly:

"We are not Igbos!"

We formed a close bond on account of the similarity of our ages and together we got up to so much mischief and of course some good. They shared the same compound with their landlords, the Abiagoms who had Emmanuel, Antoinette, Elizabeth and Margaret as their children. The Abiagoms were the first residents of the lane and had moved down from Ibadan. My twin sister was particularly close to them and would spend hours at their home. Annene aka 'Annezee', their cousin also lived with them and for years, we thought he was their brother because they treated him as one of theirs. They were devout Roman Catholics and Emma as we called him, we always looked up to; he was dignified and always had a word of wisdom for us all, he was also our football team coach. Then we had the Nwaojigbas, Okechukwu, Chukwuemeka, Adaku and Obinna who were Igbos and quite posh and very well behaved. Okechukwu and Chukwuemeka later became my mates at King's College, Lagos. Their mother was a colleague of my mother's at Seventh Day Adventist School in Abule-Oja.

I was the goalkeeper of our local team and reputed to be a basket case because of the many goals that passed through my 'goal posts' when I kept. While my younger brother, a much better footballer played the defence. Callistus who had sturdy legs and Annene with a slender physique were attacking players and Sylvannus played whenever there was a need for substitution. We always dreaded meeting *'The Balogun Bombers'*; the team had hardened boys as footballers but we had no problem defeating the Are-Ago boys who had Maxwell Dundun a slender willy and talented player in their team. Bassey Amaku whom we constantly hailed *'Bassssseeeeeaay'* was a regular visitor to Sadiku Lane and honorary member of our team. However, the Abudu Street boys that constantly featured as defending champions. One season my brother and I decamped to Ebun Street where my cousins, the Atewolguns, 'Gbenga, 'Dapo and 'Wole lived, and joined their football team. We spent a significant amount of our time with them, had many sleepovers there and it simply made sense to play for their street. The Sadiku Lane boys did not take too kindly to our perceived treachery.

It is at Number Nineteen Ebun Street, a massive white building which contained a collection of six flats with extensive boys quarters at the rear, resting upon a row of garages, that we fell under the influence of Peter 'Femi Ogunsakin. He and his siblings had only recently arrived from England and stayed with their cousins, the Lasebikans. Peter who was about three years older than us was very adventurous and brought a lot of life to our otherwise mundane existence. We constructed make belief houses from discarded carton boxes we even made attempts at constructing a 'go-cart' from the disused pallets we found around the garage areas. It is fair to say initially we were in awe of Peter and I identified with him, Fola, 'Bunmi and Ife because they had also lost their father. The truth is that 19 Ebun Street was a concrete jungle that sat on the edge of swamps and therefore prone to flooding because of blocked drains caused by its proximity to the site of the local refuse dump. It had to take someone of Peter's ingenuity to transform it into a vista of fun and adventures.

However, it was my friendship with Adewale Mosaku who lived on the top floor flat of Number Nineteen that blossomed and with time I became close to 'Bukola one of his three sisters. She attended Holy Child College at Obalende, not far from King's College, Lagos so her mother who worked for British Caledonian on Lagos Island would offer us a lift to our schools on alternative days. On other days, we would share a lift with Fola Odetoyinbo in his mother's taxicab. Fola and his brother 'Bayo were also recent returnees from the United Kingdom, lived opposite the Mosakus and it was convenient as they attended St Gregory's College, Obalende opposite Holy Child College.   There was also 'Dapo Ogunmakin, the boy from flat four who possessed the golden voice and always serenaded us with classics from Presley. He sought against all odds to pursue an ambition in the performing arts, he was a distant relative of Sunny Ade the Juju music maestro and was convinced success resided in his genes.

But it was not all fun and games at Sadiku Lane; we set up tiny patches of gardens where we experimented with the planting and harvesting of beans, yams and vegetables, we played with sand and built castles and we created mock political parties and contested elections in our make belief world. In those elections, all children were entitled to vote, I emerged as President of the lane, and for a brief period, the title 'Presido' stuck with me.

I can still remember vividly in the month of February 1976, I was playing on the sand pits of Sadiku Lane with Callistus and Sylvannus, when the tragic news of the assassination of General Murtala Muhammed and his Aide-de-Camp Lieutenant Akintunde Akinseinwa filtered through the airwaves and panic filled the air. The voice of Lieutenant Colonel Bukar Sukar Dimka intruded into the airwaves with him signing off with a dry sense of humour:

"We are all together."

The death of the 37-year-old General, possibly Nigeria's most charismatic leader sent shockwaves through our very fertile minds; we were swept with the frenzy calling for the head of General Yakubu Gowon the former Head of State, who Murtala Mohammed had overthrown months before. My first real awareness of Yakubu Gowon was from our neighbour and 'uncle' 'Femi Ayeni who constantly referred to him as 'useless', this I believe was in reference to the General reneging on his promise to hand over power to the civilians. At the time the government pushed out the propaganda that General Gowon master minded the coup. The aftermath led the government to name many streets including the main international airport after General Murtala Muhammed in an attempt to immortlise him. It was during General Muhammed's era that *'retirement with immediate effect and full benefits'* became a popular refrain to the many public servants who were abruptly dismissed. It is claimed that the wave of dismissals and retirements led to over 10,000 public officials being summarily dismissed or retired on the grounds of inefficiency or corruption.

Chief P.C. Asiodu a former 'super' Permanent Secretary explains in vivid terms what occurred:

> "10,000 people were relieved of their positions within a period of two months without due process, without query and answer. And later on, when the Pedro Martins Commission of Enquiry examined it and found that more than 99 percent of the civil servants were gone. However, the swashbuckling decisiveness made Murtala the darling of the Nigerian public, he captured the latent idealism of Nigerians at the time but hid the long term damage of that decision to relieve so many Civil Servants of their positions."[3]

Through sheer coincidence, I became schoolmates with Zakari Mohammed, Murtala Muhammed's elder son and his daughter Zehila came to live with us in Nottingham during her University of Nottingham undergraduate programme. She had a striking resemblance to her Mother, Mrs. Ajoke Muhammed whom we met when she visited our home to thank us for looking after her. At King's College, Zakari aka 'Mesi' was quite boisterous and excelled in goal keeping. He had curly hair, was diminutive but rather chubby, I recall an encounter he had with Ladi Lawanson aka 'Lawi Pepper' on the last day of term in the late 1970s. Zakari was our senior by a year before he succumbed to repeating a class. Anyway, Lawanson ignored all conventions requiring him to offer respect towards him because he felt his life had been made a misery.

He challenged Zakari to a duel behind the laboratories, Zakari was furious, he abandoned all caution and walked straight into the trap Lawanson had laid for him. 'Lawi Pepper' hid behind one of the pillars supporting the science laboratories and carefully timed a series of connecting slaps on to Zakari's face as he emerged and before he could recover, Lawanson fled off and away into the safety of the departing school bus. Lawanson got away with it but confided with many that he was dreading

---

[3] Asiodu, Philip (2011): *'Main reason Gowon was toppled, by Philip Asiodu'*; Interview of December 31, 2011 by Bashir Adefaka [Accessed on 10th March 2013 from http://www.vanguardngr.com/2011/12/main-reason-gowon-was-toppled-by-philip-asiodu/]

the start of the new term, when Zakari would mobilise his classmates to teach Lawanson an unforgettable lesson or two. Fortunately for 'Lawi Pepper' in the next term, 'Mesi' was repeating the class and was now his classmate so the opportunity for retribution was lost forever. Ironically in later years, they would become in-laws when 'Lawi' married his sister for a period.

I also had the privilege of marrying Lieutenant Akinseinwa's wife's sister, further 'cementing' my proximity to 'power'. King's College was the home to so many children of the ruling elite and usually children of the assassinated and coup plotters mixed freely together with not a hint of bitterness. It was also the home to those from less privileged backgrounds; this allowed them to mix with children of privilege bringing the meaning to brotherhood.

Anyway, with time the paths of Callistus, Sylvannus and Annene diverged as we went off to various boarding schools but I am certain we left an indelible mark on each other.

At home, we had a verandah, which led, into our sitting room and into an adjourning bedroom. The confined space looking out into the streets was dominated by two benches, which sandwiched a long table. A patio door led into the sitting room and my brother with the assistance of his friend, a neighbour, Sawendo once contrived to smash his own head into the glass of the door necessitating panic from my mother and twin and a rush to the emergency department of the University of Lagos Health Centre for several stiches to cover his gash.

This was the scene of our weekday tutorials, which we described as 'lessons', it always started at 4pm and ended at 6pm prompt! I really disliked my mother's penchant for insisting that we had these lessons. I reasoned they were unnecessary and that after school, we ought to be left to our own devices. My cousins, the Atewologuns were also part of these 'despised' lessons where Mr. Dabo a teacher from the local Seventh Day Adventist Primary School and colleague of my mother's held fort. I told my mother that I was not happy with the arrangement of extra tutoring and she promised to consider my request. In my mind, I interpreted that to mean I could now withdraw myself from any future lessons. On the next day, I linked up with Nnanna in his ground floor flat for some time of fun and games while the lessons continued with my twin and brother.   When my mother returned and discovered what I had done, she summoned me upstairs and gave me a serious spanking and even my cries of protestations were to no avail.   My first revolt had only lasted for an evening and there was to be no repeat of this antic for a while to come.

Our first cousin Temilade Olajide lived with us for a while but had to leave under a cloud.   She was a princess and her father later became the 'Olusi' of Usi-Ekiti, the paramount ruler of my mother's hometown.   Her mother whom I never knew because she died before I was born was my mother's elder sister.   Temilade had an elder sister Titilayo they were the closest we got to royalty.

The highlight of our stay at Abule-Oja was our tenth birthday, which was marked in in relative grandeur.   My mother invited all our friends from all over Lagos.   My uncle, Chief Adeagbo Odeniyi acted as the 'photographer' with his newly acquired Polaroid camera and my mother baked and made a huge cake patterned into two equal halves with different coloured icing.   The pink half for my twin and the blue half for me, and it was all presents galore for us.   We both felt like a queen and king with all the attention focused on us.   One of the books I received as a present was *'Jekyll and Hyde'* a curious choice I thought.   I tried to read it but found it was simply incomprehensible at age ten years old.   However, I had fun with my twin playing with the chemistry set we received as a present.

In later years my Uncle, Chief Odeniyi suffered grievous injuries from an armed robbery attack whilst out late at night and lost the use of one of his eyes, his handsome dark features were slightly affected but his generosity of spirit and the warmth he exuded did not diminish one iota.   I dare say till his death a few years ago he remained a shining light in the firmament.

Callistus, Annene, Sylvannus and I became very entrepreneurial and during the holidays, we would create magazines and comics and sell them at a price.   We constantly devised moneymaking schemes but in one holiday, I went too far.   St. Dominic's Church, the main Catholic Church in Yaba always had an annual raffle draw to raise money for good causes.   It relied on its parishioners to sell the raffle tickets to their friends. On this occasion in 1978, I collected a bundle of tickets from Callistus sold it all and then decided the lure of the money raised was too much to ignore! I simply pocketed all the cash raised from the sale and treated myself to few packets of shortbread biscuits and a variety of sweeties. It was only later when I became a Christian that repentance gripped me in the heart and I was compelled by my conversion to return every stolen kobo to unsuspecting relatives and friends, it certainly was not my best hour.

Mr. Abiagom, Eman's father was the first 'DIY' man I became acquainted with, as a landlord he was very much hands on. He carried out all the repairs to his property. He was a very pious, reserved and kind man, I suspected he was very wealthy but he was not the showy type. He was a devout Catholic and on a few occasions, he rendered to me his own version of the history of the Catholic Church. His wife, whom we called 'Mamma Maggie' was a no nonsense lady, but was very kind to me, I would look forward to the lifts in her Renault as she dropped me off at King's College, Lagos on her way to Leventis Stores where she worked. She later retired but invested her efforts in selling kerosene oil and crates of fizzy drinks. Like us, they had dogs as pets and it was not uncommon to find dogs playing in the environs. In later years, we became her tenants and she would always permit me an indulgence in the use of her land telephone to contact and receive calls from my many friends.

In 1976, the Adenijis and the Akapos replaced Nnanna's family as our neighbours on the ground floor flat and with time, I had a few encounters of my own with them. I being the inquisitive one always wondered what a trickle of hot water might feel like as it slithered down the back of an unsuspecting child. I emptied our kettle of hot water but was careful to leave just a little drop or two for my next experiment. I spotted my potential victim Maria, the five-year-old daughter of our neighbour from atop the stairs and quietly inched close to her and then emptied the trickle of hot water down her back. As the dribble of water made contact with her skin, descending and slithering down the contours of her back she flew up, bursting into hysterics and fled into their flat, screaming that I had scalded her! On receiving the distressing reports of my latest antics my mother dragged me into her bedroom and inflicted the cane on me, teaching me the lesson of my life. My experiment with pranks had gone so wrong; I discovered prank playing was not to be my forte.

Mr. and Mrs. Adeniji who had two daughters 'Bukola and Joke for a while they provided some deliverance to my transport conundrum when I was a young first former at King's College, Lagos and he was responsible for offering me my first job at UBA on the Lagos Island whilst I was at University. He was a dark tall, reflective man with some traditional marks carved into both cheeks, pleasantness was his hallmark and his wife was a very kind lady, very lightly complexioned.

By 1977, the flat on top of ours was completed and the Ikweles moved in, their son Andrew became my brother's friend. For a considerable time Mr. Chris Ikwele, a manager at the Manufacturers Association of Nigeria (MAN) caught a dashing figure as an eligible bachelor as he constantly indulged and surveyed the terrain of beauties about town. James and Stephen cousins of the Ikweles came to live with them and I became acquainted with them, it was through James I was for a brief moment introduced into the world of funny magazines of the adult variety, there was a stash of them hidden in their flat.

In time Brothers 'Niyi and 'Shina, students at the University of Lagos came to live with the Adenijis at the end of the Lane. My mother had engaged both of them to tutor me in Mathematics but they became more than that to me, they were my early mentors. Brother 'Niyi was very slim and spotted an Afro style on his head while Brother 'Shina aka 'Obi' was shorter, darker with a nicely trimmed moustache. They were both exceptionally brilliant and left their mark at the Faculty of Engineering, University of Lagos. I loved to hear their tales of the antics of their lecturers such as Professors Adekola, Awojobi, Aderogba, Okon, Ogunye and Susu.   There was one lecturer who they happily regaled the terror he inflicted upon his students by telling them before each examination:

> *"I thought your examinations were going to be difficult but now I know its going to be disastrous!"*

Initially Chief Adeniji did not live on the lane, however, his first wife and his many daughters, which included 'Pero aka 'Pereee', Moradeun and some of his sons 'Degbola, 'Gboyega, Wemo and 'Gbite boy' stayed there while the top floor of the building was under construction. I must confess the ladies; his daughters caused a bit of a stir on the lane and attracted many boys who fancied their chances of extra-curricular engagements though I am not sure they achieved any success. In later years the Chief relocated to Abule-Oja and he was able to offer my brother and I regular car lifts to King's College, Lagos on his way to Shell BP on Broad Street where he was contracted to work as a security consultant. The Chief was an indigene of Shagamu and was reputed to have thirteen wives and numerous children and he was a ranking member of the Ogboni Fraternity, the Olori Apena.

A constant and soothing visitor to our Abule-Oja flat was Mrs. 'Foluke Adetugbo the wife of Professor Abiodun Adetugbo, our old neighbour at the University campus staff quarters, CT36 (later named Nanna Close). She had an illustrious pedigree had studied in the USA and was from Ibadan. She always arrived in her red Datsun coupe car with one goody or the other, never forgot our birthdays, always lavishing us with snacks and sweeties. She really made our lives so bearable, I remember the wrist watches she bought for us from England at my mother's request and our many St Michael's underwear she helped my mother purchase. The underwear lasted me for many years even into teenage years. She was a shining angel sent to us from above. I was close to her first son Adewale whose intellectual curiosity always intrigued me and at the time, he seemed like a walking encyclopedia of knowledge. We shared a lot of information from Time magazine, which we regularly purchased. She had two other children, Adenike and Adeyinka, we unfortunately lost Adenike to a mysterious illness in the early 1990s.

In the fourteen years we lived in Abule-Oja we witnessed much transformation, though we had the luxury of modern toilet facilities we were subjected to the sight of weekly chores carried out by the night soil men who we referred to as 'Agbepo'. These masked men dressed in brown khaki and shorts visited some dwellings around in other streets in our area. They held a broom and carried out the job of clearing pails of human waste in the dead of the night from the many mud dwellings that dotted across Abule-Oja. These dwellings did not have running water or modern toilet facilities so human waste was excreted into a container or bucket, and collected on a set day of the week. They always carried the buckets precariously on their heads, it always seemed that it would trip over with the contents spilling on to the road.

Many rumours abound that a few rogue 'Agbepos' sought out their enemies with their brooms and pails and ensured they were desecrated with its contents. Even though it was a nightmare to encounter them many sometimes teased them at their own peril with names such as *'onishe'*, *'agbepo'*, *'ibeji'*, *'eruewo'*, *'omo adelabu'*, *'show boy'*, etc. and they always gave the chase but mostly we avoided coming into contact with them. In due course many of the clay caked roads became tarred and gave the settlement of Abule-Oja a new lease of life.

These are wistful reflections on my sojourn at Abule-Oja and the indelible associations I formed there. Many people are constantly surprised with my ability to utter a few important phrases in Ishan and Igbo even though I might mangle them tonally. These were learnt from Callistus, Emeka, Okechukwu, Sylvannus, Annene, Lizzy, Maggy and Eman (of blessed memory). That simply is how profoundly those relationships have influenced me and continue to shape my quest for my country Nigeria.

'OLUPONNA, THE TOWN OF MY FATHERS'

The summer of 1972 was a traumatic time for us. It is from here that the memories of Oluponna, my hometown are carved on to my mind. This stemmed from our first visit to bury the remains of our father. On 27th May 1972 I recall that after a long and exhausting journey, starting from the University of Lagos, College of Education Auditorium, where the remains of our father was laid in state, we arrived in the dusty and rustic town nestled at the bottom of the larger historic town, Iwo. Our entrance into the town, with the hearse moving ahead at snail speed was greeted by melancholy in the wind and with unspeakable sorrow, enveloping the atmosphere. The journey had been very long and arduous because of the extensive convoy of vehicles that followed us all the way from Lagos. We met our uncle Mr. Mathew Oladejo Ojedele at the Faculty of Education auditorium, and I was taken aback by how utterly broken, inconsolable and bereft he seemed as his eyes were bathed in tears, flowing freely as he wailed uncontrollably at the sight of us.

The remains of my father, lying in the wooden crafted coffin placed at the front of the auditorium, dressed in pure white lace material appeared as if he was in a very deep slumber waiting to be awoken. However, this was betrayed by the sight of cotton wool inserted into the nose and ears of his remains, presumably for protection from moisture. Oluponna the land of my fathers possesses a rugged and gentle undulating terrain characterised by smooth relief in the landscape. On that day, the collective out pouring of our grief appeared to exaggerate the features of the town.

Once we arrived at Oluponna, I remember most the feeling of overwhelming thirst and hunger. Whilst the adults at the funeral service wailed uncontrollably, all my siblings and I wanted to do was eat snacks, drink water, and have some refreshments. Aunty Asunke my father's sister was detailed to look after us during the service. Later that night we made the thirty-minute journey and returned to Ibadan to stay with the Odeniyis. We stayed there overnight to prepare for the farewell Sunday service at St Peter's Church the next day, my memory of that night remains virtually non-existent but I am sure it must have consisted of more sorrow, tears and wailing.

My mother had assured us that our father's remains would be embalmed and preserved and we would be able to go and see him anytime we wished. However, when we got to Oluponna the next day to our utter shock and horror the grave had been covered up and cast in freshly made cement. My mother's grief laden reaction was to attack the grave and try to remove the cement. My uncle, Oladejo Ojedele and others intervened and prevailed on the widow engulfed in grief to let go. This was the background to my early memories of Oluponna, the town of my fathers.

We made another brief visit to Oluponna in 1976 in our nicely attired 'aso oke' to bury our grand uncle Ojedele, the one we knew as *'Grandfather'*, and we were hosted by our uncle Chief Lawunmi. However, in 1977 Chief Adeagbo Odeniyi convinced my mother to let us join his family for Christmas in Oluponna. He had just completed an expansive bungalow with lots of room and acreage at Idi-Obi, the colanut farmstead in Oluponna. My mother relented and allowed us to join them and this began the annual ritual of spending our Christmas holidays at Oluponna. My uncle's father had been a successful cocoa and produce farmer and cocoa trees encircled the land where the bungalow was built. The compound was littered with fallen cocoa pods. Once thinking it would taste like chocolate I ventured to break open a pod in order to devour the contents. The taste was disgusting! It was very bitter very much unlike the Bournvita cocoa drink I was used to consuming. It was later I discovered the sweet taste of the drink came from lots of processing.

At every Christmas holiday, we followed a familiar routine when we arrived, my aunty, Mrs. Odeniyi would arrange for us to be taken to our family compound at *'Ile-Olota'* to visit our relatives. At the family house, a bungalow built from mud, with no electricity and laid out in the traditional *'face me I face you'* style, we would spend time with them, usually it was with Uncles Popoola Ojedokun and Ojekale in awkward silence scratching around our minds for what to say. This was the house where the three of four brothers, my grandfather and grand uncles, Ojedokun, Ojekale and Ojedele lived. Ojelade had chosen to return to Alaya, a small settlement bordering Oluponna, due to a family tiff. The Ojelades eventually converted to Islam. The house was not grand but it was an adequate bungalow sandwiched between a warren of mud houses and homesteads of so many other relatives like the Akinyeles, Lawunmis,

Idowus, the Alawodes and the Alajikis on three different sides and connected by a narrow maze of crooked lanes running among the houses.

It is only now that the Ojelades have reunited with the other members of the family after many years of silent strife. Later on my father's elder brother Uncle Samson Ojedokun, Papa Iyabo retired from Ibadan and made the house his residence. Polygamy was predominant during my grandfather's era so my father had quite a few half brothers and a half sister. The town is divided into about 60 compounds some of which are, 'Ile-Aro' where the Odeniyis come from, 'Ile-Alara' where the Adiguns come from, Ile-Olukoun where the Fagbures come from and 'Ile-Baale/Oba' where the traditional ruler comes from, Ile-Akeyo, Ile-Odunfa, Ile-Oosa, Ile-Jagun, Ile-Arojo, Ile-Molosu Ile- Olodes, Ile-Aroomo-Jogunle Ile-Akinniyi and the rest which are namely compounds like: Adi; Agbodorogun; Arewewenu; Apago; Moye; Gbetu; Akeyo; Jagun; Olota; Gbenro; Akuru; Arinoje; Animashahun; Agba; Alagba; Ikumopos; Molosu; Ajimagbo; Eleye/Balogun; Olukohun; Olorombo; Akeye; OjaAro Ogunle; Ekerin/Onla; Iyalode; Ejemu; Oloro; Aloba; Aluku; Lagbaja; Onibata; Akili; Lagesin; Olode; Okuloro; Alawo; Elegu; Berele; Bara, Ologbo, Parakoyi, Odofin and Odunfa.

In Oluponna as with many of its neighboring towns, compounds and not roads were the most important elements in the town plan. Each compound was the visible expression of a lineage or extended family. It is suggested that the congested and haphazard pattern that exists in part of the town was as a result of the settling of refugees from the Yoruba Civil Wars.[4]

In Oluponna, a large part of the day was spent in the open where everyone ate, drunk, and talked in the full view of everybody else. It was simply because the rooms were so hot in the daytime therefore it made sense for most of the life in the compound to pass on the open veranda or yard. Also quarrels and rebukes took place within the full hearing of neighbours. Each individual's weaknesses and vices were open to the observation of others. These had some advantages because people outside the immediate family were interested in its members and their welfare of course it made

---

[4] Gulger, Josef and Flanagan, William G (1978) Urbanisation and Social Change in West Africa: Cambridge University Press: Cambridge

exclusive family life in the Western sense impossible for only a limited amount of privacy is possible.

After the completion of those formalities we were set free and let loose on the green grass of my uncle's compound to play football with 'Seyi, Eyitayo and 'Tope. Various friends and relatives from around the town joined us in many of our football games. In one of those games, Seyi aka 'City' in his attempt to execute the perfect kick fell awkwardly and broke his leg, necessitating an early return to Lagos and an abrupt end to our holidays in Oluponna. When we got bored with football, we would rent bicycles in the town and ride round it at great speeds. On other occasions, we will go to the Oluponna Community High School past the Fagbures' residence, an imposing one story building on the outskirts of town and try to learn how to drive. Mr. Gab Fagbure who was married to my father's cousin, an Alawode, he was a doyen of journalism and had been a commissioner in the old Western State. He was strikingly tall over 6 feet 3 inches, bald with grey haired and chain-smoked. He was reputed to be one of the first to visit the palace of the Alaafin of Oyo, the historic King of what remained of the ancient Oyo Empire with his shoes firmly encased on his feet. At that time, no one entered the presence of the Alaafin with any type of footwear.

He was very articulate and together with Dr. Benjamin Abimbola Adigun, my father's cousin, they were regular visitors to our home at the University of Lagos staff quarters. Mr. Fagbure's father had been extremely wealthy and enlightened so even though his son Gab who was older than my father bore no traditional marks. Mayegun Hotel, the only hotel in the town, near Idi-Obi was a place we visited to partake in snacks and drinks and relax to music, it was owned by Chief Dairo a cousin of Chief Odeniyi and a member of the then Oyo State House of Assembly.

Christmas eve was always interesting with fireworks on display and fired in all directions. We were obliged to visit the Church for nativity plays and a late night service. The next morning we always attended the customary Christmas Day service at St Peter's Anglican Church. The Church had now been transformed from what it was at our last visit. It was grander, bigger and better and the floors had now been smoothened out with proper pews added. Everyone dressed in his or her new clothes called *'aso odun'* sewn and bought specially for the Christmas occasion. There were lots of singing and dancing in the Church as we sang lustily in Yoruba language the chorus over and over again to the melody of drums:

"Odun ti a bi olugbala araye. Kresimesi odun de, odun alayo.
Ko san gbogbo wa. Kan so gbogbo wa sire loruko Jesu ..."

Outside at the side of the Church, was the cemetery and my father's grave was prominently built of white granite marble with the inscription under a cross:

"Dr. Olasupo Ojedokun, B.A., MSc. Ph.D., ...here he rests after
life's fitful struggles..."

These words were prepared and inscribed by my grief ladened Uncle Adeagbo Odeniyi. There was always the tinge of sadness as we passed by and stopped to offer our respects.

The celebrations on Christmas Day revolved around, food, drink, music and dance. Every home in the town provided a feast and we visited different relatives around the town. Many slaughtered and cooked chicken, others goats or turkeys and the wealthiest cooked cows. In those visits, you really had to pace yourself, or after the first two visits, you were completely full to the brim.

The drummers were always out in their full force drumming and singing praises to their potential benefactors. They used the talking drum, whose pitch could be regulated to mimic the tone and prosody of human speech. Its body was covered with two skins connected by leather strings, which allowed the player to tweak its pitch by pressing the drum between his arm and body. These drummers were very skilled and adept at playing whole melodies with accompanying phrases. They always undertook their research, so they knew what songs to sing or what beats to drum and what praises to offer to the many unsuspecting passers by on the streets. For instance if you were a lawyer, they would drum and belt out words to the effect:

> *"Barrister, Lawyer, Barrister, Lawyer…...the son of the soil, the mighty one, the one who is going places…."*

In a society where much credit was and still is ascribed to titles and status it always worked, with egos enlarged, people usually parted with wads of cash responding to the praise and flattery with the sequencing of their lower and upper limbs, moving rhythmically with varied and intricate dance moves in the middle of the street. It always amazed me how the set of lively movements on the streets came to resemble a dance.

During the holidays the pace of life at Oluponna, a town of about 30,000 inhabitants was slower but it was for us the children a carefree life, consisting of play, eat and sleep while the adults busied themselves with affairs of the Oluponna Development Association (ODA). 'Seyi my cousin was always full of life and a practical joker, even as a teenager he was a carbon copy likeness of his father, while Eyitayo was always serious minded and brooked no nonsense. 'Tope was delightful and gentle with a brooding silence, Oyinkan was always very sweet and kind and I had a soft spot for her. 'Mobola was a tomboy and the soul of the party and because she was born on Christmas Day, there was always a double celebration, and my other cousins, Eniola, Olaolu, Oyeleye (of blessed memory) were simply a pleasure to be with. They had a cousin called Adewale, who happened to be mixed race, his mother was of Irish ancestry, who lived with them. The holidays always stretched into the New Year. But there was a particular year when our holidays were cut short because of the death of one of our cousins, the first son of Chief Lawunmi, in a tragic car accident while travelling to Oluponna from his Ogbomosho base.

On reflection it is suggested that Yorubas, the tribe with whom I bare the closest affinity has one of the richest, enduring and perhaps, the most sophisticated way of life on the continent of Africa but I have no doubt that other Nigerian tribes would suggest and they are even more entitled to boast about the same. The Yoruba way of life is described has being embedded in its culture, with claims that it has continued to survive and remains irresistible, I believe only time will tell.

'ILU IBADAN'

Ilu Ìbàdàn, the city flanked by seven hills, which is said to have emerged when bands of Yoruba renegades following the collapse of the Yoruba Oyo Empire, began settling in the area towards the end of the 18th century. The attraction was its strategic location between the forests and the plains. Its pre-colonial history centered on militarism, imperialism and violence. The military sanctuary expanded even further, when refugees began arriving in large numbers from northern Oyo following raids by Fulani warriors. Ìbàdàn grew into an impressive and sprawling urban centre so much that by the end of 1829, Ìbàdàn dominated the Yoruba region militarily, politically and economically.

In the decade of 1970, the decade of my adolescence it was quite usual for me to lay claim to Ibadan as my city of origin. This was because it was home to the football club I adored, IICC Shooting Stars International and it was just 25 miles away from my home town Oluponna. The football club captained by Samuel Ojebode and with players such as Best Ogendengbe, Musashiru Lawal, Kunle Awesu, Moses Otolorin, Felix Owolabi and Segun Odegbami was the team to watch, because of the sleekness in their moves, the lacing together of their passes and pin point accuracy of their shots. They were the first Nigerian football club to win continental honours, however, there was an intense rivalry between them and Rangers Football Club of Enugu.

Ìbàdàn or in its name in full, Ilu *Ẹbá-Odàn* is the city at the junction of the savannah and the forest which lays claim to being the third largest metropolitan geographical area in Nigeria. It is in this city we spent many of our childhood holidays. It later became my own refuge from the times of trouble at Ile-Ife. It is a city, which has a tropical wet and dry climate and a lengthy dry season. By the time I fell in love with the city it had acquired a population of about three million people. It is a city that has such localities as Ojoo, Agbowo, Dugbe, Yemetu, Oopo, Oniyanrin, Challenge, Molete, Oke Oba, Aroro, Idi Radio, Ajibode, Afilala, Olanla, Ikereku, Akinyele, Oje and Beere. On one occasion, we visited Dugbe market courtesy of my aunty Mrs. Ojedele to be kitted out in the latest fashion, for Dugbe was the place to shop. It was the city where my father met, courted and married my mother. It was the city where my parents completed the final stages of their education before they left Nigeria for the shores of England.

Initially in the early 1970s, it was with the Odeniyis that we spent most of our early holidays at their Idi-Ape residence in Basorun, Ìbàdàn. In 1971, my father had proudly displayed a portrait of his cousin, Adeagbo Odeniyi's newly completed house and promised to take us there during the holidays. After my father died, we continued to spend our holidays there and it was from there that my mother attended some catering school to improve her skills in that area.

However, in 1974 after the Odeniyis moved away and relocated to Adeniyi Jones in Ikeja, Lagos, it was with my uncle Ojedele that we spent our holidays while in Ìbàdàn. We stayed at Ago Taylor in Ìbàdàn while he was serving as a senior civil servant with the Western and later Oyo State Government. My uncle was very reserved and it is said he remained locked in the grief brought about by the loss of his closest companion, his cousin, my father. I am convinced he would have made more progress, surpassing that of becoming a Permanent Secretary had the tragedy of my father's loss not befallen him. The two cousins were indeed like twins, born around the same period, sharing the same bed, hobbies and indeed friends. They attended the same primary school, same secondary school, Offa Grammar School and the same University at Ìbàdàn.

My cousins, the children of Uncle Oladejo Ojedele, Ajibola, Kikelomo, Mojisola, Morunranti, Ope and Babatunde aka 'Tune' all made our holidays with them very lively. They packed a sense of humour with an uncommon wit and all spoke the Ìbàdàn 'dialect' of Yoruba. Their mother's devoutness was never in doubt and for a while I drew close to her because of her Christian faith. Kikelomo later joined my twin at Ile-Ife to study Physics; she was a very early starter, gaining admission at age 14 years old! In 1994 tragedy hit us so hard when we lost 'Tunde aka 'Tune' to ravaging illness of Typhoid Fever.

Later on in 1978, the Ojedeles moved into a sprawling but near completed house built and which nestled at the bottom of a hill in Idi-Ape, Basorun a few metres down the road from the Odeniyi's my other cousins. There was always something interesting to do while in their home. My uncle was very close to Mr. Babajide an indigene of Iwo town, who worked at the Oyo State Sports Commission so he would always take us to visit him. We always came back with some gift or souvenir and he would take us around the Liberty Stadium, the first of its kind in Africa. When we were at Ago Taylor I had little sense of dress code for church so once I attended a service with my cousin in my brown imported stonewashed hot pants, which left little to the imagination! When my uncle and aunty returned from some travel they were aghast wondering why I had worn what they described as *'Sokoto pepe'* to church!

At age seven in, 1973 I also remember fondly when my uncle was posted to Sagamu as a District Officer, we spent some holidays with him in his sprawling official bungalow. Once at the urgings of the housemaid my siblings and I ventured into town, and we got lost. We became consumed in a desperate panic, and simply went round and round various alleyways and roads only to become more confused. Thankfully, we hit a stroke of luck when we recognised a car we had passed and made our way home in complete relief. While we were lost panic was coursing through my mind for several minutes thinking that we would be kidnapped and it would mark the end of us and no one would ever find us.

In time in the 1980s, the Odeniyi's home became more of a second home to us. I credit my father for this, when he was alive he always took us there to spend our holidays while he sneaked off to stay with his many cousins. So we were used to staying with the Odeniyis and it is there I became very good friends with the Aboderins and Ladapos. The Odeniyi's earlier move to Ikeja in Lagos had meant closer proximity to us in Lagos and we spent many more holidays with them there. Chief Odeniyi like Mr. Ojedele had attended the same schools with my father but diverged for his 'A' Levels to attend King's College, Lagos only to rejoin them at University College, Ìbàdàn.

In 1978 I remember very fondly being driven to Ibadan by Uncle 'Kola Ojedokun (of beloved memory) in Chief Odeniyi's official Toyota Land Cruiser through the uncompleted expressway of Lagos – Ìbàdàn. We were about the only car cruising effortlessly on the highroad. At the time, it was a marvel of construction and it cut down a journey that was about three hours to one hour. We were on our way to spend holidays with the Ojedeles and my Uncle Odeniyi had been kind enough to lend us his car. At that time, Chief Odeniyi was Commercial Director of West Africa Portland Cement.

My twin sister, however, choose to spend most of her Ìbàdàn holidays after she gained admission into the University of Ife with our cousins the Idowus. She had formed a close bond with 'Ronke when they attended Federal Government College, Oyo and developed a close friendship with Ike. It was incidentally with 'Ronke that she spent most of her last days on this earth.

I may not lay claim to a homestead in Ilu Ìbàdàn but I am at heart an Ìbàdàn boy, I am a life long supporter of 'Shooting Stars' (Up Shooting!) and will gladly answer to: *"Omo Ìbàdàn kini show?"* Ironically, my twin also married Ademola Laniyan an Ìbàdàn man.

'THE BEGINNING'

The Portuguese explorers were so enchanted when exposed to the sandy shores of the place called 'Eko' that their first instinct upon disembarking their ship was to christen it, *Lago de Curamo*, the name for lakes. The modern day Lagos remains a unique little jewel in the West Coast of Africa. It is bounded on the west by the Republic of Benin, to the north and east by Ogun State with the Atlantic Ocean providing a coastline on the south. It is blessed with a total of 3,577 square kilometers; however, 787 square kilometers is made up of lagoons and creeks including: Lagos Lagoon, Lagos Harbour, Five Cowrie Creek, Ebute-Metta Creek, Porto Novo Creek, New Canal, Badagry Creek, Kuramo Waters and Lighthouse Creek.

It offers a mix of charm and history of the Portuguese and Brazilian embroidered with Yoruba culture. The warmth of Lagos and her people make it difficult to resist falling in love with it. With water splashing and lashing around shores of Lagos, it a city of life, for water wherever it is found sustains life; it also gives hope and opportunities to those who live near it. That is why our adventures to Mars, beyond our planet, to go where no one has gone before cannot fully commence until we find a way to transport water there.

The origins of Lagos though interwoven with myths remains unquestionable Yoruba and some clues can be found in its 'Oriki'; the literary genre used to inspire its people is recited below:

"Eko akete Ile ogbon
Eko aro se se majae ilu eko KO ya bu omi suru mu
Warm, Eko, aro mi sa legbe legbe
Eko o ni baje o
B'oju o ba ti Ehin'gbeti, oju o ni t'Eko"

The direct translation is:

"Eko, the Island of wisdom

Eko, a land bounded by seamless flow of waters

An Island of non-diminished heritage and values

As much as commerce never cease so does Eko remain the citadel of innovative enterprise."

So I found my feet in the midst of so much potential for life, surrounded by so much vitality in a city influenced by Portuguese and Brazilian architecture. A city, which received its wealth from the economic boom, that came from being Nigeria's capital and its vitality from the smattering of night parties that dotted across its landscape. This is a city with a climate characterised by tropical wetness and dryness bordering on monsoon climate.

It is in this city that I took my first political steps. I can recall my recent visit to Lagos, everything felt frozen in time, not much had changed and some decadence had set in. The roads have improved with a dose of sanity injected but it remains congested with traffic, which emits ever more increasingly potent fumes from gridlocked vehicles. There are many more pedestrians struggling for very limited spaces. In many respects, it resembles organised chaos and the earlier attempt by Governor Lateef 'Kayode Jakande to provide a tram alternative was frustrated by the military regime of Major General Muhammadu Buhari that took over the governance of Nigeria in 1983. The past Governor Raji Babatunde Fashola rekindled this dream with a tram project called the Blue Line which was completed in 2023 by Governor Babajide Sanwo-Olu. These are where my nascent dreams matured; here is the backdrop to my beginnings, the beginnings of a journey of discovery.

At our Akoka, University of Lagos home by 1971 we enjoyed the luxury of riding to school in a 1970 version of the American Chevrolet Caprice Kingswood, Estate wagon, a black one and a white one; the engines purred as it moved along the wide roads leading to our primary school. They were the biggest and most expensive cars in the whole school and this made me feel very special. We were never wealthy enough to afford two Chevrolets, but my father had become the acting Director-General of the Nigerian Institute of International Affairs (NIIA) and with it came perks of office such as official cars. The cars were donated to the Institute courtesy of the Ford Foundation. I remember his driver, Umeh, his infectious smile, the lightness of his skin and his smart military bearing which made me suspect he was ex-military.

Once my father indulged me by allowing me to sit on his lap as he drove and playfully encouraged me to feel the steering of his car, he loved playing pranks; he was full of fun and life. You could always hear his deep sonorous voice bellowing out and resonating through the walls of our one storey home when guests came to visit, he would tease them several times in Yoruba language saying:

"Ema wo le!"

Which meant:

"Look at the ground."

He told me his ambition was for me to become an engineer so I could become a creator and an inventor. I did not become an engineer in the traditional sense, but an engineer determined to create a space for social transformation. My father's rise had been meteoric and quick, from his appointment as a lecturer at the University of Lagos in 1968 to the pinnacle of the Institute in 1971. In the University of Lagos, my father was reunited with his mentor Professor A.R. Aderibigbe who maintained his close relationship with us even after his death. At the Institute he was credited with initiating a programme for the Institute of interdisciplinary research, symposia, and lectures, and the publication of monographs and surveys, with emphasis on African affairs, a legacy which continues till today.

My mother recalls that I was very inquisitive as a child and my early memories seem to corroborate this. I can remember shortly after we returned from England to Lagos, pointing at every item of furniture in our new home and constantly asking in my heavy

South London accent repeatedly:

"Daddy did you buy it? Is it yours?"

I can remember how my father packed so much dynamism and achievement into his short life. I still have fond memories of how he bought second hand car after car, playing mechanic only to be frustrated because his and his brother 'Lawale's attempts at repairing the various cars proved futile. I can recall the elaborate picnic we had in the bushes of the University of Lagos behind where we lived. At heart, my father was a village boy and he always sought to re-create the nostalgia even in the serenity and orderliness of the campus. On that occasion, we feasted on roasted yam dipped in red palm oil with palm wine to cleanse the palate and for a brief period, we journeyed back to village life whilst anchored firmly within the sophistication of the campus. As time went on, we saw less of him as his new job at the Nigerian Institute of International Affairs took more of his time.

He grew in sophistication and became a tobacco smoker, purchased a pipe and acquired a beard. He started wearing a thickly rimmed pair of glasses his wardrobe was transformed with neatly cut suits replacing his casual clothes. The man seemed so indestructible! He was looking ever more distinguished and important, a man going places. He began to feature regularly on television programmes and he began to travel around the world with increased frequency. On one of his trips to Singapore, he bought us some kites. We tried to fly the kites but they proved no match for the locally made kites made from discarded newspapers, broomsticks glued together with locally made starch. My father took enormous pride in his work and every new publication he authored he would show us even though at age five or six we could barely understand much. Once we received chastisement because we soiled one of the journals where his paper *'The Anglo-Nigerian Entente and its Demise, 1960-1962'* was published with palm kernels while playing out in the garden of our home.

"Daddy, Daddy, I have some homework and I need a pen."

These were the last words I uttered to him and his final response as he laid writhing in pain and slurring his words on his marital bed with visible darkish bloodstains on the covers, was:

"Look in the top drawer, I am not feeling too well".

In a few hours my mother and her sister rushed him to the Lagos University Teaching Hospital, Idi-Araba (LUTH) where he passed on at 2.45 pm. Even in 1972, the short distance between the two campuses was made even longer because of the unnerving winding chronically chaotic traffic between the two. In the end, the brave and sacrificial attempts by his colleagues at the University who raced to Idi-Araba to donate blood were futile.

My father, a practical joker had pretended to die so many times before. Arriving from work, he would drag himself up stairs to the edge of his bed slumping, exhausted and pleading with us to race down the stairs to get him scraps of bread before he died of hunger! If we delayed, he would proceed to shut his eyes, pretending to be dead. However, this time it was real! All of a sudden, our home was turned upside down and in turmoil, suffocating with grief and all the framed photographs covered up or turned backwards as many mourners from far and near arrived. The event was very traumatic and unsettling for us, but life moved on with trepidation.

Eventually we had to move out of our home, away from the well-ordered life and glistening manicured lawns of the University campus to share my mother's sister's home. The three bedroom terraced accommodation with a garage and a boy's quarter came with my father's job and we had exhausted the six-month's period of grace allowed by the University. It was a life of relative comfort; the University provided all the beddings, crockery, cutlery, cooker, refrigerator and furniture. We had Mr. Ige with his sons Abayomi and 'Dayo on the right as immediate neighbours and the Adetugbos on the left. Other families such as Akinsetes, Orimolades and Adalemos lived opposite us in the expansive cul de sac.

I remember the generosity of the Akinsetes who took us into their home for a week whilst there was mayhem caused by mourning at ours. It was here I was introduced to the delights of a cereal, Weetabix, it was always served with hot milk, sprinkled with sugar and I loved it. Mrs. Akinsete was a doctor and lecturer at the Lagos University Teaching Hospital and Dr. Alaba Akinsete who later became a professor was a lecturer in the Mechanical Engineering Department (now of blessed memory). Mrs. Akinsete also became a professor and for the short while we stayed with them, spoiled us and made sure we were distracted from our grief. It also did me little harm because she had a beautiful daughter, Abiola whom I was fixated upon at the time. The nanny reported my newly acquired interest but Mrs. Akinsete simply asked her to leave me alone. At home, we were used to cornflakes and I can vaguely remember the congealing of the hot milk when splashed all over it, as it was drenched in the bowl.

In the University campus near our staff quarters were two very extensive fields where play and bicycle riding dominated the evenings. It is here you found most children running around without a care in the world. It was around this field we learnt to ride our newly purchased Raleigh bicycles; a gift from Colonel Ogunkanmi and for a while suspended all anxieties. Yet, the university architecture also presented a ponderous form because of its preponderance of concrete, which contradicted its maritime environment. We moved into my mother's bedroom after my father's death and woke up each day to the flashing red lights that came from the top of the white coloured huge iconic water tower, reservoir, shaped like a mushroom but with a top like a rounded ball that dominated the skyline, which you could see from the windows of her bedroom.

Out on the fields as the wind transported the fumes from the insecticide spray towards my direction, collapsing in a heap, contorting into an embryonic form I grabbed my face, yelled in exaggerated fashion, playing dead. This was 1971 on the University campus and we were, children all gathered, delighting in fun and games at the open space beside our terraced houses. My attempt at a prank soon descended into utter chaos and panic as I resisted all the attempts at revival, intent on prolonging the drama. Soon the very worried children I was playing with summoned 'Uncle' Olu, the

Adetugbo's helper to the rescue. Shaking me like a broken reed he tried to revive me but to no avail. Before I realised it, I was lifted up and thrown into the waiting car, which moved at high speed towards the University Health Centre! On the way there I realised I had gone too far this time but still persisted in the pretense, thinking it would get into more trouble if I recounted. We arrived at the Health Centre, and I miraculously revived, the nurse gave me one look and asked me to jump up and down a few times and then I was discharged. This time I got a way with it, but for how long?

Less than six months after my father's death we left the University staff quarters. Departing from the campus meant we had to start all over again, my mother had found it increasingly difficult to find suitable accommodation near the University so her sister and her husband offered us temporary accommodation. We all moved in to stay at their home until we found a suitable flat. However, it was not an easy one, it was Ebute-Metta which was farther away from the campus it was a densely populated part of Lagos near swamps and infested with blood sucking mosquitoes. We moved into their four-story building where on each floor dozens of families lived in a *'face me I face you'* style. They were also known as *"face me and face trouble" or "face me and face wahala."* They were tenement buildings with the rooms being no more than 10 x 10 feet square metres. This was a form of architecture where a group of one-bedroom flats have their entrances facing each other to form a compound with a main entrance leading into a square in the middle, however ours had the added complication of several flight of stairs.

This was a very common architectural style in Ebute-Metta; the rents were low and they were popular with the average Nigerian because of their affordability. All shared a single toilet and bathroom facilities every morning was a daily nightmare, waking up so early at dawn, in order to beat the queues of families waiting to bathe and relieve themselves. We became inventive, using potties and only venturing to wash late at night.

In January 1973, I recall watching the Second All African Games whilst living there and enjoying the intense competition and rivalry of participating nations. My mother took on three jobs to ensure we continued with the best quality education and with the help of Mr. O.K. Atewologun, her cousin, we eventually moved to a slightly better and fast developing settlement of Abule-Oja.

In all those difficult years the cushion of generosity provided by my Uncles now all late, Odeniyi, Adigun, Ojedele, Ogunkanmi, Adetugbo and Atewologun bolstered us through our challenges. I was glad that at least now, we only shared our flat with just one family. Our new neighbours, the Ayenis were Ekitis like my mother and we all got on like one big happy family. My mother was a teacher, a secretary and a caterer. We were now neighbours to her cousin Mr. Atewologun who had children who were similar to us in age and he treated us like his own.

My mother's father, Pa John Adeniyi Noble was a trained tailor, quite tall and lived until he was in his 90s. He had acquired his surname name whilst working with the colonial masters as a servant; the story was he inherited the name because he conducted himself like nobility. I remember him as a strikingly tall man with regality his second nature. The distance of over 325 kilometres away in Usi-Ekiti did not stop him from being my mother's rock in those times of unremitting grief. My mother tried all she could to reassure us and I always craved her attention, her softly spoken voice, her enduring hugs, and of course, we could not forget her savoury cooking. She also ensured we cultivated the discipline of writing to grandfather, to update him on our progress and other matters of interest. All these projected a sense of security and stability. My mother was an exquisite cook and was famed for being one of the first to master the art of cooking fried rice in Nigeria. Many times we retreated into the comfort her cooking and home baking provided and offered. It was very soothing to her as it was to us. I can still remember her immediate response to my father's death was to retreat into the kitchen and bake various tasty pastries.

Memories are aroused of my mother, a strong and fearless one, attempting to stand up to soldiers during a traffic incident on our way back from school only to be rescued by the *'messianic'* actions of my uncle, Professor 'Biodun Adetugbo. In 1973 the Professor of English, then a Senior Lecturer, on that humid mid-week afternoon, at risk to his own life fought the rabid soldiers to a standstill. The incident dragged on rather late into the evening before it could be resolved with my uncle ending up in hospital and we at Lion Building. After it all, we thought we had the next day off school, but my mother still insisted we continue with our routine.

The memories of my father are now somewhat distant and what I know intimately about him seeps through the recollections of my mother, uncles, aunties, from the pages of letters and the records of research he undertook before he died. I can remember the many stories from Uncle 'Lawale Ojedokun about my father. My father was the second surviving child of his father Ojedokun there was the constant spectre of death that hovered around many families at the time leading to the loss of four of his sisters who did not survive into adulthood. His father, Ojedokun had four brothers, Ojedele, Ojekale and Ojelade and they were the sons of Ojeleye. Bilikisu Alajiki, his mother was a tall proud woman, a Muslim convert, she died in the 1950s not too long after the birth of my uncle, Ayoku Adeleke Ojedokun. Uncle Ayoku bears a striking resemblance to my father and because he never knew his parents, his brother, my father became his surrogate. My early memories of Brother Ayo as we called him, now the University Librarian of Bowen University, Iwo, are of a generous and kind teenager dishing out to us two or three pence as pocket money after ensuring we did our homework. He always emphasised hard work and always asked whether we came first in the class examinations! He was a stickler for form and procedure. Today with a height of over 6 feet with his shoulders slightly stooped, I sometimes feel he walks as though burdened by the memory of the lingering loss of his elder brother.

Anyway, it is from the scraps of facts woven together by my Uncles Oladejo Ojedele. 'Kola and Ayoku Ojedokun that I learnt my ancestors were itinerants who moved from town to town in search of greener pastures. They belonged to the Yoruba traditional '*cult*' of masquerades and the guild of masque dancers and acrobats. The guild was different from the practice of ancestral worship, which was firmly established in Yorubaland through the egungun. I am not sure they were very successful because they later settled on the edge of Oluponna in a hamlet called Alaya as subsistence farmers. However, an ideal kept them moving, the ideal of a better life for their families. Later after the death of the patriarch Ojeleye all the family except Ojelade moved into the Olota Compound at the heart of Oluponna to reside with their in laws, the Akinyeles and Lawunmis and with time they became assimilated and settled as part and parcel of the life of the town.

In Yoruba land everyone and compound has an 'Oriki', a kind of Yoruba literary genre used to inspire people. It is usually in oral form and in a form of poetry, consisting of songs of praise; it provides clues to one's history and identity. In search of my identity, I learnt that the Oriki of the Olota's compound where my ancestors settled is:

> *"Omo a so igbo di ile, so igbe di igboro Babaa mi a so aatan di oja*
> *Omo a mo agbara kan ile agba, a mo tere kan ile Olota, Omo*
> *Akinjogbin ni iwoye.*
> *Ewe kigoke ogan eni goke ogan yoo fi ile iya han mi, ile iya lookan ti*
> *babanbe ni tewure*
> *Omo okuta meta ode ilota, okan ko mi lese dabo, okan wi pe kin*
> *maa rora okan ni nigba ti nko mo ona kini mo wa se lode ilota.*
> *Olapolubu omo ina awo ti njo geere omo ina eesan a fi aiko o jo bula.*
> *Omo ateni wijo ki tata ta oro ma baa ta sile.*
> *Omo omu igba re oja fi eti ko ila wale*
> *Olalomi, iwo ni iyeru okin, omojoolofa mojo - omo abisu joruko ijakadi*
> *loro ofa. Olofamojo loluponki, oluponki ore Eko; Eko tara Ibadan o ri*
> *je to nbifa e leere."*

I have translated it into English so that we can get an appreciation of it:

> *"A child imbued with unique capacity for industry and enterprise;*
> *As he is turned a forest into habitable haven; so did he convert a*
> *forlorn forest into humongous community;*
> *My progenitor, who, thorough creative ingenuity turns a wasteland*
> *into vast marketplace enterprise;*
> *A man of valor who came through the ancestry of the ancient; he is*
> *of the Olota and Akinjobin descent in the homestead of Iwoye;*
> *A glorious descendant of the tripartite stone that fills the landscape*
> *of Ilota;*
> *Of these three stones, one welcomes me; another cautions me tread*

carefully; and yet another question the reason for mission to Ilota without a compass."

I learnt that my paternal forefathers had their origins in Oyo Ile from the Akpotoma Compound. They left the old town of Oyo with Prince Olufioye when he lost his bid to become the Alaafin (King) of Oyo. They initially settled at Igborike a small town between Ogbomosho and Igbeti, then moved on the Gbongan to found a new town and then via Sogbein, a small town near Osogbo from where my ancestor, my great great-grandfather whose name remains forgotten moved with his drummer to Alaya a hamlet near Oluponna. Ojeleye, his son had four wives and upon his death, all his children dispersed to their mother's ancestral homes. I like to believe the rumour that they migrated all the way from the North of Nigeria a century before. This seemed to be backed by an account of our origins that suggests we settled in the town of old Oyo and then left with the Prince into exile.

My father was tall for his generation, about 5feet 10inches, charismatic and very reflective. I am told that my father grew up working the farm with his first cousin Oladejo Alamu Ojedele until their elder cousin Chief Alani Lawunmi and one Mr. A.A. Ogunrinu rescued them at age nine and insisted they enroll at the local St. Peter DC Primary School in 1945. I sometimes wonder where his path would have ended if he remained on the farm, would he be with us today? After attending St Peter's School, Oluponna, Christ Church School, Mapo, Ibadan and D.C. School, Araromi, Iwo, in 1953 and 1954 when they went off to Offa Grammar they never had the protections that shoes offered and their uniforms were all bought on credit. My father and his cousin then proceeded to attend Nigerian College of Arts, Science and Technology. They both attended University College Ibadan on Federal Government Scholarship, then part of University of London. My father obtained a 2nd Upper Class honours degree in History and my Uncle, Oladejo initially admitted to study Mathematics but completed a degree in Geography, his performance affected by the loss of his mother and then as his so often the case with siblings their paths and their destinies diverged in differing directions.

In 1965, my father won a Commonwealth scholarship to study International Relations at the London School of Economics. Through dint of hard work coupled with sheer brilliance, in the space of three years he acquired a Masters and a Doctorate in the subject, specialising in Nigeria's economic relations. Eager to fulfill the promise of his generation, he rushed back to Nigeria in the throes of a vicious civil war and after some contemplation took up a faculty position with the University of Lagos. From there in 1971 he was appointed acting Director General of the Nigeria Institute of International Affairs, Victoria Island, Lagos.

Growing into adolescence was met with a seeming familiarity that many Nigerian dignitaries worthy of mention knew of my father and it extended beyond our borders. As evidence of this, a portrait of my father and President George Bush Senior assumes a place of pride in our home in England. Mr. George Bush then the United States Ambassador to the United Nations had paid a courtesy call to him at the Institute in 1971. He was also kind enough to send my mother a condolence telegraph when my father passed on. What was it about Dr. Olasupo Aremu Ojedokun, his personality that meant in four short years he was able to enter into the sub consciousness of many?

He bequeathed little in terms of material wealth but left a brand new olive brown coloured K70 Volkswagen sedan car. The name "K70" referred to the fact that the engine had a power output of 70 PS. It was an expensive car to run and it was not the best for top speed and acceleration, nor for fuel consumption, and the K70's indifferent fuel consumption became an increasingly pressing issue because the car's production run coincided with the 1973 oil price shock. We had a squeezed income so my mother could not afford to keep it for too long. He left a few newly purchased suits and other discarded clothes and a trunk box. He also left a good name, which opened a few doors for my siblings and I. The trunk box contained a treasure trove of documents and it was to become my most valued possession and one of my escape valves from this world. It was where I could dream dreams and imagine how great my father might have become if he had lived just a little longer.

Years later after I had returned from England and to my horror I was informed that termites had with the passage of time decimated most of it and eaten up any trace of his memory. The news hit me so hard and for months I grieved the loss of so many intimate documents from my father, it was as if I had lost him all over again. Before the destruction of those documents I spent most of early my days going through every file, immersing myself in every detail of history it concealed. It was my romance with these files and many of his books that introduced me to a world of politics and possibilities. Another visit to Nigeria, however, established that some of those documents survived and may now rest in the residence of my mother's late sister, 'Mama Taiye' at Mowe outside Lagos.

To all who cared to listen I would show off letter exchanges between him and Chief Obafemi Awolowo, I would devour contents of his letters that expressed anxieties about his and our future. But from it, I learned he had a confidence and the makings of a man who would have gone on to *'Speak Truth to Power'*. He had already become a regular newspaper columnist. I recall while he was alive, he would fascinate us before the video age with television recordings of himself on current affairs programmes, we would wonder how it was possible for a man to be in two places at the same time.

I was only six years old when my father passed away to the great beyond. We spent many nights sleeping in our mother's bed and she comforted us by telling us *'Daddy'*, my father had gone to *'Summerland'*. I spent years haunted with so many questions about him and the circumstances of his death.

> *"Why did he die early? What killed him? Will we see him again? Will my mother die next?"*

To me he was the enigma who occupied the space in my dreams and the one who for years I dreamt of his return home in triumph and glory! I simply could not settle down because my father and my hero was missing, and nothing my mother or relatives uttered could erase that single, immutable truth. I felt so starved of his attention and craved his warmth, so every other relationship to the outside world felt unspeakably hollow, and the effects suffocated me. My face always presented a forced and fixed grin constantly betraying my mood and my tongue usually felt too bloated to utter any words. With time because of the several sleepless nights these induced, my mother moved my siblings and I into her own room at our Abule-Oja flat as a temporary solution but in fact the three of us never left her room till we turned eighteen.

In the early 1975, my mother fell very ill and was admitted to Lagos University Teaching Hospital for weeks. It was as if our nightmare was being re-lived all over again, we felt very anxious and for many moments contemplated our fate as possible orphans. The main relief at the time was the Odeniyis who made arrangements for us to spend every weekend with them until my mother was well enough to be discharged from hospital. The weekends were usually spent visiting the Apapa Amusement Park, where we rode various rides and forgot about our worries.   During the weekdays, Mr. O.K. Atewologun arranged for us to be taken to school and picked up afterwards.

We normally had cereal for breakfast, the small kid sized Kellogg's variety boxes. At my suggestion, my siblings and I decided to devour the contents of the cereal as a snack in the night fully aware that in the morning we would have nothing for breakfast. The morning came and there was only the milk I had prepared but no cereal, we then proceeded grumpily to the Atewolguns for our regular lift to school. Mrs. Atewologun noticed our mournful looks and guessed something was up. She placed us under inquisition, whilst I stuck to the agreed line that we had had our breakfast, my twin, Folashade interjected, broke ranks, contradicting me and confessing we had had nothing to eat. Aghast at the revelation, Mrs. Atewologun prepared some eggs and bread and then summoned Mama Taiye my mother's younger sister to establish why she had subjected us such to deprivation. She was of course rendered speechless and unable to provide any answers since she was unaware of our antics. No one really shared with us what strange affliction had been visited upon my mother, but thank God in a few weeks my mother had returned to full health.

The spoken accounts my relatives gave could not sufficiently explain why or how my father died. Weeping uncontrollably with my eyes constantly red and sore, my heart always yearned for something more but no one could tell me what it might have been like had my father lived. I remember Colonel Alimi Ogunkanmi one of my father's close friends who had been paralysed from gunshots he sustained during the Nigerian Civil War at Owerri in 1969, now wheelchair bound, investing so much in our happiness, purchasing expensive Raleigh bicycles for us. Yet none of the gifts offered the much sought after succour, my mind was constant with throbbing for even fun and games provided me no release from my seeming torments, it was a recurring nightmare for a while.

Like great figures in the pages of history books, my father became an attractive prop in my own story, a remote figure with a pure heart, the mythical stranger who did so many great things in his lifetime but a prop to me nevertheless. This was demonstrated through a vivid encounter in my First Form at King's College, Lagos, I had a tussle with a mate and all of a sudden, I blurted out crying:

"Is it because I do not have a father? …"

Taken aback my classmates gathered around, and were remorseful, they enquired when his death had occurred when I told them it was five years before, they walked away, miffed and berated me for being unable to let go. Reflecting back, I know this was not simply an unending grief but my anguished cry for help, help needed to navigate the weight of expectations now bestowed upon me by my admission to King's College. In those days when my grades were not so good, when I was left behind by my classmates and in the face of my twin sister's relentless advance my mother would summon the memories of my father and the weight of my history to will me on. She would state almost 'prophetically':

"They are watching us to see whether we will succeed."

I always wondered about the significance of those words.

The only antidote I found to the vacuum inflicted upon me was a constant retreat into the world of drawing and sketching; I became some sort of artist. In that world I could re-live life with my father featuring prominently. I would take some comfort of how I thought the world ought to be. To me, art was to become the prop and crutch against times of uncertainty. I became very moody and withdrawn and some interpreted it as my natural inclination. In Primary Two at a time when my twin's companionship might have helped soothe the pain of our loss, we were wrenched apart and sent to different classrooms. I remain puzzled at the reason for separating two grieving twins who had just lost their father. I guess in those days people just did not understand grief or the close bond that twins had. I grew up as a lone ranger attending an exclusive primary school, University of Lagos Staff School, always retreating into and preferring my own company. The loss of our father marked us apart from other classmates, we became to some, an object of curiosity mixed with pity. They wondered what we had done wrong to have deserved the loss of our father? It all seemed to me as if we were to blame.

My father was suddenly thrust into my consciousness at a celebrity debate organised by the National Council for Women's' Societies (NCWS) at King's George's Hall Onikan, Lagos. I was on the same team with retired Major-General Henry Adefope as his co-debater ranged against Dr. Christopher Kolade and some Queen's College student. Major General Adefope (of blessed memory), a medical doctor had served in Obasanjo's regime as a Federal Commissioner for Labour and later for External Affairs while Dr. Kolade was previously the Director-General of the Nigerian Broadcasting Corporation and now the Commercial Director of Cadburys. After the debate Mrs. Emily Aig-Imoukhuede, one of the organisers of the event approached me and asked me if I was 'Supo's son, when I confirmed it, in excitement she raised her voice, saying she knew my father very well and continued:

> "We always expected him to make a First Class and it was a surprise that he narrowly missed it...."

To most places I went people had stories or anecdotes to retell about him and it is these that made him come alive to me. His memories began to fill the vacant space in my mind.

Through many anecdotes I picked up from my uncle Chief Adeagbo Odeniyi, my father's cousin and closest friend, I learnt so much about his leadership qualities. The Chief, the 'Agbakin of Iwo', played a significant role in our lives; he ensured that we were connected to our roots in Oluponna and was generous with us to a fault, he always took care of us as his own. Through my mother, I discovered the Chief was an alumnus of King's College and we developed another common bond. As I matured in years, I acquired my father's old clothes and shoes and wore them with a conviction that it would draw me ever closer to him. It was as if I was seeking to wrap his identity around my own.

I flinch with embarrassment as I recall an incident that occurred when as part of the Old Boys executive I visited Sir Ademola Adetokunbo to brief him on the preparations for the 75th anniversary of King's College, Lagos. I was in the company of Otunba Adeniran Ogunsanya and Mr. Allison Ayida, they had finished speaking and the learned retired Chief Justice asked for my opinion. I leaped in with excitement trying to remind the judge that he had worked with my father as Chairman of the governing board of the Nigerian Institute of international Affairs while my father was at the helm. Sir Adetokunbo without batting an eyelid responded and said:

"What an interesting connection."

Apparently that was not the connection he was seeking from me but I was too engrossed in discovering my father's real identity to notice.

In the celebrations that year, we invited Mr. S. O. Wey as the guest speaker. He had previously chaired the panel set up to review the workings of the Nigerian Institute of International Affairs (NIIA) while my father served as the Secretary. The panel was set up in 1970 to re-organise the NIIA by the Federal Military Government of the then Major-General Yakubu Gowon. The Institute had been funded in most part with grants from Ford Foundation and The Carnegie Corporation. The completion of the report led to the enshrining of the Institute being in law in August 1971 and its being taken over by the Nigerian Government. The reasoning behind this was that funding should be guaranteed and not reliant on foreign donors and whatever alternative sources of funding acquired should continue to ensure its character, as an independent, nonpolitical and non-profit-making organisation remains unchanged.

The review established the following as the new objects of the Institute:

> *"(a) To encourage and facilitate the understanding of international affairs and of the circumstances, conditions and attitudes of foreign countries and their peoples.*

(b) To provide and maintain means of information upon international questions and promote the study and investigation of international questions by means of conferences, Lectures and discussions, and by the preparation and publication of books, records, or otherwise as may seem desirable so as to develop a body of informed opinions on world affairs.

(c) To establish contacts with other organisations with similar objects.

In order to achieve these objectives, the institute was charged with promoting the scientific study of international politics, economics and jurisprudence, and providing facilities for the training of Nigerian diplomats and personnel and those of other countries whose vocations relate to international affairs."

Mr. Wey who delivered the King's College anniversary lecture had served as Head of Service and Secretary to the government during the time of Prime Minster Abubakar Tafawa Balewa. Immediately I sensed the connection with my father and I approached him and we agreed to meet up at his Ilupeju home. When I visited, Mr. Wey, he was so down to earth, he invited me into his bedroom for discussions and I enjoyed reminiscing with him over the life and times of my father. He was one of those who began to allow me to gently unwrap the enigma that was my father.

I learnt from the various accounts given about my father that his memory would never die, and it enveloped me where ever I went. Chief Phillip C. Asiodu a former Super Permanent Secretary under Yakubu Gowon told me that he knew my father and his loss so early was a huge blow. Mr. Asiodu always fascinated me by the way he spoke fluent Yoruba and he regarded himself as a Lagos *'boy'* despite his parent's origins which were in Asaba. He became a Federal Permanent Secretary at the age of 31 and was prematurely retired from service in 1975 when he was Permanent Secretary, Ministry of Petroleum and Energy.

Mr. Justice Mahmud Babatunde Belgore, my father's 'school father' when they attended Offa Grammar School, was the Chief Judge of the Federal High Court. He was a very kind and generous man who provided my friend, Pedro and I accommodation in the boy's quarters of his 31 Cameron Road, Ikoyi official residence during our Law School year. He used every opportunity to introduce me to dignitaries such as His Royal Highness the Emir of Ilorin and a few others as the son of Dr. Olasupo Ojedokun. The Judge was of Fulani tribe from Ilorin with links to the aristocracy and he could trace his ancestry to New Bussa near Sokoto. Whilst culturally Yoruba it was obvious, he still bore the features, traits, height, complexion and stature common to so many Fulanis. His cousin who later became the Chief Justice of the Nigerian Supreme Court, Justice Alfa Moddibo Belgore, was a regular visitor to his residence and once impressed us with his mastery of Fula language and knowledge of their ancestry. It was a period of much fun and I got to know one of the cousins of the Belgores and a sister to my classmate 'Femi Suleiman. 'Bisi, my law school classmate who had skin, which appeared dipped in chocolate and with a certain degree of royal bearing in her posture.

It was a similar story in my encounters with Mr. Allison A. Ayida the Head of Service and Secretary to the Federal Military Government under General Olusegun Obasanjo and who later succeeded Otunba Adeniran Ogunsanya as the President of KCOBA. I remember the courtesy accorded to me by Dr. Lateef Adegbite, the Secretary-General to the Supreme Council of Islamic Affairs in Nigeria at his CMS building Lagos office when he discovered who my father was. It is with time I learnt to rely on his name and the connections I thought it could bring me. To me, this was all a long ponderous search for something, a search for his identity and ultimately mine.

In the search for his identity I stumbled across one of his letters written to Professor 'Kunle Iyanda in 1971. The professor later became the Provost of the Polytechnic Ibadan and Director-General of the Nigerian Institute of Management. In the letter, he was detailing his anguish, about the frustrations he felt with the slow pace of change at the Nigerian Institute of International Affairs. It was in the letter to him, that at age ten I came across the word *'disentangle'*.

I believe my father continues to represent an ideal, and ideals never die, but precede action for change as Chief Chukwuemeka Odumegwu Ojukwu suggested. What was it in my father's DNA that meant an impoverished gangly boy, without shoes; rustic looks and a face that was carved with slightly lacerating designs of many tribal marks that destined him for brilliance and potential greatness? What is in his story and mine that signifies that if we can make it thus far, then our country ravaged with so much conflict, so much underdevelopment, and so much corruption can still make it?

I remember that over snacks I had several lively conversations with my adopted uncle, 'Wole Ayeni, a neighbour who had taken over the tenancy from his cousin Uncle 'Femi, with whom we shared our flat. Uncle shared the flat with us for financial reasons. My mother's finances could only extend to three rooms while his covered two other rooms. We shared the bathroom toilet and kitchen facilities but in reality, he rarely cooked so we had full reign of the kitchen. He enlightened my political consciousness with constant discussions on many topical issues. It was from his regular purchase of newspapers, Tribune, Sketch, Punch, Concord and the Daily Times that I became addicted to current affairs. I had always loved reading newspapers but prior to my closeness to 'Uncle', I was always drawn to the sports' section. He would regale me with stories about Nigeria's first republic, about how he adored Chief Obafemi Awolowo and in response, I would tell him of my admiration for the Rt. Hon. Dr. Nnamdi Azikiwe, the first President of Nigeria. We spent many nights arguing about the merits and demerits of our respective heroes.

With time, I have come to accept the words of F. Scott Fitzgerald:

> *"Show me a hero and I will write a tragedy."*

Shouting:

> *"Kayode, Kayooooode…"*

Many times my mother would have to drag me away from those discussions because she thought I was neglecting my studies.

Uncle 'Wole's basic thesis was that with Chief Obafemi Awolowo as President, Nigeria could attain great heights, while my position was that only Dr. Nnamdi Azikiwe was capable of reuniting the nation. I am afraid with time my views modified and as time passed my *'hero worship'* of *'Zik'* diminished and I eventually moved over to become a wholehearted supporter of Chief Awolowo. Later, Uncle 'Wole became a clerk (Senior Executive Officer) at the National Assembly just a few metres from King's

College. This had dual advantages; it meant regular lifts to school but also access to the National Assembly buildings. I could have regular access to the chambers of the National Assembly and observe *'democracy in action'*. I would listen to and watch Senator Aja Wachukwu who was a marvel to behold, a huge solid man with a mastery of debates, there were other giants like Senators Obi Wali, Jonathan Odebiyi, 'Banji Akintoye, Oke, Uba Ahmed etc. With a predicted regularity, I devoured the Hansard of its proceedings, which he readily made available to me.

It was as if time and space began to converge turning my previous misfortune into something more tolerable and politics becoming an antidote and even a source of obsession with Uncle 'Wole as the midwife. I suspect these encounters left lasting impressions on me. In 1983, this influenced the beginnings of my own political story at King's College, Lagos. By then Major General Muhammadu Buhari and his co-travellers in the military had truncated the Nigerian democratic experiment and we were back to the uncertainties characterised by military governments, however, it seemed my own search had certainly just began.

At University of Lagos Staff School I was known as and called 'Kayode, pronounced as 'Kaa-YOW-Day', a short form for 'Olukayode' and many assumed my initials began with the letter 'K'. By my Third Form I had come to resent this because I felt the initial 'K' distanced me from the identity of my father, Olasupo who had 'O' as his first initials, I was determined to reclaim 'O' as my initial, 'O' for Olukayode. Therefore to everyone who asked what my name was I simply told them it was 'Olu' and with time it replaced 'Kayode. Everyone including my mother was encouraged to call me Olu, it was only my twin sister who resisted the urge and stuck to what she had always known, *'Kayode'* and all her children inherited that habit from her.

'PASTOR'

Whilst it was courtesy of 'Gbemi Kehinde and Victor Amokeodo, my King's College classmates that I acquired the coronet 'Pastor' it was Ayowale Ogunye my good friend who 'consecrated' its usage during the summer school. The summer school was where we received the extra tutoring at the University of Lagos Faculty of Education during the long July to September holidays. It was open to the children of university staff or members of the public with some hint of association with the University. At that stage, it was my ambition to win over every youth for Christ and to witness the gospel to anyone within sight and the summer school was certainly rich for the pickings.

Initially under the influence of Apostolic Faith denomination, I foreswore the watching of television or anything that smacked of pleasure but with time, news and current affairs programmes lured me back towards the small screen. I also had indelible associations with Lattie Williams and 'Biyi Mabadeje and you could not avoid the television screen if you visited their homes on the University campus. I enjoyed my time with Lattie who at a point acquired an air rifle. I developed the practice of accompanying him on his ventures into the bushes of the University of Lagos to shoot at any creature that strayed into our view. He was also known to shoot a few wandering dogs causing them only slight injuries, but that was Lattie, a 'dare devil', for you.

With time in the late 1970s/early 80s I set up the Campus Christian Organisation with 'Tunde Oderinde, Ope Fagboungbe, 'Wole Eperokun and a few others as members. Bro 'Tunde Oladunmiye became our Patron and Mrs. Eperokun (of blessed memory), the wife of the University Registrar became the Matron. We acquired a cassette player/recorder courtesy of Brother 'Tunde and listened to Christian based messages and then went about seeking to do some good. We were able to acquire abundance of gospel tracts from the University's Faculty of Education home of Mr. William F. Kumuyi, a Mathematics lecturer who was then of the Apostolic Faith but later became the founder of Deeper Life Bible Church.

The highlight of the summer school was always the end of term party held at the University's Student's Union buildings, Akintunde Ojo Building. But the teachers, the organisers of the summer school always held the prospect of its cancellation over our heads like a sword of Damocles to compel good behaviour.

To begin with I did not do disco parties like many of my friends, but later I found it was possible to go to these parties with the objective of preaching and saying a prayer or two from the safety of the venue's entrance, standing as a sentry with whoever was there. The boys and girls just thought me rather odd, but I found relevance and comfort in it. There was also the grand party of 'Tunde Ojo whose father was a Professor of Law and his mother a senior government lawyer, held in their top floor flat off Ozolua Road on the University of Lagos Campus. 'Tunde had agreed I could lead in prayers and I had geared myself up to say the opening prayer; I was all set to go when some of the girls protested and that attempt was aborted to my huge disappointment. However, with time, I built a strong network of friends from Queens College, Yaba and among them was Chidinma Ekwueme. A few boys became acquainted with me with the faint hope that I would become a facility for their liaisons with the girls.

As 'pastor', I undertook a number of 'preaching engagements' in school and without. The height of my *'preaching engagements'* was in 1980 when I engaged a bevy of beauties from Queen's College, Yaba, including Iyabo Obasanjo at the Tafawa Balewa Square Racecourse. They had come for the October Independent Day secondary schools' marching rehearsals. I simply spoke about my faith, what I believed in and fielded a few questions from the girls. The boys appeared rather silent and I always wondered why?

Later that year I took Ibadan by storm; my late uncle Mr. Ojedele (later installed as the Baba Ijo of St. Peter's Church, Oluponna) had invited us for summer holidays in his partially completed 6-bedroom palatial residence in Idi-Ape. I had acquired a Yoruba bible and imagined that I could gain mastery enough to start preaching in Yoruba but this proved to be very ambitions. I had collaborated with my aunty and summoned the entire family to a session of preaching in the large and expansive sitting room. All my cousins, Ojedeles, Ojekales and my siblings were gathered but my words and sentences were laboured and halting, exposing my inadequacy in the Yoruba language. We had always spoken to one another in English and it was only from eleven that I developed some confidence in speaking it. In any case, my uncle joined us on his return from work and ended the session with his rationalisations about religious extremism. I left the session with a feeling of disenchantment and failure.

'PANAFISM'

My hands were raised up towards the heavens, suspended in a clasp, standing bedecked and resplendent in pure white silky *'Danshiki'*, a black fess cap tilting upon my head and a pair of black trousers providing the contrast.   Standing upon the central table, I responded to the boys' excited chants of:

'Panafisssssssssssssm, Panafissssssssssssssm, Panafissssssssssssssm.'

with retorts of:

'You are Carried' 'You are Carried!'

I continued deploying flaming rhetoric, followed by a crescendo of sounds, which transformed into yells of *'Yankari', 'Yankari'*. The yells sounding like some melody sung in the Hausa language did not matter because I milked and relished it. In scenes reminiscent of rock stars, I was dominating the dining hall, the venue, of the campaign trail's climax. The hall had been the scene of so much drama, where prefects held sway, where prayers were said and was one of the oldest and more historic buildings in King's College. On the top floor lay the Hyde Johnson's House, the first boarding house in the school. King's College, Lagos had a great history and tradition which could be traced back to 20 September 1909 as King's School before being transformed into a 'College', it has maintained its original site on Lagos Island, adjacent to Race Course now renamed, Tafawa Balewa Square. The origins of the School's philosophy had always been a conservative one, one designed to maintain the status quo:

> *"To provide for the youth of the colony a higher general education than that supplied by the existing Schools, to prepare them for Matriculation Examination of the University of London and to give a useful course of Study to those who intend to qualify for Professional life or to enter Government or Mercantile service."*

Anyway, it was at this venue in this bastion of conservatism, the dinning hall, in 1983 that I made my final campaign speech, which was embroidered in rhythm, sprinkled with quotations. It began with the uttering of the following words:

"Boys and girls, ladies and gentlemen, fellow compatriots."

With the opening line borrowed from my debating routine, my voice ricocheting against the dinning hall walls, I drove the boys into heights of uncontrollable frenzy. In measured tones, I sought to define 'Panafism' as:

"The making use of pen and paper, supported with facts and figures in achieving an objective with the application of other means where inevitable".

To them the words, *'other means where inevitable'* were code words for radical action and they loved it. Then I carefully positioned myself, tilting my head, allowing me to introduce more rhythm into my speech. In the words I laced together, I promised to go everywhere, any length, up to great heights and into the furthest depths to protect the rights of the students. My speech was unashamedly welfarist in content and minced no words in reference to the *'powers'* that be. It was as if I was seeking an open confrontation with *'power'*. On top of the central table where I stood I proceeded to reassure the crowd gathered that I would be no ordinary Secretary but a 'people's Secretary'. My campaigning ability, the ability *'to Speak Truth to Power'* had been horned through the last few years of class-to-class proselytising of the Christian gospel, which earned me, the nickname 'Pastor'. It was not unusual in the earlier days for 'Gbemi Kehinde, Ayo Onafeko, Ayo Oyewole and others to hail me with the words:

'Esa ami Pastor, ani esa mi Pastor!'

I am not sure they were ever able to decipher what I was about, for certain they knew I had acquired the habit for turning the other cheek when physically attacked by my fellow classmates and that I had foresworn the pastime of chasing girls. It was always a temptation for them to see whether 'pastor' would actually turn the other cheek when slapped and many times, they got the proof that I would.

71

My intrusion into the realm of politics was certainly not accidental but was due to a constellation of events. On reflection, I realise my previous experiences conspired to make this happen. I had observed that even when I was proselytising, God made it possible for people to listen with rapt attention. I noticed that it gave me some sort of rapport, identity and self-confidence. This sowed within me a deep hunger to voice out my inner yearnings and to articulate my ideas. At a recent reunion of classmates from my old primary school many said they were unable to recognise in me, the potential for the garb, my response to them whilst reflecting, was that when:

"When I found Jesus I found my voice."

I believe my discovery of the Lord Jesus Christ accounted for the major transformation in my life. I am certain that without him I would still be a shivering, moody and nervous wreck in front of any crowd.

Bibi Paiko my campaign manager and the Chairman of the 'Panafism Orientation Committee' was a dark, slightly tall boy with an ample bulk. He possessed an easygoing manner, which endeared him to many. He spoke fluent Yoruba language even though he was from the North of Nigeria and he would always tease me in the Yoruba vocabulary with words to the effect:

"Panaf you need to settle me with some cash o!"

I always left his presence ribbing with laughter. He was very effective in ensuring that my message and ideas were floating around out there in the school. There were others who helped me spread the message like 'Wale Babatunde my childhood friend, whose staunch support I will never forget. His mother was a very close friend of my mother's. They had both grown up in Usi-Ekiti where Wale's maternal grandfather had served as a Priest. It was with great sadness that I learnt that a few years after we left the school both of these remarkable stalwarts had lost their lives in tragic circumstances. It was more poignant in 'Wale's case as I had met up with him in King's College a few weeks before he died.

The message was that *'Panaf'* was not like the boys of old, but was a more professional, sophisticated and disciplined campaigner, determined to leave his mark on the scene and in the annals of King's College history. He was prepared to tread the path where other candidates had been unable to follow; he was prepared to deploy and advance oratory and rhetoric to great effect, to propagate and to raise the level of debate in order to introduce a new ideal.

I encountered some barriers to my newly found ambition, which included institutional opposition from some School Prefects and established convention. However, I choose to defy convention that restricted the running for the Office of Secretary to the Students' Council to Lower Six Formers. Having meticulous studied the Student's Council's constitution I duly submitted my nomination papers daring the powers that be to exclude me from the process. I was in my Fifth Form; I had previously been elected the Assistant Secretary before the PKC aka 'Bingo' suspended the Council. In response to the suspension I had spent a year traversing what seemed like the length and breadth of Lagos meeting with Old Boys like Mr. Akintunde Asalu (a previous Secretary of the Students' Council), Alhaji 'Femi Okunnu (The first Secretary of the Students Council), etc.

Alhaji Lateef Olufemi Okunnu had served in the government of General Yakubu Gowon as the Federal Commissioner for Works and Housing, he was known for his trademark bow tie and his dark glasses, he had very light complexioned skin and indulged in his love of BMW cars. He owned an iconic silver one, a 1973 BMW Bavaria 3.0S Sedan model with registration LX 1. It was rumoured that he always shipped it aboard for its annual service. One of his notable contributions to the school was the construction of a squash court; Alhaji had used his good offices to facilitate its construction on the grounds of the school. However, by the time I was admitted to the school, the squash court had also assumed an alternative purpose, it was the place where scores were settled, where fists and kicks reigned and an arena that encouraged the settlement of disagreements. It had the advantage of being secluded so that any pummeling of your victim was carried out without any unwarranted interruptions.

I recall an occasion where John Ogwo challenged our local champion Gbemi Kehinde to a duel in the squash court when we were in Form One C. Gbemi was diminutive in stature but broad and sturdily built and an experienced street fighter, he could fight dirty, grabbing all bodily parts in plain sight. In John Ogwo's case he was very tall and possessed exceptionally long legs and his arms had an extended reach. The date and time was set for the duel and many boys took opposing sides, we felt that Gbemi would come out on top. However, using height and reach and his knowledge of the martial arts, John Ogwo decimated Gbemi, gave him a lesson or two and for a while this comprehensive mauling subdued Gbemi, it was quite an upset.

I recall my first experience with Alhaji 'Femi Okunnu in 1983. In search of him, I had initially gone to his old office on Wakeman Street, Yaba, near Sabo a Lagos suburb where his legal practice was based. I was advised that he had relocated to Number 3 Karimu Kotun Street on Victoria Island, Lagos. He extended great courtesy to me by writing to me on his letter headed paper and scheduling an appointment to meet with me on a later date. It was a letter I showed off to friends and family with great aplomb.

When I got there on the scheduled Sunday at 12 noon for the arranged meeting at his newly constructed home/office in what was then a newer part of Victoria I had to wait till 4pm to see him in his octagon shaped office painted in subdued version of green. I did not mind the long wait for this was the beginning of a professional relationship with the law firm of Alhaji 'Femi Okunnu & Co. In 1989, he was kind enough to offer me the opportunity of undertaking my Solicitor's Articles in his firm. He would share with me stories of his 'socialist antecedents' and described himself as a *'Socialist with a conservative tinge'*. He was an immensely devout Muslim who loved people of all religions. I believe the fact his family had a mixture of Christians and Muslim may have been a factor in this. Alhaji approached me at the KCOBA dinner at Eko Hotel in 1990 and enquired about my future plans. I confided in him my decision to return to England but he urged me to reconsider and come and work in his firm. It was a kind offer but one to which I had to decline. In later years, he served as the President of the King's College Old Boy's Association and became a Senior Advocate of Nigeria. The meeting with the Alhaji was part of my intent on convincing the Old Boys of the need to urge 'Bingo' to rescind his suspension of the Students' Council. I also wrote to the President of the King's College Old Boys' Association (KCOBA) to highlight my concerns.

Thankfully, the Council was now reinstated and I was convinced that I as *'the deliverer'* deserved the ultimate prize. However, a classmate, a friend and a Prefect presented as my stiffest obstacle. He was the coolest boy on the horizon; Emmanuel Obe aka *'O Reggae'* a class act, handsome in every respect and a heartthrob to the many teeming admiring secondary school girls he met while playing basketball for the school. It was his charisma I had to contend with, he was one I respected and one I hoped never to run against.

Emmanuel 'Wale Obe's story was similar to mine, our paths, almost identical for we had lost our fathers so early but now we were on opposing paths. His father had been serving as the Nigerian Ambassador to Senegal when he drowned in a swimming pool. Obe and I had a close but eclectic relationship. Then there was the likable and photogenic 'Tunji Omole whose intrusion into the race we felt could cause an upset. He was very charming and possessed an infectious and disarming smile, there was something of a radical edge about him. He was a scion of the Brewery magnate and philanthropist Chief Lawrence Omole from Ilesha.

My early experiences of Students' Council election campaigns came from the cartoon posters drawn and posted on the school walls with outlandish claims like *'Hulk says Uncle Joe is the rightest man for the job.'* They were usually jolly and jovial affairs and many of the junior boys with an artistic flare were recruited to sketch and design some of these posters. It was a privilege to be chosen and seeing my own artwork displayed on school walls was a source of immense pride. But my campaign for the Office of Secretary was novel and influenced directly from my understanding of Students' Union politics, it was a novel approach and I perfected a tactic I had used in my previous campaign, issuing a full-fledged manifesto and churned out regularly *'typed'* articles cum press releases, explaining what 'Panafism' was all about. I remember that I sketched and designed a giant campaign poster of myself with my eyes bathed in optimism projected towards the heavens, a clue I believe of where my help came from, the creator of heaven and earth.

In an election strategy reminiscent of Nigerian Students' Union politics the 'Panafism Orientation Committee', the campaign group I set up, ensured that every nook and corner of the King's College campus, the toilets, the showers, the kitchen and the dormitories had a poster that just contained the bold inscription 'PANAFISM'. There was a refrain that even when you were 'blocking' (using the toilet) you saw 'PANAFISM', in the showers while taking your wash it was 'PANAFISM', when you woke up early at dawn you saw it. Everywhere you looked there was the inescapable fact of 'PANAFISM'. The effect of this was that 'PANAFISM' became a buzzword, one you could not escape from. We went as far as planting many boys in the dinning hall to herald and proclaim loudly 'PANAFISM' when the campaign was officially declared open.

My *'political mentor'*, Panaf Olajide Olakanmi, the President of the University of Lagos Students' Union, from 1982 to 1983, had tutored me extensively. I was in the habit of visiting his office or room in 'Baluba Kingdom' unannounced. We had formed a close bond in the University canteen over many meals and he was always generous to me with his time. It is to him that I owe the ideology, 'Panafism'; it is to him I owed my initial political strategy. My campaign was therefore different and seemed better planned than those of my contemporaries, I thought it ran like a well-oiled insurgency. The result of the campaign was a testimony to the fact that I won with 609 votes to my nearest rival's 103 votes. But upon sober reflection I now believe I won not because of fancy things I said but because I gave voice to a story and an ideal that the boys could claim as theirs. I sowed within them a hope that their lot could be better, that together we could make a difference.

Now with victory attained, my eyes danced around in self-confidence as I shifted and became transfixed on what I considered to be the ultimate prize, power. The sheer size of my mandate meant there was always the temptation to exercise power in an undisguised and indiscriminate fashion. But this was just the beginning; on the morning after my victory, there was none of the customary honeymoon period that you could expect. I met with Mr. Fabiyi, the London educated Chairman of the Students' Council who had recently returned from England. He was a Lagosian but was unlike the conventional Nigerian teacher, he was constantly bristling with ideas and was very effervescent. In our first meeting in the Biology Laboratory's side office, he sipped his cup of tea, peered at me from behind his glasses with his slightly crossed-eyes, slithering in opposite directions as he congratulated me. I could sense from observation that he was trying to unravel the enigma called 'Panaf'. It was obvious he had followed the campaign closely and he added he was my fan but made it clear the PKC, Mr. A. A. Ibegbulam was very concerned about my victory and was on the warpath. Later in that day as expected, I received an invitation to meet with the PKC in his office.

'WITH GRITTED TEETH'

In the briefest of moments, in my febrile mind I wondered how I should respond to the PKC's invitation. Senior boys before me had nicknamed the Principal 'Bingo' because they felt he always barked out orders indiscriminately, they were used to Mr. M.O. Imanna, his more restrained and under stated predecessor and the stable but brief interregnum provided by the Acting PKC Mr. Akinruli aka 'Ire' who years later in the 2000s became the substantive PKC. I came to a resolution with gritted teeth to face down the PKC. I was certain that he was aware of all my not so 'clandestine' meetings with the King's College Old Boys and I had no doubt that he considered me a rabid and infantile radical, an unyielding non-conformist and one who needed to be reined in.

However, I bore a heavy weight upon my mind, it was the clear electoral mandate I had received. The mandate provided me with fortification and confidence, and allowed me to draw strength from my convictions, summoning political capital I had just acquired as I marched through the rows of classrooms on my way to see the PKC. I reasoned I had come a long way, from the uncertain first former who was grief laden to a confident teenager with the destiny of every King's College boy entwined with his. I had arrayed myself in my best whites, a short sleeve shirt and white pair of matching trousers. I ascended the two floors of the staircase, went through the administrative offices and emerged into the outer office of the PKC. His confidential secretary confirmed I was expected, the cream coloured painted wooden doors in patio style flung open to reveal the PKC seated at his desk wearing a black bean coloured suit and a crimson coloured tie carefully resting on his matching sparking white shirt. The PKC was a diminutive man with slightly bulging eyes and a pronounced forehead accentuated by his receding hairline. He observed me slowly through the top of his glasses, perched precariously on his nose and with the nod of his head, he acknowledged me, as I remained standing in his presence. I felt the tension in the room, it was palpable and one could slice through it with a knife.

The PKC dressed resplendent in his dark blue coloured academic robe on top of his suit worn traditionally at all assemblies had earlier that morning officially announced 'Rotimi Ashley-Dejo aka 'AD99' and myself as the Students' Council's Assistant

78

Secretary-elect and Secretary-elect respectively. As I approached the stage where all the teaching staff sat, to receive the customary congratulatory handshake from the PKC, the formality of the moment was punctuated with shouts of *'Panafisssssssssssssm, Panafisssssssssssssm'*. The hall rang out with affirmation of my ideology and the PKC was left in no doubt about the popularity of my mandate.

The PKC's office was a room situated in what looked like an 18th century attic. From the outside, it had pretentions of grandeur and it had in the early 1900s served as some staff residence. As the meeting progressed in his office, I was disarmed by his conciliatory gesture towards me. I studied his face intently as he spoke; he impressed upon me the need to be responsible in my new role and assured me that he looked forward to working with the new Council. The tension drained out of the room as I sank back in relief and then choosing my words with care, I responded by explaining my priorities and indicating that I looked forward to the fulfillment of my electoral mandate. It appeared that Mr. Fabiyi's warnings had proved to be exaggerated for now in fact it was a damp squib. 'Bingo's' calmness had denied me the opportunity to display my much-vaunted *'revolutionary credentials'*.

We got down to the business of steering the affairs of the Council; I decided from the onset that I needed an office, a secretariat where we could establish the machinery for delivery. The room adjourning the old tuck shop under Hyde Johnson's House, adjacent to the dinning hall and beside the common room met with my approval and I simply appropriated it. In times past it served as the store room of the tuck shop but we painstakingly transformed it to the new secretariat of the King's College Students' Council. I acquired two tables and two chairs for 'Rotimi Ashley-Dejo and myself.

In consultation with the Chairman of the Council, I summoned the first Council meeting. All the councillors, representing class forms, various clubs and societies were present resplendent in full school uniform, the senior boys robed in their *'magical'* blue blazers, white-striped blue ties and others with white coats. The President of the Council, the PKC was present to inaugurate the Council and swear in the new officers. After giving a speech declaring the new Council open, the PKC departed and left us to get on with the business of constituting the *'government'*.

"Point of Orderrrrr, Point of Orderrrrrrr, Mr. Chairman! ...."

These were the staccato of words that rang out from various corners of the lecture theatre ricocheting against the walls. There were intermittent pauses in between as councillors struggled to catch the dancing eyes of the Chair; from the front where I sat, it was impossible to discern where all the sounds were all coming from. The theatre normally used as the classroom of the Lower Six Biology had been transformed into the Council Chambers. It was a room designed with concrete elevated floors, placing each row of desks on a different level and at its front was a huge oak, immovable table with a hand washbasin where the officers of the Council sat.

The elections were held into the various Council Committees, Finance, Games, Health, Information and Social. The Finance and Social Committees were always the most sought after and keenly contested because of their revenue generating potential. It was rumoured that these Committees had been the scene of many scandals. The members of Committees were duly constituted with the election of various Heads. Emezie an old friend of mine, who had earlier contested with me for the position of Assistant Secretary, emerged as the Head of Cabinet. Ntima, the Head of Finance, my close ally and a member of the 'Panafism Orientation Committee' Olugbemiga Serrano was elected the Head of Information Committee and Musa K a veteran of Mckay House Head of Games Committee. In line with the arcane constitutional provisions of the Council, I became the Cabinet Secretary. I maintained the records of the Cabinet deliberations and summoned its meetings in conjunction with the Head of Cabinet. The new Cabinet members took their seats at the left hand side of the Chambers towards to entrance facing the Chairman, the Secretary and Assistant Secretary of the Council.

In my earlier discussions with Uncle 'Wole Ayeni who was a Clerk of the Nigerian National Assembly we had already foreseen the potential for a power tussle of some sort. He pointed to the ambiguity of the Student's Council's constitution, a blue coloured booklet, which lay in the fact that it provided for the Head of Cabinet to assume a role akin to that of a Head of Government but left the position of the school's elected Secretary in what seemed to be a position of a glorified clerk of the house. In other words, it seemed I was simply a civil servant of the Council. However, the clues to the powers of the Secretary's Office lay concealed in a provision for regular liaison with the PKC and another provision to act as Chairman of the Council in the absence of the substantive Chairman. We concluded the constitution had sown the seed for future conflict, however, I had a clear mandate to deliver a manifesto rooted in welfarist goals from the students and I was determined to deliver.

In my detour into memory lanes littered with the experiences of my predecessors I realised that they also operated under the same constitutional provisions with little difficulty. We had Telema Princewill aka *'Printe…. Alacrity'*, very charismatic and a Cadet Unit Commandant, as Secretary and yet there was no crises with his Cabinet. We also had 'Tunde Akinrinmisi and who seemed to have cordial relations with his Cabinet. So why was it going to be different in my case? What was in my make up that would ensure that planted deep within me was the propensity for domination? I sometimes find myself transported to another realm thinking maybe at those times, in my early youth I was trying to compensate for my lost years in school or my failure to be appointed a prefect. The truth is that I was reserved and aloof towards those who had become my classmates and in my pride, I sought to keep what I imagined to be a respectable distance.

In any case that was the conundrum I faced, but also there was a certain arrogance that convinced me of the justness of my position. I believed that after the role I played in the struggle to get the Council reinstated and with the possession of an overwhelming electoral mandate, the boys owed me all. I had been on the Council for five years as a councilor and knew the constitution quite intimately and I was determined to use it to the advantage of my constituents. I faced a discernable tension between power and service. I knew my time was limited and I was determined to achieve a lasting legacy in the time that I had left. I was convinced that the time for delivery was at hand!

'POST TENEBRAS SPERO LUCEM'

I saw my assumption of office on the Council as the affirmation of my identity and linked it intrinsically with the exercise of power. However, subsequent events proved there was more complexity to the issue of my identity.

In 1984, it was three months into the Council year and I had it up to my neck with what I considered the constant snipping and display of *'petty politics'* from my cabinet colleagues. My ego had become exaggerated by my proximity to power and I reasoned that since Panaf Olajide Olakanmi had schooled me in the art of student union politics I could not allow these *'young upstarts'* to upstage me. In my musings, dripping with arrogance, I thought and asked:

"What did they understand about politics?"

At the time I thought it was all about 'Panafism', an ideology, but upon reflection, I now know it was more about the exercise of raw power and some remorse begins to creep in! My subsequent doctoral research, focusing on *'Speaking Truth to Power'* confirmed what was an inconvenient truth about me in those very early stages of my political life.

Post tenebras spero lucem means, *'After darkness a hope for light'*, Spero Lucem: *'A hope for light'* was the motto that the founding fathers bequeathed King's College, Lagos. All of us who were privileged to have sauntered through the gates into King's College, were drilled with the idea, that no matter the hopelessness of our circumstance, the barriers we faced, no matter what path we had trod before, that at the end of it all lay hope.

On my first day in King's College, Lagos I arrived in my mother's cream coloured iconic Volkswagen Beetle and stepped out into a morning air filled with clouds of dust created by the Harmattan breeze. The Harmattan has sometimes been described as something that comes with terror and menace with a strong naked touch of nature poisoning the cold morning. The morning of that day certainly felt like that. Earlier in

1974, my mother had sold the K70 Volkswagen sedan my father bought because of the incessant mechanical problems it caused her.

In the imported version of the Volkswagen Beetle, she acquired was one of the most iconic cars ever produced, it was a classic and it had so many myths woven around it. I remember the rattle of its air-cooled four-cylinder engine and the feeling of having my ankles cooled by the floor-level heating vent. The seats were covered in black mock patterned leather. We called it *'Ijapa'* a Yoruba word for tortoise. This reflected the strength of its bodywork but also the ponderous but assured manner in which it moved when driven on the roads of Lagos. There were rumours that it could leap over the ditches but for my mother it was simply a workhorse, a utility vehicle. The car was almost always filled up with cartons of beverages and provisions she purchased for the buttery she ran and managed.

With my mother in tow, we were confronted with the brooding presence of Mr. Njoku the head security man who prised the gates open. He was a very serious character, spotting some wildly growing whiskers, had pronounced 'K' shaped legs that seemed to constantly knock against each other as he walked. He always carried a menacing black coloured baton. I paced myself and walked through the gates on 5th December 1977. On that day, I was oblivious to its immaculately kept lawns, its neatly arranged classrooms and its well-stocked library. What beguiled me was not its long and chequered history, what excited me was not the first class facilities it possessed, what amazed me was certainly not its record of academic excellence. It was the exercise of power exhibited by the prefects, the charisma of the School Captain Obineche, the tall light complexioned boy with Afro cut, and the opportunity to appropriate one's democratic right from an early age. At a stage when the military rule was still a feature of the Nigerian life and we could not vote for our own government, in King's College we had that right. It was much later that I appreciated the diversity of the varied origins of its students was what really made the school truly unique.

I was happy to be re-united with all former University of Lagos Staff School pupils, Afolabi Omidiji aka 'Wheezee', Oluyinka Olutoye aka 'Toy', Dolapo Ogunmekan, Akitayo Ojo, Ayodele Onafeko, 'Segun Alawaiye, 'Folarin Ososami, Ayorinde

Oyewole, Omotayo Johnson, Joel Ugborogho, Anthony Uduebo aka 'Ebo', 'Tola Durojaiye and Joseph Ownwuchekwa aka 'JAMO'.

It would now seem that my earlier natural shyness and awkwardness only masked a deep hunger and thirst for power. At age eleven, I was moody, introverted and needy, and then only sketching and drawing pictures and cartoons would suffice. As years wore on, deep down in my subconscious, this became inadequate and I concluded that only the acquisition of power could offer me the perfect antidote. I was an average artist and liked to scribble on every desk I owned, it was a way of rebuffing any invasions and claiming my own personal space. I would draw a portrait of myself with the inscriptions: *'Oje The Power'* and *'Oje The Pirate'*. In my dream world, power is what seemed to matter. It was this that seduced me to position myself for election as vice-class captain in my First Form, winning and going on to ably assist the captain, 'Wale Goodluck.

One incident that occurred while in Form One C still rankles me. I had started the exotic hobby of stamp collecting and built up a very interesting album with a range of sets of rare stamps from all over the world. I had acquired a few sets by raiding my father's trunk boxes and asking relatives for old letters. The generous courtesy of 'Fola Odetoyinbo, gifted me a green coloured stamp album where I compulsively arranged my collection. 'Fola was also kind enough to give me some rare British stamps to enrich my limited collection. Many in my class admired it and other boys were avid stamp collectors, and it became some sort of ritual pageant to display our respective collections at the lunchtime. However, one day I forgot the album in my class desk overnight. I prayed that the next morning I would arrive in school and retrieve the collection. I was certain that it would be there for that was not the first time I had forgotten it in my desk. The next morning I searched my desk frantically but discovered it was not there. It became apparent that it had been stolen with all its prized contents! 'Fola was not well pleased when he discovered I had not been the meticulous keeper and collector he had imagined. That incident terminated any pursuit or desire to collect stamps until I returned to England in the 1990s.

With that side attraction, out of the way my fleeting affair with power was also abruptly terminated after I had a profound and unforgettable encounter with the Lord Jesus

Christ following the requirement that I repeat the Second Form. For a while, the lure and attractions of power became a distant relative as I was downcast and contemplating the misfortune of repeating a class. It is under these circumstances that I heard this boy, Nkem Animalu reading from the Bible, the book of Revelations with his slight American accent. He expounded it to those of us who would listen and after a few days he invited us to make a commitment, without any hesitation on 10th October 1979 I made my personal commitment to the Lord Jesus Christ.

Afterwards I drew very close to Ifeanyi Onah a fellow believer. Brother 'Yomi Adewale an Old Boy of King's College, was my first real Christian mentor and I received much encouragement from him but there was also Brother 'Tunde Oladunmiye a Computer Science postgraduate student who for six years was the constant mentor at my side. At the time, he was the 'landlord' to Bishop Francis Oke, the President of the Lagos Varsity Christian Union (LVCU) in his single bed Jaja Hall room. Through his role as the superintendent of the Unilag Chapel Sunday School, I eventually became a Sunday school teacher whilst at secondary school. All the due care and attention I received from him combined to make my uttermost concern the winning of souls and the total eradication of all misdemeanors from King's College. I developed an obsession with school rules and acquired a puritanical fervour. I came to believe that I alone could actively *'sabotage'* all evil and this led my classmates to nick name me *'load carrier'*. They even conjured up a chorus to capture my newly acquired zeal:

"Load don't break my back, load don't break my back."

I suspect that they began to sense that I had become ponderous and a fun killer who sought to carry the entire weight of the school upon his delicate frame.

In the midst of all these, my fascination with whom I imagined my father was grew. He wore glasses while alive so I took to wearing a pair of glasses I found strewn amongst Uncle 'Wole Ayeni's possessions. I wanted to look so much like him, with time, at age thirteen my wish was granted when an eye test at the Lagos General Hospital confirmed I had poor eyesight. Now I could look more like my father and probably acquire his first class brain and achievements!

85

As the years rolled by I became a regular feature on the Students' Council but this was simply because many boys did not want the hassle of being a councillor. I took an active part in its elections, and in 1981 became a campaign manager to Oluyinka Olutoye for the post of Assistant Secretary. I also became a keen supporter of Ayodeji Awoyingbo who contested for the same post in the following year. With closer proximity to power, slowly but gradually, the thirst for it began to re-surface. In the meantime my academic progress had stalled and I had lost another year, failing my Third Form promotion examinations. It seems from then on my love affair with power was destined for rekindling. I think it was a quest for relevance and a search for my father's memory, which re-awakened that craving and this sets the background to the rest of this chapter.

When my proximity to the Student's Council is considered, it is not difficult to understand how power seduced me and the affair was rekindled. In every Council meeting I attended, every debate was punctuated with *'Points of Order! Points of Information!'* At each meeting the more experienced councillors were able to quote in verbatim various standing orders and from copious portions of the constitution. It was an awesome spectre to behold I suspected they had crammed it the evening before. Even at that stage as teenagers in the Council, mastery of the chambers was achieved through the following attributes: quick wit, agility and intelligence. The only order of precedence required in Council debates was not seniority of class but the mastery of facts and figures. To our credit, we never exchanged blows, curses or overturned furniture as so often happens in some legislatures.

The Students' Council's constitution had a requirement that at every Council meeting the Cabinet shall submit a report of its activities in the intervening period, it also required the report to be debated upon and approved. The provision that followed made it clear that a defeat of the report would require the resignation of the Cabinet. In 1984, three months into the Council year prior to the next Council meeting, the Cabinet members advised me at the regular Cabinet meeting about their inability to prepare the required report because of the demands on their time caused by our mock GCE 'O' Level examination preparations. I understood the implications of their inaction but blinded with lust for power I kept uncharacteristically silent and refused to offer them any advice.

I was acutely aware of the constitutional provision to submit a Cabinet report at every meeting and was determined to keep this fact a closely guarded secret and only to be revealed as a weapon of offence during the impending Council meeting. I intimated my good and childhood friend, 'Emeka Nwaojigba about my intentions and as always he urged me to remain steadfast.

In a curious twist, events conspired to prevent the Council Chairman, Mr. Fabiyi from attending the next meeting due to a clash of engagements. Under those circumstances, the constitution made me the acting Chairman. The meeting was convened on a Tuesday afternoon on a day when the heat was stifling and oppressive, some portend to the actions I would precipitate. After routine deliberations in the Council meeting, responding to various *'Points of Order and Information'* we reached the climax, the submission of the Cabinet report. In a calm but calculated manner, I requested the submission of the report I knew was non-existent. The Head of Cabinet responded that there was no report and sought to explain the reason for the omission. I referred him to the relevant parts of the constitution and the implication of a non-submission. An eerie silence descended upon the chambers, as the mist settled and the implications became clearer. Then with my heart drumming with anticipation, unable to believe the Cabinet had wandered into my trap I threw the matter open for debate on the floor of the House.

It was clear to me the letter of the constitution had been breached, but it was not certain how the Council would respond. It was also unclear to the many observers how I would exercise power as the acting Chairman. The questions whirring around my mind were:

> *"How should power be exercised? Should I temper justice with mercy?"*

At that moment, I slumped back in the chair and allowed the debate to rage! However, as events unfolded in the Council it struck me:

> *"That every path to change was one, which many of my*
> *ancestors had followed before, every strategy for survival*
> *had probably been selflessly explored as they moved from*

87

town to town. Now even with my best intentions, in allowing the dissolution of the Cabinet to proceed was I not in danger of betraying them and ending up further removed from the struggles of the boys I purported to serve?"

'PYRRHIC VICTORY?'

The debate raged on for far too long into the evening, past the start of our suppertime, the siren, which dominated so much of school life, had sounded off for supper. In earlier times it was a bell that one of my seniors, Igbokwe had the privilege of ringing as the bellboy but due to technological advancements, a siren had been installed and the bell was consigned for use in the dinning hall. The tradition had it that prior to the technological innovation a fourth former was selected and appointed for bellboy duties.

There was always a lot of decorum surrounding the Council Chambers, we had to bow to the Chairman as we came in and do the same as we took our leave. It had a gallery at the back where various constituents could observe their councillors at work. In the past Council, meetings started at 3pm and lasted until late at night. This acted as a disincentive to day students wishing to participate fully in the Council proceedings. I experienced the inconveniences as a day student of having to flee a few meetings in mid flow in order to catch the last bus home or get a lift from my friend Cllr. Adebiyi Mabadeje, previously a commissioner in the Lagos State government of Nigeria. Therefore, one of the first reforms we instituted once in 'power' was to ensure the brevity of Council meetings and its accessibility to all students.

But this meeting was unusual, I was presiding magisterially from the chair (in reality this was a tool which raised the height of the presiding officer) and we were debating the fate of the Cabinet because of the non-submission of its report. The arguments went back and forth and as various councillors ploughed on with it, it eventually rested on whether we could vote on a non-existent report. I was scrupulous enough not to betray any partiality at this stage; I bided my time and concealed my intentions behind a fixed grin. All through the debate only one thought seem to matter, the opportunity to ensure my complete and utter domination of the Council. Later in life I came to understand some truth in the words of Professor 'Wole Soyinka that:

> *"… truth for me is freedom, is self-destination. Power is*
> *domination, control, and therefore a selective form of truth,*
> *which is a lie."*[5]

But at this time and on this occasion, I admit I was firmly on the side of power.

I saw my role on the Council as some sort of compensation for missing out on being appointed a prefect. The truth is I had always fantasied about being a prefect, but because I had caused the PKC too much trouble, it was never going to happen. In 1983, I had been elected Chairman of the Food Committee at the start of the first term and I engineered plans for a food boycott in protest at the continuing poor quality of meals served. I was also in constant touch with Old Boys suggesting to them that the PKC against all school traditions was about to introduce uniforms for the boarding house!

On the night before the appointment of a new set of prefects, my friend, a prefect had suggested to me in confidence that I had been recommended to the PKC for appointment. I barely slept a wink, the next morning I awoke excited and full of anticipation; I wore my best whites, fully expecting to be announced as a new prefect during the School Assembly. I was to be bitterly disappointed but was consoled that at least Akinlusi, a more deserving classmate was appointed in my stead.

My discrete inquiries about what transpired suggested I was considered too much of an unyielding non-conformist and a loose cannon to be let anywhere near the institution of Prefectship. The truth is that until recently I deluded myself that I might have been a good material for Prefectship. It was not to be, but here I was as acting Chairman of the King's College Students' Council presiding over a crucial and decisive debate, I felt I was at the height of my powers and the closest I could get to the exercise of the power and patronage of a prefect.

---

[5] Soyinka, Wole (2009): Conversations with History. Available at: http://saharareporters.com/art-life/conversations-history-wole-soyinka-uc-berkeley

The debate was dominated by Cllrs. 'Emeka Nwaojigba and 'Niran Ade-Onojobi, the School Captain and scion of the legendary Ade-Onojobi family on the side of impeachment and Cllrs. Oluwagbemiga Serrano and Ntima on the side of the status quo. The debate had reached a stalemate with neither side willing to concede any ground. I sensed the mood of the house was evenly split, suppertime was about to begin and exhaustion had set in. I felt there was no choice but to ask for a division and I called for a vote on the motion, which was framed:

"That the Cabinet report be rejected and the Cabinet resign forthwith."

The vote was taken and supervised by 'Rotimi Ashley-Dejo aka 'AD99', the acting Secretary and the results confirmed the Council was evenly split. We were deadlocked! This presented me with the opportunity I craved and the constitution became my useful ally, for it stated that:

"In the event of a tie the Chairman shall have the casting vote."

Slowly and deliberately, I rose from the chair, descended on to the floor of the chambers, pacing up and down in front of the large oak table and launched into a verbal assault on the Cabinet. I included in my speech illustrations of glowing references, recounting and cataloguing the sacrifices, I imagined I had made for the Council. The whole spectacle seemed as if I was proceeding to trample upon my colleagues while they laid prostate and to disparage them. In this unbridled display of power, this was certainly not my finest hour.

Many councillors had expected that I would offer the Cabinet a reprieve, that true to my Christian profession I would offer mercy and cast the vote in favour of them to remain. This was not to be because I sensed an opportunity for retribution, I ruled that the constitution was clear and I had no discretion but to give a casting vote on the side of their dismissal. The truth was that I was responding to what I considered an audacious challenge to my mandate from the Cabinet. I had the option of adjourning the meeting for the more neutral arbiter, the Chairman to rule on the issues at hand but I was not prepared to consider that.

What seemed like a long silence, descended upon the Council chambers, the tension was palpable. I could have sworn that I imagined from outside, howling of winds, flapping sounds of the wings of bats flying back from their insect hunting, interrupting us, as the full import of my decision became clearer. The acting Chair (the Secretary) had dissolved the Cabinet, it now seemed the words of William Butler Yeats but popularised by Chinua Achebe had been brought to life in our Council chamber:

> *"Things fall apart; the centre cannot hold; mere anarchy is loosed upon the world."*

Without providing the dismissed Cabinet the opportunity to re-group, I swiftly adjourned the meeting *sine die*. But that did not conclude the drama, it was simply the beginning of many scenes to be re-enacted in a long and drawn out night. The drama led to a direct confrontation between the prefects and I, it seemed the mask had slipped and the intoxicating aroma of power finally held me a captive. The truth was I found the fragrance of power so overpowering and so irresistible.

'ITS NOT YET UHURU'

Uhuru is the Swahili word for freedom and it became the name of a political organisation centered around the principles of Pan-Africanism, which advocated the economic and political liberation of Black Africans on both the continent of Africa and in the diaspora. It is fitting that I start this chapter exploring the illusionary nature of the freedom I thought the acquisition of power might fetch me.

The school playing fields opposite the Council chambers, where my brother, Adebowale displayed his mastery as a football defender, had long been deserted. The dust had settled and the winds whistled with tension. In the midst of this, I needed to consolidate my last move on the chessboard of power. As part of my strategy to shape events, on the way to the dinning hall, I engaged Cllr. 'Niran Ade-Onojobi, the School Captain, in a *tete a tete*. My concern was to cement my *'audacious power grab,'* I suggested to him that I needed to address the boys during the dinning hall announcements. I convinced him it was essential to inform them about the monumental changes that had occurred. Without any hesitation, he granted permission, one I suspect the School Captain came to regret afterwards.

In the dinning hall after a meal of rice garnished and layered with stew and a blend of beans and fish the bell sounded, to signal the time for announcements, the air thickened with tension as the clouds of anticipation gathered. Various prefects made routine announcements in what seemed like quick succession but I paid scant attention to them.   While this was going on, I got more impatient and I thought:

> *"…. This is my time, this is my hour, and I need to speak now!"*

My eyes danced around with anticipation and after Prefect Uzodike of McKee-Wrights' House had spoken, without warning I rose abruptly and found myself strolling to the front of the Prefects' table placed at the front of the hall. The hall was 'T' shaped and any speaker who stood at the centre could be seen and heard from the three different directions. I bore my files as a prop to indicate a sense of purpose and serious intent; I was still in my full school uniform, with a blue blazer to match. All eyes shifted towards my direction, the focus was intense, students held their gaze and prefects

93

were dazed and into a state of stupor. My voice stern and purposeful, bounced around the columns supporting the structure of the dinning hall:

> *"…. Fellow compatriots, boys, gentlemen, a monumental decision was taken tonight; the Council in its wisdom dissolved the Cabinet. It is regrettable but we must move forward. Pursuant to this all Cabinet, members are now required to hand over all Council property in their possession to the Council Secretariat. Further details will follow about the reconstitution of a new Cabinet in due course. In the meantime, all members of Committees should remain in place and await further instructions. Thank you for your co-operation."*

Immediately after the dramatic announcement the hall broke into uncontrolled chatter, I was told afterwards that the prefects' faces betrayed their fury. I could not see them because they were seated behind me as I addressed the boys. But I did not wait for the aftermath; with the same abruptness, I stormed out of the dinning hall and trod into my office to review the events of the day and to plan with 'AD99', the Assistant Secretary. 'AD99' to his credit thought I had gone too far and too fast this time, but remained loyal. After a decent interval filled with further consultations with 'Emeka Nwaojigba, Bibi and other members of the 'Panafism Orientation Committee' I left for the residence of Mr. Fabiyi to render a full and complete account of my stewardship as acting Chairman. I arrived there with the feeling that the dissolved Cabinet had already met with him.

The role of the Secretary of the Students' Council was not just record keeping; he was also responsible for conveying Council resolutions and bills to the President, the PKC (Principal, King's College) for action. It was his duty to persuade the PKC to respond to the will of the House. Prior to my taking over the office of Secretary, very few bills were ever passed but we had the distinction of passing seven bills by the end of our tenure. The bills addressed a wide range of issues promised in my manifesto and ensured that despite my obvious faults, my popularity remained high and many still greeted me with shouts of *'Panafism, Yankari!'*. Imperviously, I assumed it was all down to me, but in reality, it was a team effort. My office became a refuge for me away from times of study, a place where I could avoid the 'school's lights out', an engine room of ideas, and it also acted as the treasury where the Council funds were kept before its deposit in the bank.

My announcement had set the whole school in uproar and the boys were all in excitetable chatter, huddled together. Rampant rumours abound that I was now more powerful than the prefects. A few boys led by Sanni a fourth former approached me and enquired whether the making of dinning hall announcements would now become a routine by me. Some felt I had broken with tradition, for only prefects should make announcements they reasoned. Outwardly, I appeared supremely confident but inwardly I was pensive and conflicted, and began to wonder whether the path I trod that night was the right one. I mused:

"If my father had been around what would he have counseled?"

It was as if the air had been sucked out of me as I worried about Mr. Fabiyi. I wondered will he offer me his support or would he support the dissolved Cabinet? What of the PKC? He was not my greatest fan, would he reverse my decision and cut me down to size?' My mind exploring, was in a constant whirl!

I retreated across the long forlorn footpaths towards my dormitory in Panes' House, all scantily lit, selected a fresh change of clothes from my wardrobe. I reasoned this was the time for my trademark white '*Danshiki*', black fez cap and pair of black trousers. I reckoned if I was going down, it had to be in style and confidence. I lifted up the bucket of water placed under my bed, had a quick wash with a bowl scooping from it the water in the shower room that had ceased to function due to a malfunction in the power pump. I then wore my clothes and strode out into a dark and uncertain night. As I walked slowly, I was filled with arrogance and a stubborn streak emerged from within me for I still thought my actions had been completely justified.

I filtered through my thoughts, focused on the past, the journeys I made to Victoria Island, Suru-Lere and Akoka, all at my own expense, to get the Council reinstated. The logic replayed in my mind was while these boys were busy playing games, partaking in social endeavours, studying and doing whatever teenagers got up to I was making

95

sacrifices on their behalf. I thought these chaps were seeking to reap where they certainly did not sow. At a time when Godly counsel would have been apt, when prayer might have been the healing balm, I simply leaned upon my own strength and understanding and I certainly was not being very Christian now.

'CHAIRMAN FABIYI'

Mr. Fabiyi, a teacher of Biology was one of the most approachable members of King's College teaching staff; he spoke with a slight British affectation acquired from his years of living and teaching in England. He was the House Master of Hyde Johnson's House but his jovial nature masked a flaw. He was the second Chairman I had worked with, the first being Mr. Sanni Oni Yakubu who was also Panes' House Master. Mr. Fabiyi's flaw was his possession of a volcanic temper which when ignited saw him fire off expletives in many directions. Even a *'self-proclaimed'* radical like me did not wish to incur his wrath, but to his credit, he chaired the Council fairly and with an iron fist. Mr. Fabiyi always walked at a leisurely pace flinging his legs in front of his body and I sometimes wondered how he controlled the seemly involuntary jerky movements of his legs.

I arrived at his residence, a 19th century house built entirely from timber wood, located at the far end of the school grounds. It appeared rather imposing, in the past it had been the residence of the former Vice Principal King's College (VPKC), Mr. Odunewu aka 'Oba' who left in 1978, and later on Mr. Yakubu's, but in reality it was quite small, crammed and rather neglected. I was received calmly, immediately after I settled down into one of his sofas, he let rip and betrayed his concealed fury, he demanded to know what had happened in his absence. Initially he had the impression that I had taken the advantage of his absence to engineer a series of events, which had resulted in a detonation causing unquantifiable chaos!

At my meeting with Mr. Fabiyi, I was armed with the constitution of the Students' Council, I explained to him the circumstances under which the dismissal of the Cabinet had occurred. I displayed the minutes in front of him confirming, the facts that the Cabinet had submitted no report. After some discussion, I was able to convince him that I had done things by the book, the constitution. However, his concern shifted to how I would contend with the PKC. As I emerged from Mr. Fabiyi's house I observed that the skies were filled with darkness, complete blackness because of the moonless night. It was almost 10.15 pm I noted that very soon the siren for the *'lights out'* would sound, time was running out and the darkness was brooding!

Along the walk, on the footpath back to my dormitory I encountered some ex-Cabinet members, their faces congealed with rage, they let it be known in very certain terms that I had betrayed them. They uttered words to the effect:

"Such a betrayal will never stand!"

I smiled and kept my counsel, now, I thought was not a time for recriminations. I reflected a little and regretted the fact that my relationship with Cllr. Serrano who was now the ex-Head of the Information Committee, one of my ardent supporters had become a prime casualty of my decision that night.

I returned to my dormitory very weary but discovered that the School Captain was in the hunt for me. I was puzzled he was searching for me. The School Captain was the only student with his own private room; it was located on the second floor on top of McKee-Wrights' House, the row of boarding house dormitories facing the school main entrance. His room was sparsely furnished but at least it ensured the occupant lived in relative comfort and privacy. I went to see what the fuss was about, approached the School Captain's room only to find him waiting outside. There was no customary welcome into the comfort of his apartment; he door stepped me at the entrance to his room, evidently furious and quivering with astonishment and rage he uttered words to the effect:

"What did you think you were doing, making an announcement in the dinning hall like that?"

He suggested I had undermined the institution of Prefectship and that they were on the warpath. 'Niran Ade-Onojobi and I had history; we were old classmates from Form 2C before I succumbed to the habit of repeating. He was in the Upper Six Arts Form and I in the Fifth Form so the unspoken convention was he could not discipline me. 'Papa' as he was fondly called was a football enthusiast, previously a member of Hyde-Johnson's House and a prolific mid-field player. He had an encyclopedic knowledge of English Football and was a keen collector of many football magazines. Mr. D. Ade-Onojobi, his grandfather had been the oldest living Old Boy and

Housemaster at a time and his father attended King's College. He was therefore steeped in the traditions and history of the school.

Quietly but firmly I reminded him, that he had given me permission, one I sought after the Council proceedings. He admitted the fact but explained that he had expected I would give him space and time to introduce me and shape the context. I was frustrated and I challenged him to do his worst, stating that I was sick and tired of having to offer explanations for my actions and then walked back to my dormitory, and slumped on to my bed. As I drifted off to sleep, I knew that the next day a meeting with the PKC, my old nemesis loomed on the horizon.

The F1 dormitory where I slept was a familiar place to me; it was home to me in my Second Form and hosted formidable senior boys like Osekita, Wilson, Citizen Nwochocha, Frank Inok, Citizen Babalola, Adekola and Citizen Ayo Odunayo etc. They all had varying degrees of influence on me. These were hard but fair *'boys'* and you could not afford to betray any sign of weakness in their presence. There was also Ife Akintunde, my junior who happened to be blind but was very resilient, he was later to achieve the distinction of being one of the *'best students'* in my Law School 1989 year. I recall on a few occasions when minor infractions on my part invited punishment in the form of 'mounting' on top of my locker/wardrobe. I also recall that for weeks in January 1979 I succumbed to a strange illness that sent me to hospital on admission. I missed two weeks of school in the second term because of my mystifying and paralysing illness. The doctors after exhaustive diagnosis indicated I had a *'crisis'* and explained I was a carrier of the sickle cell anemia. My mother actually thought it was my fear of a return to the boarding house rather than my illness that kept me in hospital on admission but she was farther away from the truth.

Now I was in my Fifth Form, one of the three boys, 'Femi Suleiman, the Vice-School Captain and 'Bayo Oyesanya who had spent up to seven years at the school. I felt I had the weight of history upon my fragile shoulders. I was in the midst of boys who were at my beck and call. Keno Achakobe was always dutiful in ensuring my bucket of bathing water was regularly replenished, there was Jimoh aka 'Gawe' who became School Captain after I had left and there was also Prefect Idem Etuk, a fine Christian boy, fair, kind, but firm. My bed was situated at the front door near one of the bay windows opening up into a long veranda, which led to Harman's House on the right and the ground floor on the left. It ensured I always received a cool breeze and certain mosquito bites if my net canopy had holes in it. That night I went into a deep slumber, dreading what the PKC might have in store the next day.

'THE PKC'

The Principal, King's College was by custom abbreviated to PKC. Mr. Augustine. A. Ibegbulam, aka 'Bingo' had been a diplomat at UNESCO in Paris, he was very sophisticated and suave. He was an Old Boy and had been a teacher at the school. In maintaining control over the school, he deployed psychology rather than the brute force of the cane, to drive fear and obedience into the student populace. With the VPKC, Mr. 'Tayo Sofoluwe aka 'Ishano', the strokes and lashings of the cane came as routine expectation when you caused offence, but with the PKC you were never really certain of what awaited you. 'Bingo' bestrode the school grounds like a colossus with the weight of traditions thrust upon his diminutive frame. You crossed him at your own peril; many scampered at the rumours of his approach. Some thought I was playing a dangerous and improbable game when I took on 'Bingo'. But I was re-assured by Jacks aka 'Jakaba', of blessed memory, a previous Vice School Captain and at the time a student in the University of Lagos, that I was on the right path.

My earlier run-ins with the PKC were instructive; he once stopped me whilst I was out in the city of Lagos on an exeat from the boarding house. He beckoned to me as I strode along Tafawa Balewa Square summoning me to his parked chauffeur driven car, a cream coloured Mercedes-Benz 200 with leather seats, to interrogate me. He asked me where I had been and then questioned the legitimacy of my green coloured exeat card. I assured him the exeat was legitimate, pointing to the signature of the Master, but rather than let the matter rest he referred me to Mr. Ibaru aka *James Bond 007'*, the Senior Boarding House Master for further investigation. I was racked with nerves because the exeat's legitimacy was masked by a sinister fact; I had obtained it under some false pretenses to attend the dentist but instead had gone for my GCSE Examinations.

These were unofficial examinations, which a few adventurous Fifth Former, entered for discretely and took ahead of the official examinations as some sort of practice run for the real thing, the West African School Certificate Examinations. I had visions of Mr. Ibaru, the quintessential 'spymaster' inspecting my dentition to establish whether I had received any dental treatment. I made strenuous efforts to re-open a previous gap between my teeth to create the right appearance but failed. In any case, I was cleared of any breach of school rules but I wondered if he was out to get me. Apart from that incident, I was scrupulous in my obedience to the school regulations because I reasoned that once I decided to take on the PKC I had to dwell above board. I resolved never to break any school rules or provide the authorities an excuse to 'hang' me.

Another run in with the PKC occurred when I had the privilege of compering the lecture delivered by Justice Victor Ovie-Whiskey (the father of Anthony my old classmate), then Chairman of the Federal Electoral Commission, during the King's College Fifth Form Week. I had visited the Justice at his Onikan office and he had received me with great courtesy and bent over backwards to accommodate my requests. He had served as the Chief Judge of Bendel State before his current appointment. He was as robust in his stature as he was in his courtesy and he wore a thick-rimmed pair of glasses and bore a thick moustache.

One of the privileges of attaining the Fifth Form was the opportunity to organise a week of celebrations, which included religious services, games, lectures which climaxed with a dinner open to invited secondary school girls. I had arranged the lecture, contacted and invited the speakers, and in my view compered it rather well. I was very pleased with myself and was euphoric after the event. It was after school hours, I had my shirt untucked, 'flying' as we called it, as I glided around the school celebrating my *'mastery'* and *'triumph'*. Suddenly the PKC's voice bellowed out in my direction:

> *'Speaker of truth, speaker of liberty …. breaking School Rules.'*

Apparently, though it was outside school hours I was still incorrectly dressed. I suspected that his reaction and rebuke was in response to my extra-curricular activities, which included reporting him to various King's College Old Boys. All of a sudden, the euphoria was sucked out of me and I fell down to earth from my moment of gliding around the school grounds with a big and painful bump.

My mind wanders through to my only experience of the Fifth Form Dance, which occurred during the 1982 academic session. I had declined to take part in the Fifth

Form Dance of 1984 simply because in my arrogance I reckoned I was past it, I simply felt mixing it up at that stage was not a priority. I was originally of the 1982 set but was now two years behind having succumbed to the loss of two academic years in 1979 and 1981. In fact, I could have been entitled to attend three Fifth Form Dances if I so chose but I was not susceptible to greed of that kind. In 1982, I was in Form Three but that did not debar me from participating since they were all my former classmates. I attended the Dance not because I had desires to fraternise with the girls or gyrate to the rhythms of the music, but because I was determined to act as a spoiler preventing my mates from indulgence and exuberance of the sinful variety.

I was bedecked in my 1979 check suit, made in America, purchased for me by my Uncle Ojedele, the only suit I owned. It had passed its fashion date, the bottom of the trousers flared, sweeping all the dust and dirt in its path but I cared less at that stage. Others were more suitably attired with the fashion of the age and this appealed more to the girls. I remember incurring the wrath of 'Niran Fatunla aka 'Lakubu'. He had secreted a girl away from the Assembly Hall, the venue of the Dance into one of the deserted classrooms near the basketball court availing him of the darkness of the night to engage in a particular manner of fraternity. I had had my eyes on him all night and I trailed him to the rendezvous point then at the top of my voice like a latter day John the Baptist, I announced my presence by screaming:

"It is a sin, leave her alone, it is a sin!"

My intervention put paid to Lakubu's intentions and desires, but he was sure to repay me with a merciless beating after the weekend was over. I am not sure 'Lakia' with whom I later re-united with at the Faculty of Law, Obafemi Awolowo University ever forgave me for the incident. It is with regret that we lost him, Lakabu a few years ago.

I was due to preach at the Fifth Former service organised for the Sunday preceding the Dance and had received a lot of advanced billing. I had prepared my message and looked forward to preaching a message sprinkled with some brimstone and fire. However, it seems the planning committee had developed cold feet and decided that the PKC might consider it inappropriate for a 'serial repeater' to take to the rostrum. The only problem was no one remembered to advise me about the change. The change of plan hit me like a thunderbolt when I saw S.K. Anguwa raise himself from his seat and stroll down from the Assembly Hall stage where we were seated towards the rostrum to deliver his prepared message. I sat there with my classmates, stony faced, seething throughout the service feeling very betrayed!

In the morning after the dissolution of the Cabinet, the PKC invited me into his office to provide an account of the events from the previous day. It was apparent that he had been well briefed and I was expecting the worst. Armed with what had become my constant companion, the constitution of the Students' Council and the minutes recording details of the momentous event, I explained to him that my role had been that of an impartial Chairman who gave the casting vote on a motion put before the house after it was deadlocked. The concealment of my true motives continued, assuring him that I had neither instigated nor mobilised anyone and could not be blamed for the negligence of the Cabinet in failing to fulfill its constitutional duties. He listened intently and was very reflective, he advised me that he would arrive at a decision after making further enquiries. Later in the day, he confirmed that the constitution had been followed and that the Cabinet remained dissolved.

On this occasion, the PKC had impressed me as a fair-minded man and it seemed that his perception of me was slowly being transformed and vice versa. I sensed he began to see me as a *'radical reformer'* rather than a *'rabid radical'* and he appreciated the clear mandate I had to deliver lasting changes to the Council. The dissolution was confirmed and the scene was now set for the election of a new Cabinet and my 'dominance' of the Students' Council. I now thought that at last I could *'form'* a Cabinet in my 'own image'. Immediately a Council meeting was conveyed and Cllrs. Akufo, 'Dipo Akinla, Britus of blessed memory and Oyewunmi were elected and constituted into the new Cabinet. At the first meeting of the newly constituted Cabinet, I advised them that my time was limited; I meant business and was determined to deliver. Cllr. Dawuda Britus my fellow Panes House member and previous Ikoyi Run winner was elected the new Head of Cabinet.

It seemed I was at the height of my powers and it felt intoxicating to be adored by many and sundry. The unrelenting chants of *'Panafism'* and the usual chorus of *'You are Carried!'* were never distant from me trailing me all around the school. In all the adulation, I sensed I could do no wrong and that *'my people loved me'*. The complete and utter 'domination' of the Council by the 'Panafism Orientation Committee' was now in place; at least that is what I reckoned. But this reckoning was to be brought down to reality with a serious incident. The incident led to my arrest and detention at the Lion Building, Lagos, the zonal Police Headquarters.

Today, I believe most of the traditions associated with the office of the PKC have faded, as acutely observed by my classmate 'Niran Ade-Onojobi. The aura accompanying the office has been lost and the allure, the beauty and glamour of ceremonies such as the 'Speech Days' which saw the PKC and staff all bedecked in academic gowns of various shapes and sizes have ceased to be a feature. The well started green military uniforms borne by the cadet are now replaced by ill fitted blue safari suits masquerading as uniforms.

'ARREST AT DAWN'

The arrival of dawn with the streaks of orange light seeping through my dormitory windows roused me back into reality. It was the last day of the second term in March 1984 and as an early riser, I had already taken my shower and was ready to bedeck myself in the full school uniform before taking a brisk walk down to the office. It was part of the regulations that on the last day of term and the beginning of term all boys wore the full school uniform. I had barely placed my feet through my pair of trousers when one of the younger boys ran into my dormitory to announce to me that my office had been broken into! The night before I had placed over four hundred naira, some of the takings from the tuck shop into the office safe. We had set a budget in the Council to fully furnish the common room in fulfillment of the last of my campaign promises.

I dashed down to my office at the other end of the school under Hyde Johnsons' house adjourning the dinning hall to establish what had happened. I was panting, as I got nearer the office, the appearance of the broken and mangled locks of the doors sent a surge, spasms of shock across my face and induced a chill into my marrow which cascaded down my entire body. I noticed the doors had been wrenched open, I rushed towards the safe where I had kept the money and *'lo and behold, it was not there!' All gone, vanished into thin air!* I gasped in shock! It was steadily becoming apparent as the clock ticked away that we had been robbed! Words were an inadequate description for how I felt, I was deflated, King's College boys were not supposed to be thieves. Thoughts flashed through my mind:

"What mindless person would do this to me? Me a man of the people."

I reasoned:

"I thought my people loved me?"

How naïve I had been, many must have noticed, that trade was brisk and booming in the tuck shop. We had also organised lucrative film shows and a number of fund-raising events, so it did not take science of the rocket variety to establish that the

Council coffers were full to the brim and it was ripe for the picking. Prior to my tenure, the tuck shop had become derelict and had been abandoned and we resorted to purchasing our snacks over the school wall near the kitchen from junior staff quarters. Nego a dark-skinned attractive girl, with beautifully enameled features, a daughter of one of the junior staff was on standby to sell various snacks. She was very popular amongst the boys for a few other reasons. We also had hawkers in front of the school gates. 'Mango' the very dark skinned boisterous bald headed ice-cream vendor was the most notable. 'Mango's pastime as he perched on his ice-cream bicycle seat was to get into altercations with day students at the school gate. It is suggested that his stance was a pre-emptive action against the attempted pilfering of his stock and constant provocations from the boys. These altercations were so frequent that I always wondered how he ever made any money. If we were lucky at lunchtime a vendor, Mrs. Osokolo, the mother of Obiora, one of my classmates came in as a vendor of delicious and tasty meat pies and cakes, delivered in her light blue coloured Mercedes Benz 200. The pastries supplied were devoured like *'hotcakes'* by the hordes of hungry boys in hot pursuit.

The truth was that we had planned later that day to bank all the proceeds accumulated. I immediately alerted Mr. Fabiyi to the incident, he came running out, swearing left, right and in all directions and his legs flailing all over the place. It seemed on this occasion that he was going to combust! I was half dressed and completely beside myself and I had to wait at the scene of the crime.

The PKC was duly informed as he arrived on the school grounds. He came to inspect the scene; he did not say much and advised me that the police will need to be informed. Within what seemed like minutes the detectives from the CID at the Lion Buildings arrived. Yusuf Suleiman, one of my trusted aides, a brother of 'Femi Suleiman, a few other boys and I were rounded up as suspects and ordered to stay where we were in front of the scene of crime. We were now officially suspects, the policemen got down to work and started dusting down the common room and the office premises for fingerprints and then we were matched off to the Lion Buildings, a few metres from the school in a single file. Lion Buildings did not have pleasant memories for me because years before we had visited it with my mother when we went to report the soldiers' brutality on my uncle, Professor Adetugbo. The whole school gazed down at us as we matched through the footpaths, past the Council Chambers out of the school grounds through the gates and off to the Police Station.   I could not help but wonder:

"Which of the boys would betray me like this?"

It was the unkindest cut. We arrived at the Police Station and the process of obtaining our fingerprints and interviews was to last the next few hours.

In the space of six months, I believe the boys of King's College, Lagos through its Students' Council had risen to great heights and had transformed their lot.   They had starred their problems in the eye and confronted each and every one of them.   We now had a fully functioning Council, the production of the Mermaid (College Magazine) had began under the editorship of Kingsley Eze after three years in abeyance, the tuck shop was brimming with life and had become a source of constant revenue.   We had also started the refurbishment of the common room and we had a Council Secretariat, a small office, which housed the Secretary and the Assistant Secretary.   The threat of boarding house uniform had abated and the quality of the food had vastly improved. We organised a successful Students' Council Week with Mr. Akintunde Asalu invited to inspire us.   We had proven that we, even as boys could take responsibility and govern ourselves.   It seemed I had found my enduring purpose and power had now replaced sketching and drawing which had been my past retreat.

But in a boarding school with over 300 students, there was bound to be a few bad apples that would exploit our good fortune and turn it into misfortune. I do not think I was remotely a suspect for the cowardly crime but the investigation had to follow its course and attempts had to be made at elimination in order to establish the culprits. I had left the office very late the night before, so the crime must have occurred in the dead of the night when all and sundry were in deep slumber.

After seven hours of standing in the Police Station suddenly, we were told we were free to go, what prompted this I do not know but I have my suspicions, I believe they were closer to home. Even as I write today, there are one of two names that spring to mind and I suspect bear responsibility for that cowardly crime. I do hope they can at some stage in their lives come to terms with what they almost destroyed.   They almost truncated a dream, but our dreams of progress, of good triumphing over evil had been implanted over a century ago when the King's College, Lagos motto was established as *'a hope for light'*. The dream has always been certain to succeed because it contained the word 'hope' at the very end of it.

By the time, I left the school all the funds we lost had been replenished through more innovative schemes. Akufo, the Head of the Social Committee and I were privileged to visit Chellarams on Broad Street, Lagos, an electronic cash and carry shop to purchase a brand new coloured television set for the common room. I suggest this was a hallmark of *'Panafism'*, not power for its sake, but power to deliver and to transform. There was massive jubilation as we returned to the school in a taxi with a brand new television set. I may have been intoxicated with power, vindictive in deploying it, but I consoled myself that it was surely for the greater good of King's College. Later in the year, there was to be a complete rapprochement between the PKC and I at the *'Speech Day and Prize Giving Day'*.

'THE RETURN FROM EXILE'

It took some concerted effort to convince my mother that a return to the King's College boarding house would do me any good. She was concerned that my last experience in the boarding house led to multiple examination failures culminating in the loss of two years. I marshaled my arguments and reminded my mother that my twin, Folashade, was already at the University of Ife enjoying the life of a Law student. I queried the basis that led to her denial of a right I considered inalienable and over time with sustained pressure, she relented. I am convinced that it was a combination of the weight of evidence; the soundness of my logic and my impudence that made my mother relent.

During my time in exile away from the boarding house in the land of the day student, I was determined to play a full and active role in the life of the school. As I matured a little in my Christian journey, I acquired the nickname of 'Pastor'. The accompanying popularity began to creep into my head and I felt that if I was to acquire more status and relevance then contesting for office of some kind would not be a bad start. In my first Third Form, I was elected class captain for two consecutive terms, only to be retired by the class teacher Mrs. Umenyi on account of my increasingly poor academic performance. Victor Ogwai was my replacement and it was a huge blow for during that time, the taste of power was pleasant, but I learnt the hard way to serve by example.

I can recall that many times when my errant classmates downed tools and refused to clean up the classroom I would take up the task and sweep the classroom clean and wait patiently to visit retribution on the offenders at the opportuned time. Typically, my duties where simple, maintain order in the classroom and represent the class to the teachers. It was a role from which I learnt so much fairness, integrity and responsibility.

The Arts teacher, Mrs. Inko-Tariah had noticed me during that period as an above average art student. This led to me my entry as a school representative for the National Arts competition. I was also invited to design, sketch and paint the scene of a cricket match on the background wall of the school stage in readiness for the *'Annual*

Speech Day and Prize Giving Day'. It was indeed an honour and privilege because that year the President of Nigeria; His Excellency, Alhaji Sheu Shagari was the guest of honour. I assumed that there would be a prize, *'Service to College Life'* awaiting me as a reward for my artistic efforts and that I would have the opportunity to shake the hands of the President. However, that year I was not awarded a prize; but in the following year, I would proudly received my 'overdue' prize.

The convention was that only Fourth Form boarders could contest for the position of Assistant Secretary of the Students' Council but I would not be held back by convention. I had studied the contents of the constitution and I was quite clear that the provisions did not debar me. Prior to the time, I had been intimately involved in many campaigns either as a designer of posters or a campaign manager for Oluyinka Olutoye aka 'Toy' and a supporter of Ayo Awoyingbo aka 'Awo'. At that time my mother was not prepared to countenance my return to the boarding house so I took the bull by the horn and threw myself into the ring and my nomination was dully accepted.

In the meantime I had spent my exiled period as a day student following the University of Lagos Students' Union politics and attending their annual celebrations and commemorations. I immersed myself in the lingo and culture of student unionism and followed its politics. I also got very close to Panaf Olajide Olakanmi having being introduced to him by Hakeem 'Kayode Johnson, an engineering student of rare distinction. He, Panaf, lived in Mariere Hall aka 'Baluba Kingdom', his hall was also known as *'the bottle breakers'*, he taught me the rudiments of politics and offered to sponsor my political adventures. I learnt from him the initial art of political writing and slowly to the horror of my Christian mentor, Brother 'Tunde Oladunmiye I became more political and less Christianly in my attitude. I produced over four hundred copies A4 write-ups where the ideology of Panafism was espoused and every student at the school was given a copy. I also unleashed on the boys periodic press releases. I think I may have become some sort of phenomenon at the time.

I contested against the handsome and photogenic Emezie (later Head of Cabinet of the Students' Council), and won with about 238 votes to his 73. On the Sunday night, the day of the Speech Night I had to stay over night at the school. I still cannot remember how I convinced my mother to let me sleep over. As a result of the votes, I was elected the first day student to become Assistant Secretary in the history of the college while Ayo Awodein was elected as Secretary. After the ceremonial handshake, 'Bingo', the PKC decided to suspend the Council for reasons yet unexplained and it was from here that the struggle began.

My return to Panes' House F1 dormitory was not plain sailing, I had arrived a week late to the boarding house and Jimoh aka 'Gawe', had taken over the bed space near the entrance beside the front bay window of F1. In a nod to tradition, I simply requested him to move but he stubbornly refused! It was the tradition that senior boys occupied the bed spaces closest to the windows but my late arrival had given 'Gawe' the opportunity to establish some sort of claim to the space. The atmosphere was constipated with anger and I was reduced to a rendering of the history of King's College, Lagos, which I am sure must have bored him. I referred to tales of how I had been admitted years before he dreamt of applying to the school. He would not budge and then I reckoned, it was time to deploy the big guns. I *'summoned'* Olaleye aka 'Baba Leyi', the Prefect and Panes' House Captain and pleaded with him to enforce the *'rule of law and precedence'* in my dormitory, to prevent a breakdown of law and precedence. After a stiff talking to from Olaleye, 'Gawe' relented and found he had no choice but to effect compliance with tradition. He later came to give me the full respect I craved. I settled down in my new corner, selected a choice of side lockers, identified a junior boy for water fetching duties and set down to sketch out my plans for the total domination of the King's College's political scene.

We had been used to food of the highest quality except for 'Eba', grated cassava meal, which we avoided in our numbers. Then suddenly in the later months of 1983 things changed, the food became deplorable and we were expected to accept it with meekness. As far as I was concerned, the Head Caterer had become a bit of a law on to herself, the food was becoming increasingly inedible and we had been subjected to the indignity of banana milk. I was of the view that this could not stand because the milk had a awful taste and no one drank banana milk. I dug deep into history, because I heard of the strike of the previous generation and of the heroic roles played by 'Emeka Odumegwu Ojukwu. I reasoned that if Ojukwu a mere Second Former at the time could be a major protagonist in a strike then so could I.

I crafted a powerful letter, full of bombast, and wrote to the PKC threatening a food boycott if things did not improve. I made it clear it was unacceptable that boys should be treated to such quality of food. I gave an ultimatum for the withdrawal of the offending milk and demanded improvements be made to the quality of food. I suggested any failure to heed our demands would lead to us abandoning all attempts of eating the meals prepared by the school kitchen. This was an unmistakable threat to go on a hunger strike. Only Bibi Paiko and 'Dayo Oleolo were party to my letter and as I was determined to face down the school authorities. It led to a confrontation with 'Bingo' in his office.

'FOOD THE SUBSTANCE OF OUR STRUGGLE'

After receiving the letter, the PKC summoned all the members of the Food Committee to the *'ivory tower'*, his second floor 'attic' office. The office stood at the peak of the school grounds with a wind vane on the top of the roof. The vane had an ornament sitting on the peak of the roof with a large flat area designed to rotate and point into the wind. Under the ornament was a fixed section, which showed the four main compass points: North, East, South and West. The vane was mounted on that location so that the compass points could reflect the reality of the weather, and the ornament turned freely so that whichever way its head was pointing indicated the direction the wind was coming from. It seemed that in reality the tower was the barometer of the prevailing mood in the school and offered clues to the mood the PKC was tending towards.

It was a building that had its origins in the early nineteenth century and it was not always a pleasant place to visit. Threats of *'I will send you up'* always sent shivers down the spines of many boys. On this occasion I was bullish and feared very little, I was confident that a clear and dignified articulation of our position would win the day and subdue the PKC.

I joined other members of the Food Committee as we filed into the office of the PKC. We all stood at full attention and then the PKC comfortably seated with his eyes darting from face to face, requested a clear and concise explanation of the contents of the letter. When the PKC set up the Food Committee, I am certain he did not expect *'infantile radicalism'* of any sort. It was supposed to be a consultative body and nothing more. I had been elected Chairman and 'Dayo Oleolo emerged as the Vice Chairman. 'Dayo was the voice of moderation and reason, where I sought confrontation, he encouraged dialogue, where I relished *'hell and fury'*, he counseled heavenly peace. However, my head was filled with heroics of the infantile sort and I was determined not to shift an inch in our encounter with 'Bingo'.

One by one the PKC picked off the members of the committee with most admitting that they knew nothing of the contents of the letter written in their name. It was now time for me to enter the fray. Then I admitted full and material knowledge of its contents indicating full responsibility for it. I suggested to him that our position was simple, the food had deteriorated and I wrote the letter to forestall a breakdown of 'law and order'. I continued the exaggeration and mischief making, stating that some wanted a strike, and many others desired some 'action'. 'Bingo' expressed dissatisfaction with the tone of the letter and advised me to watch my step. It was clear the PKC felt we were skirting with danger but he appeared to be bidding his time. We were all dismissed from his presence and I was convinced that I was a marked 'man'. However, I was glad after that, the offending banana milk soon disappeared from the menu.

After the meeting the Head Caterer invited me to a meeting, she was very bitter and angry, she was convinced I was accusing her of pilfering foodstuffs. She gave me a detailed account of the catering budget and seemed to suggest the fault lay elsewhere. Over the next few weeks the food improved remarkably and from then on, I had an open door to the kitchen and her office. I felt word had gone round that there was a 'loose cannon' in town.

After my encounter with 'Bingo', I became convinced that should the suspended Council be resuscitated then it would need a 'deliverer'. There was some element of delusion in my thinking but I was convinced that positive action could bring changes to the 'running' of the school. But more fundamentally, my struggle for the Council's reinstatement was about a process of self-discovery of remembering the dream of my ancestors before me, the dream that told them that their lot could surpass that of the generation before them.

I believe that it was after much pressure from some Old Boys that the PKC decided to restore the Students' Council in early 1984. He appointed Mr. Fabiyi as Chairman to replace the mercurial Mr. Yakubu who had been transferred away on promotion to another school. At the initial stage, I was disqualified from contesting for the Office of Secretary because I was a Fifth Former. However, I took the argument to the authorities, explained that their action was a breach of the constitution and they relented. But during that time I now believe that a few boys were approached by 'the powers that be' to run for the Office of Secretary to the Students' Council to forestall me.   With the constitution on my side, I duly submitted my nomination and re-constituted the 'Panafism Orientation Committee'.   Bibi became Chairman and Citizen 'Emeka Nwaojigba was Vice Chairman with, 'Bayo Oyesanya, 'Wale Babatunde aka 'Babat', Olugbemiga Serrano, Citizen Adegbesin, Shettima, Obasanjo Fagbemi, Ken Ekwueme and Mohammed aka 'Baba Mut' as members.   It was a highly disciplined and efficient campaign committee and they mobilised in any way they could.

It was after I resumed office as Secretary of the Students' Council that as time passed the PKC warmed towards me.   I honestly cannot remember the turning point but I do know that Mr. Fabiyi was my constant ally.   I believe that the PKC soon discovered that I could be passionate about the *'truth'* and I did not necessarily seek confrontation for its sake.   I also believe a good word or two was put in on my behalf by the many Old Boys I interacted with in pursuit of various grievances.

When I completed my 'O' levels at King's College, the PKC issued me a gushing testimonial, which read:

> *"He matured and mellowed with pleasing results with time."*

I can only conclude that he convinced himself I had changed.   Throughout my nascent political career, I hope that in the pursuit of power, I never betrayed my principles but I cannot say that with any certainty.   However, I agree that eventually I had to reach an accommodation with power in order to consolidate certain gains.   In culmination of our rapprochement, the PKC awarded me a prize at the 1984 *'Speech Day and Prize Giving Day'* for *'Services to College Life'*: *'…for being an effective and dedicated Secretary of the Students' Council.'*   Curiously I was given a book, a biography of Robert Mugabe, then the Prime Minister of Zimbabwe and who later turned into a brutal dictator was there a coded message there?

In concluding this chapter, my reflections lead me to state that, if during my forays into politics I achieved anything good for the boys at King's College, Lagos it was a team effort.   If, however, I made some errors, the fault lays entirely with me and me alone.

'A BLAST FROM THE PAST'

'Present past and future form one mighty whole;   shining forth

emblazoned on one muster role;

When the call is sounded all must answer, "HERE!"

Voice and bearing showing neither shame nor fear;   pointing to our

honour with untarnished stands.

Bright as when we took it from our founders' hands.

This shall be our watchword, "Always play the game."

Sound the old school's praises trumpet forth her fame.

Though of many nations we will not forget.

That we all are brothers with a common debt.   Let us pay by

giving as we forge ahead.

Service to our living. Honour to our dead.'

The boys always sang the third stanza of the King's College school song gustily. On many public occasions the boys emitted in a deep loud roar a particular word at the end of a verse, which evoked a consistent response akin to a frightened cat jumping out of its skin, the verse was:

'When the call is sounded all must answer, "HERE!"'

When sang it frightened many of the unsuspecting audience witless because the boys always roared the word: *"HERE"* at the top of their voices. The fright and the shock it induced literally made them jump out of the seats.

Whilst I was not the loudest amongst my contemporaries, I always had some suspicion that I could debate a little and was itching to be on the debating team. Starting from my First Form I had followed the debating exploits of various secondary school boys and girls on the regularly televised *'School's Debate'*. I felt great pride and very fulfilled when in 1983 I was finally chosen to represent the school as the Chief Debater. Obasanjo Fagbemi a Third Former was in the second chair, he had wooly textured

117

hair and was an impatient and fiery radical who later contested for office on the Student's Council after I had left the school.

It was at the King's College Society that boys like Bawa, Jacks aka 'Jackaba, 'Tunde Akinrinmisi, Idemudia Guobadia and many others cultivated their debating skills, however, my case was different. I do not believe I had the naturally facility of oratory, but years of preaching class-to-class and a few school-to-school allowed God to hone my ability to lace together a sentence or two and maintain a quality of rhythm that arrested the attention of many, compelling them to listen. Over time I had learnt to weave and spin words into a great tapestry and with adequate embroidery, which many considered as art. This was a remarkable turn around because in primary school I was timid and very shy, and public speaking was nothing natural to me, it was simply something I learnt, acquired and mastered over time.

On one of such debating outings I arrayed myself in the navy blue King's College double-breasted blazer. The blazers when worn made King's College boys stand out smartly and it was suggested that some boys who joined us for the two year 'A' Level programme from other secondary schools believed in its vaunted *'magical'* qualities. The myth was that it attracted the ladies in the same way nectar from flowers attracts the bees. Therefore, they found every excuse to adorn themselves with the navy blue blazer when outside the school.

On one Thursdays during the week when we had a debating encounter with one of the local secondary schools, I neglected to shave so spotted a moustache and was heavy on sideburns. Whilst the chins of my classmates shone brightly with innocence and was soothing to touch, due to *'older'* age mine was beginning to experience the ravages of the regular shave of tufts of hair that kept on appearing. Unknown to me, Mr. 'Tayo Sofulwe, the VPKC, now of blessed memory, was on my trail, he was parked somewhere on the route to the debating venue and suddenly emerged from nowhere, pulled me aside and in his snappy manner announced to me that I was in serious trouble for not being clean-shaven. This was my second serious encounter with Mr. Sofoluwe! He ignored by limp protestations and asked me to report to his office the next day. I knew there could be only one result from a visit to his office, the partaking in six of the best from his cane.

I simply went to the debate, performed my best and resolved to ignore 'Ishano' as he was nick named by the boys. I reckoned I could get away with it and he would soon forget about the indiscretion I considered minor. A few days later, he accosted me in my classroom and dragged me into his office. Once there he suggested that I had deliberately ignored his direct request and proceeded to administer the cane on my buttocks. I took it like a man, straightened my tiny frame and promised myself that I would never allow it to happen again.

Many talented boys and girls enriched the Lagos debating circuit, however, there was a particular student, Odutola whom I feared, he was in fact 'the master' in the art of speaking. *'The Best Speakers Contest'*, an annually televised event and the climax of the debating season was fast approaching. In 1984, I was entered as the King's College representative and I was simply considered a *'no hoper'*, and one who was there to simply make up the numbers. The event was held at the National Museum, Onikan, Lagos in a thatched roofed building with an open courtyard in the middle, it was called the Museum kitchen. The Museum courtyard where the kitchen surrounded was always used as open-air theatre, which brought it to life. It provided a place to eat the best of Nigerian cuisine, watch Nigerian plays, and listen to Nigerian music.

It was not long before I was invited to speak on my chosen topic *'Africa'* by the baritone voice of Mr. Osiolukoya the debate master. I had prepared for the day by studying various techniques of oration, the persuasive, informative, humour/entertaining, actuate, and inspirational. Citizen Jawando, an Upper Six Former was on hand to coach me. Using the skills of voice repetition, modulation and adopting a tilt to my frame for effect. I spoke into the microphone with precision, sustaining and unrelenting rhythm filled with cadences:

"Africa, Africa. Africa…. Land of hope and glory…."

Succession of eyes skirting around, I paused before launching further into my speech. With use of pace and deliberation, I began to draw the attention of the audience and then command it and slowly but surely something remarkable happened. Out of about 40 participants I was suddenly a contender and was in the race to become the *'Best Speaker'* of Lagos State, I did not win, but I came in as the second runner up. The organisers announced at the end of the completion that due to the closeness of the results for the first time in history, the prize, a bursary of three hundred naira would be split amongst the winner and the runners up, however, that was the last I heard of that promise.

That day I learnt a valuable lesson that the power of the spoken word is undeniable and I believe in the words I found somewhere on the Internet that:

> *"At all the great crisis and hinges in history, we find great speeches which swayed the outcome. Great speeches have motivated citizens to fight injustice, throw off tyranny, and lay down their life for a worthy cause. Words have drawn meaning out of tragedy, comforted those who mourn, and memorialized events with the dignity and solemnity they deserved. Words can move people to risk life and limb, shed tears, laugh out loud, recommit to virtue, change their life, or feel patriotic. By weaving and spinning words into great tapestries of art, a man can wield an almost god-like power. Of course, even the most malicious leaders have known this and sought diligently to hone this skill for nefarious purposes. The power of speech can be used for good or evil and comes with great responsibility. Those who uphold virtue and goodness must be prepared to speak as masterfully as those who seductively and smoothly seek to convince the public to abandon its values and principles."*

The skills I acquired from debating bolstered me in my budding political career at university, but some of my contemporaries today feel that I am a talent lying redundant, refusing to get his clothes wet. However, I have a different take on it, I believe that at this moment I am called by God as a servant to the Nations I am not called to govern, but to serve and that is why I at the present time I remain in ministry that seeks ways to transform students and nations. I suggest that placing too much emphasis on one gift to the detriment of others is a recipe for dashed hopes. But I am convinced that as I established in my doctoral thesis that I can *'Speak Truth to Power'* and make a difference. Therefore, I write today not to glory in the past but to critically examine my beginnings, to establish whether there are parallel lessons I could extract and apply to my country and the nations within it.

I end this chapter by reflecting on another stanza of the King's College, Lagos school song that goes forth:

"This is what they teach us in the good old school

Only by obedience may you learn to rule

If you fail look closely seek the reason why

You have power to conquer if you only try

Others went before you and attained the light

Where they wait to cheer you victors in the fight."

'IN THE BEGINNING IT WAS NOT SO'

I was strutting towards our home, a four bedroom flat nestled on the 2nd floor in a greying building on one of the dusty, clay caked streets of Abule-Oja, a small suburb of Lagos, suddenly from the verandah of the first floor my cousin Taiye stuck her head out screaming with delight:

> *"'Kayode, 'Kayode…. You have been admitted to King's College,*
> *your admission letter was found under a pile of washing! ……."*

I bounded up the gangway of stairs and got to our first floor flat to confront the contents of the letter. Stunned and in utter disbelief, I grabbed it and stared at it; It was indeed my letter of admission into King's College, Lagos. Pondering to myself, I thought this could not be real, for it was two months into the first term and I had already resigned myself to my fate at CMS Grammar School, Bariga, the oldest Nigerian secondary school. A few months before then, we, my twin and I had been due to resume at Federal Government College, Akure and Federal Government College, Ogbomosho respectively. I did not think you could be admitted into two Federal Government schools at the same time.

In what seemed like a bolt out of the blue, my mother announced after *'the game was set and matched'* that she had changed her mind. In later years she explained to me that she had reasoned that both of the schools were new, miles apart we were to become the foundation students which meant she would run the gauntlet of regular travel miles a few times a year! It took Professor 'Kunle and Mrs. Iyanda a whole night at their University of Lagos staff quarters' home to persuade and cajole me to accept the option of attending the CMS Grammar School. However, my agreement was to come with one condition. The agreement carefully negotiated late at night was I would go to the Grammar School until the resumption day for the Federal Government College. The only uniforms I had were the green and white of the Federal Government College I therefore had no CMS Grammar School uniforms so an approach was made to Mrs. Akinluyi, the British born Caucasian CMS Grammar School Vice Principal and wife of Dr. Akinluyi. She provided me the dispensation to wear coloureds for a day or two. I started at CMS Grammar School a week later than my other classmates but was embarrassed on the Assembly lines by the same Vice Principal who seemed to have forgotten about the dispensation she had given. My twin who was the more stoic one, had with minimal fuss simply settled into Methodist Girls' High School, Yaba for a year before her transfer to Federal Government College, Oyo in her second year.

Later I discovered that my mother was unable to follow the terms of our agreement. I was, however, in good company with my cousin 'Gbenga Atewologun, 'Deji Adeogun, Ayodeji Awojobi, 'Dayo Akinosi, 'Femi Parse, 'Deji Adeogun, 'Femi Meshe and Ayo Odunsi. Ayodeji was possibly the most brilliant mind of our generation; he was simply a .22 calibre mind in a .357 magnum world. He was admitted to King's College, Lagos but his father the legendary Professor Ayodele Awojobi, the youngest Doctor of Science ever, a CMS Grammar School alumnus and a social critic, had encouraged him to go to CMS. At school together with my cousin we went regularly to purchase fried plantain and fried yam with spicy sauce as a side, *('Dodo and Dundun')*. We also attended Mr. Dada's lessons at the staff quarters after school hours with my twin joining us from Methodist Girls High School, Yaba.

In the meantime I was unable to resist the urge to dupe one or two boys in school under the presumption that I would soon depart before they discovered my true character. Sanyaolu, who had a tall burly frame, a strapping boy of thirteen years old was one of the boys who fell victim to my small time scam. He was not well disposed to me when he caught up with me; he roughened me up and issued a few ultimatums. There was no hiding place for me now, I had to stay in the Grammar School and face the music and the wrath of the boys I had duped, there was to be no saving by the school bell.

At the school, there was the brutality of Papa Mose, our Music teacher who carried a heavy cane, so thick it could pass for a rod. There was something Dickensian about him; he regularly used the cane to inflict punishment for every perceived minor indiscretion. It was as if he was always searching for an excuse to apply the cane. He belonged to a school of thought that believed fear and intimidation was the best way to educate a child. He was reputed to have bruised many students to submission. I was once a victim of his brutality simply because I failed to understand the point he was making during a lesson. On that occasion, he dragged me to the front of the classroom and got two of my classmates to place me on the table in front of him and spread my legs, as I lay faced down! He then proceeded to apply the cane on my buttocks. I lay writhing in pain; the strokes caused me a tingling sensation that pervaded my entire frame as he repeatedly applied the cane. Papa Mose must have been in his late sixties but he was a law on to himself!

Now I was faced with the surprise late admission into King's College, Lagos and there was much to comprehend. Whirling around in my mind was the thought that it was not my kind that got admitted into KC, I was not the sharpest of brains, I was merely average, I was neither very confident, nor special.   I heard from Mrs. Adenugba at primary school that *'block heads'* never made it to King's College, for she had on a few occasions referred to me as a *'block head'*.   There were boys more fitting and worthy than me. So, I am convinced that God at that particular time ordered my footsteps and ordained it to be so.

I turned up at King's College, Lagos on the 5th of December 1977 and after the completion of formalities we were led to the newly formed Form One C classroom, which was situated in a new extension block near the basketball court. It was obvious the classrooms had just been constructed from the smell of fresh paint that caused the atmosphere to be constipated. Initially we were only seven in the class but as the academic year progressed our numbers increased to twenty-one. I remember 'Bayo Oyesanya, John Ogwo, 'Femi Jaiyesimi, 'Wale Goodluck, Joel Ugborogho, 'Dokun Thompson, Charles Ikpeme, Valentine Onyia, Raymond Njoku, the enigmatic 'Niran Fatunla aka 'Lakubu' also known as 'Lakia', 'Gbemi Kehinde, Eseku, Tokunbo Balogun, 'Bunmi Akinremi, Alufohi, Omotayo Johnson aka 'Caga', 'Bunmi Akinremi, Enahoro 'Dodo', Gabriel Ebvota and Salman Akram a boy from Pakistan as my first classmates.

The first year was not very remarkable I was simply getting to grips with the reality of KC and constantly had to pinch myself to establish whether I was in the real world or fantasyland. I had only one scrap noteworthy to recall, it was with 'Wale Goodluck, we had a disagreement and we challenged each other to a duel. Spontaneously we decided to settle it with our fists, in the middle of the unseeming tussle, Citizen Junaid from the top of Harman's House dormitory emitted in a deep loud roar: *"Come Here"*, to us. The 'A' level students were always referred to as 'Citizens', and it was a title that preceded their surnames. At King's College there was never the informality of referring to each other by our first names, we were always on surname terms. In any case, he had witnessed the whole incident; he gave us a lecture on the evils of fighting and then punished us by asking us to kneel before him. I was so scared and after the incident, I promised myself I would never succumb to temptation of fighting.

In the first year I was elected a councillor to the Students' Council and witnessed first hand democracy in action during the Students' Council elections into the posts of the Secretary and Assistant Secretary. We usually ran the gauntlet of many senior boys who were bent on fagging us into submission. We were teased that we entered or gained admission the school through the kitchen gate on account of our late and unusual admission.

For the day students amongst us, the school bus offered a respite and a refuge from the harsh realities of *'fagging'* and the daily torment that senior boys delighted in inflicting on us. We were entertained with a menu of jokes and it was not unusual to hear Victor Amokeodo bellow out repeatedly *"Bus Corner Sirrrrr"* to gain the attention of the driver as we got nearer his stop. 'Dayo Oreagba aka 'Natty Gba' and 'Ladi Lawanson aka 'Lawi Pepper' were boys you could not mess around with on the bus and mischief was their main occupation. Form Two boys like Shonubi and Dibia tried to maintain order but we simply humoured them. We had the opportunity to have breakfast and lunch in school and witness some of the dramas of the boarding house. The breakfast, which we paid 10 Naira a term was rather elegant, consisting of soft and succulent slices of white bread, eggs boiled to perfection and prettied with some spicy stew as complements. There were of course lots of kettles of tea to go with it and milk and sugar in plentiful abundance, it was certainly not the meal to miss.

On one such bright morning in 1978 during breakfast, the then Vice-School Captain, Felix Onwuka was furious with some senior boy, and so he took to the front of the dinning hall and during announcements threatened in his unique accent and booming voice:

> *"There is a certain form four boy in this dinning hall, he thinks he is very heady! If you think you are heady, come and confront me!"*

125

It became a folklore for a few years afterwards as boys recalled the incident in jest for it was the strength of his Igbo accent, which sheathed the meaning of his words rather than the content of his threat that made it so hilarious. Every new day in King's College brought a new revelation. By the end of the year I was itching to get into the boarding house for I was convinced, that was where all the action lay. In the second year, Kelechukwu Mbagwu, Seyi Oguntomilade, Sheu, John Olufawo, Kiladejo, 'Niran Ade-Onojobi, Emmauel Obe aka O Reggae and a few others joined the class to raise our numbers to the requisite 35.

But of course, my actual beginnings before King's College, at the Grammar School and Staff School lay in my mother's womb, which I shared for nine months with Folashade, Feyisara, my twin. She was born first, she was the natural leader of us two, boldness, style and determination were her hallmark. She was not afraid to tell me of my numerous failings and did not suffer fools gladly. I owe the richness of my beginnings to the fact that I am a twin and yet less than a century before we were born, in parts of Nigeria we would have been killed because of that fact.

I have never been so proud, never been so strong than when I led in front with my younger brother bearing the coffin of Folashade, Feyisara my twin on the way to the earthly resting place of her remains in Maidstone. In fact, I insisted it was a rite we must fulfill, that in it we might find therapy. That we will meet again I am certain, that she is in eternal rest I have no doubt. It is her departure that has inspired me to begin the search for my identity, to go back to my beginnings, one so radically altered and affected by her absence.

'DELUSIONS OF POWER'

It was my entry into the boarding house that sowed the seeds of conflict in my mind. In October 1984 at the interview for admission into the Sixth Form at King's College I was very conflicted, I pictured in my mind that I had some unfinished business at the school's boarding house and thought the post of School Captain was my natural *'destiny'*. But when I gave more consideration to the narrowing academic gap with my younger brother, Adebowale, also a student at King's College, which could disappear I quickly renounced my quest for the *'delusions of power'*. I had passed the interview conducted by Mr. Abiola, the Hamman's House Master and History teacher and was sorry to decline the offer of a place for the Sixth Form.

It was not easy but there was the irresistible beckoning of University of Ife. It was an opportunity to rejoin my twin sister after years of separation, one that dated back to primary school. In preparation for University, Panaf Olajide Olakanmi had provided me with some 'tutorials'. He was clear in his advice, I had to seek peace with power in order to succeed in politics. It meant mellowing on my Christian profession in order to succeed politically. In a parody of the scriptures he urged me *'to seek ye first the kingdom of politics and suggested all other things will be added unto me.'* I reluctantly agreed with the *'master'* for the lure of office seemed worth it all.

It was in my second year at King's College that Anthony Ovie-Whiskey introduced me to realities of boarding house life. He was a fellow member of Panes' House and stayed in the dormitory next to mine. He kept me well informed on how to avoid pitfalls and traps. However, he never seemed able to avoid them himself. He was constantly on a collusion course with trouble. 'O Whiskey' as we called him was fun to be with, there was not a bad bone in his body, he never intentionally caused harm to anyone and was a sportsman of great distinction. I liked 'O Whiskey' and I resolved that my immediate future would be bright with him around. He quickly introduced me to Eric Umeh and together we lurked around the school grounds in our free time.

The boarding house opened up a new vista for me, but it was clear it would be no plain sail with the demands of bathroom work and the dormitory duties. On every Sunday evening at 4pm after a sumptuous meal of Jollof rice (tomato coloured) with choice pieces of prime beef or fish with only the rest period (siesta) intervening, there was the much dreaded bathroom work all junior boys had to contemplate. My duty was to clean the blocked urinals and I hated it, the stench and the fumes it produced were lethal enough to cause a bout of nausea and vomiting.

During the weekdays we had the morning inspections by the prefects who ensured that our duties were completed to their satisfaction, failure in this respect was punished with lines of imposition and an instant recall from the dinning hall during breakfast. I missed so many breakfasts simply on account of my *'imperfectly'* completed bathroom work. In the background was always the deep resonant voice of 'Folayan Osekita, the school's Cadet Unit Commandant to the stern and brooding demeanor of Frank Inok and the philosophical musings of Citizen Nwochocha who had a twin brother, there was much to observe and learn. Citizen Odiri Oteri was a quiet one but you dared not mess with him and Citizen Babalola rarely smiled at us. Citizen Ojeyinka on account of the similarity in our names attempted to take me under his wings, Citizen Odunayo impressed me with his Christian faith and my distant cousin Citizen Abayomi Ogunkanmi another Christian in McKee Wright's House always kept an eye on me. However, it was to be Uka, a Fourth Former that I became close to for a while. Citizen Odunayo, quick to the sprints later became Pane's House Captain.

Towards the end of my first term Christmas holiday disaster struck! Suddenly my entire frame was convulsed with stinging pain and I was unable to move around and lay immobilised in my bed. My mother rushed me to the University of Lagos Health Centre where I was placed on admission for two weeks. The hospital proceeded with a battery of tests to establish what the matter was but my mother became convinced that it was due to some ill treatment I received in the boarding house. She thought I feared returning there because of bullying. In the end under relentless and sustained questioning, I placed Ukah in the frame and unfairly gave him up. Unfortunately for him, Mr. Ibegbulam had just resumed as the new PKC and was looking for an example to make. Ukah received a suspension and the way was clear for my return to the boarding house. The only revelation that was brought to our attention by the Health Centre was that I was a carrier of the sickle cell gene, AS. A regimen of drugs was prescribed for me, however, a year later when I found Jesus I began to operate on the basis of divine health and discarded the drug regimen. Anyway, this became my get out of jail card and I was excused from grass cutting and a few other strenuous chores that characterised life in the boarding house.

The legendary 'Tolani Opaneye, the Vice School Captain and Panes' House Captain was just in F5, a few dormitories from mine. He was a diminutive sportsman that many feared and you knew never to cross him. He could subdue a dinning hall into silence with stern looks and repetition of sentences, which resembled a chant. There was the School Captain, Terrance Onyewuenyi, enigmatic, handsome and cool. He was soft spoken but he packed a gentle authority, lots of charisma and athleticism into his lean frame. When he ventured into your presence charisma flowed rapidly towards him. I remember his announcement where he referred to '*Standards are falling*', which was to become *a tour de force* and a source of inspiration to many of us. It was much talked about for months and had a profound effect on the school.

In the year 1978/79 Prefects like, Onyewuenyi, Opaneye, Adeola, Ayanlowo, Adesanwo, Olorunsola (before he left for University of Lagos), Oaiah, Osugo, Longe, Okafor, Okoneh, Owosina, Orette, Onasode, Soneye, Rosanwo and a few others dominated the scene. I once incurred their collective wrath and I blame my good friend 'Wale Goodluck. Goodluck was a day student at the time and he had some punishment inflicted upon him for some minor indiscretion. He was required to write up some imposition but he was lost for words to write. I noticed his dilemma and decided he was worthy of assistance. I was close to Citizens Balogun and Sokan and I was in the habit of ease dropping on their '*gists*' so I had gathered from my memory the various nicknames of the prefects and Sixth Formers. I relayed all these names to Goodluck suggesting that it would make his imposition much more interesting and hilarious. 'Wale proceeded on my advice and prompting to write in many of those nicknames at my dictation and submitted it but the matter did not end there.

After Goodluck submitted the imposition, the prefects read it and stumbled across all the mischief contained within it. Under sustained interrogation, Goodluck gave me up to the prefects. I was to experience the most sustained of corporal punishments you could imagine. I was made to rest my shivering frame against the wall, stretch out my arms and then made to pretend I was sitting on an imaginary chair. This was alternated with my kneeling down with both hands raised above my head. For what seemed like hours and hours unending, I faced the music in the Prefects' room and nothing of my pleas for a prerogative of mercy came to anything. The prefects taught me a lesson I would never forget. I believe Goodluck being a day student was able to retire to the relative comfort of his home.

After that, I learnt to watch my step and take things steadily. Later on, we faced the boarding house initiation, a rite of passage that every new boarder had to pass through. You were required to entertain the boarding house audience with all kinds of performance acts during a Saturday evening; any disapproval meant you were subjected to taking brine under the supervision of the prefects. It was brutal, as the salt filled half the glass and was mixed with water. As the victims were compelled to pour the brine down through their throats and their stomachs filled up with the salty solution, it created a nauseous feeling and triggered bouts of vomiting all over the school. However, before that you were required to recite the 'fag pledge', which started with the words:

> *"My name is ……….. I come from the bush village of ………. where people do ………… I am a fag, a dirty stinking fag, I am to be seen and not to be heard, as from this day I promise to discard all my rustic and outlandish behaviour and to become a true King's College boy."*

This was followed with a roar of *'sure!!!'* from the audience and then the hapless boy continued:

> *"With your kind permission I beg to entertain you with…………."*

Emmanuel Obe and I had decided to put on a joint act that evening, most of our classmates were determined that the tall and handsome Obe would not escape drinking brine and by allying with him I would simply be collateral damage. Our act was simple and unsophisticated; I passed Obe on the stage, bumped into him and then he gave me a whack on the face! I found myself flat on the floor writhing in pain but this elicited a huge roar of applause! It meant we escaped the torment of taking brine and it seemed that our destinies had converged at least for the night. By sheer coincidence, Obe and myself were to repeat exactly the same classes due to failures in examinations and we were drawn close together by mutual adversity.

'Ewati! Ewati!'

I repeatedly taunted Umeh in the classroom as he sat down concentrating on writing the imposition he had been subjected to. My call was one reserved for boys who were at the regular receiving end of the punishment of impositions and it meant *'beans lover'*. All of a sudden, his face contorted with rage and he clinched his fists until his knuckles clicked and then without warning, from all directions, a flurry of blows landed on me in quick succession. Umeh had decided he would use swiftness of his blows to silence me up once and for all. I was stunned into cowardice and simply stood there receiving the punches in the rope-a-dope Muhammed Ali fashion but there was to be no miraculous come back! 'O Whiskey' who was observing from the sidelines urged me to respond in kind but I retreated behind the excuse that as a 'Christian' I did not believe in revenge. The truth was far from that, I was scared of the injuries Umeh might inflict on me if I decided to engage him in a duel, surrender was the best option, and something I duly choose.

'ISHANO STRIKES A NEW NOTE'

It was my friend and classmate, Asuquo Ibok Esq., a Prince of the South-South in Nigeria that conjured the nickname 'Ishano', one with which we christened the new *'Sheriff'* in town. This was Mr. 'Tayo Sofoluwe, the new Vice Principal King's College (VPKC Academics), who spoke very quickly, had a very fiery temper and was easily combustible, he did not suffer fools gladly and was quick to draw on his constant companion, the cane, whenever offences were committed. He was also in the habit of inflicting collective punishments, dishing out impositions without a sense of proportion.

On one such occasion, there was slight murmuring in the Assembly Hall while awaiting the arrival of the PKC. This was the first of the Assemblies held twice a week. 'Ishano's' response was to *'sentence'* the entire school to an imposition of lines; everyone was to write *'half an hour'*, two thousand words for creating a 'disturbance'. There was complete and utter outrage from many senior boys including I and we threatened not to write the imposition. This game of cat and mouse continued for a few weeks until all of us refuseniks were ordered to his office and flogged with six of the best. The man had stamina, he was after all a squash champion with a very strong forearm and he deployed it to his best effect as he whipped us all.

What amazed me about the man 'Ishano' was what appeared to be the sharpness of his memory in all matters concerning me. Before he administered the cane on my buttocks he called out my name, *"Ojedokun!"* knowingly and with a grin on his face and went on to administer six of the best strokes, I winced from the pain and took it as a *'man'*. Thereafter after much pressure from my mother who discovered the corporate punishment from my brother, I relented. But I still felt it was unfair to sentence the entire school to a collective punishment, to me it seemed an act of arbitrariness.

I must, however, hand it to Mr. Sofoluwe, he complimented the PKC very well and brought some needed discipline to the school. I later discovered that the reason he had a sharp memory as far as I was concerned, was because he had been my father's contemporary at University College, Ibadan in the 1960s. He revealed this to me during a chance encounter after I became an Old Boy, indeed, what manner of man!

I saw no contradiction in being radical and yet conforming to school rules, I simply found no attraction in breaking bounds or committing indiscretions of varying sorts, it was simply not my style. Yes I loved the aroma of the succulent and freshly baked bread laced with suya (barbecued beef) which, wafted through the dormitories as the various couriers clandestinely delivered on their errands. However, the lure was not tempting enough. Some might, however, detect some hypocrisy here, as I was not averse to partaking in the fruits of such indiscretions, consuming the odd loaf or suya purchased by those breaking the school bounds or *'tearing gate'* as we called it.

I am convinced that my Christian Faith had a lot to do with this. I am also convinced it was this belief that gave me the moral fibre to fight and rise up against unfairness and injustice wherever I sensed it. I simply found it impossible to remain silent when the many were suffering that is why I found it so perplexing that for a while, in the face of the glaring injustices presented in Nigeria I was unable to *'Speak Truth to Power.'*

As I conclude this part of my school boy adventures I am inspired and humbled by the words of an old friend and classmate at King's College, Dr. 'Femi Suleiman who wrote these kind words about me:

> *"Most especially I remember you as a very independent and resilient person. You were never laid back when it came to making your views heard and you never backed down in the face of opposition. I remember you very clearly as one of the few students who were totally of enviable good character, morally upright (paaaaaastor) and of good cheer! You were indeed a shining beacon, one of the most visible and outspoken guys of our time. These traits I'm sure have persisted and bloomed. Knowing you has been inspirational."*

I return to the challenge presented by William Wallace who holds that we owe a duty of constructive and open criticism:

> *"To speak truth to power, not to hide our knowledge in obscurely erudite terminology, nor lose ourselves in scholastic word games, nor speak truth in secret only to each other."*

I am convinced that like my itinerant ancestors before me:

> *"Each generation must discover its mission, fulfill it or betray it, ..."*

My ancestors discovered their mission, fulfilled it and did not betray it and now I must tread that path of fidelity to my generation as my forbearers trod before me. What are the implications for my nation, my country and for their destinies? As I tread through this path of life, the eerie silence of my twin, Folashade pursues me like a moving cloud into the present, making even more poignant the words she spoke in times past.

'THE CADET UNIT'

Through the various clubs and societies King's College, Lagos provided us opportunities to explore our hobbies and past times. It was also an opportunity for self-improvement and broadening our horizons. Like clockwork every Wednesday afternoon, the school gates were locked at closing time to prevent day students from scampering off to their homes. All students were required to join and participate in the activities of a chosen club or society. There was a vast array of clubs and societies, ranging from the Photographic Society, Cadet Unit, Stamp Club, Boys Scout to the King's College Society, Junior Literary and Debating Society and many more.

By 1981, the Cadet Unit was by far the most popular and oversubscribed club. In earlier years you could only apply to join the unit once you became a senior boy, however, with time boys from all forms became eligible to join. My early memories of the Cadet Unit are of Prefect Isaiah Abu who was the Commandant and Regimental Sergeant Major (RSM) assisted by, Folayan Osekita, Yusufu Pam and Noel Inyang. The members of the unit were quite formidable always impressively kitted with bayonets and rifles. Every Tuesday night cadets prepared for the parade of the next day in the evenings, pressing their uniforms with hot irons ensuring the starch in their faded green uniforms made it stand out. Each of their boots was carefully polished and shone so brightly with a reflective glaze covering it. The brass on their uniforms was also meticulously polished.

Attendance at the Cadet Unit parade was always summoned with the call from the bugle sounding the *'Reveille'*, which was usually blown out from the verandah of Hyde Johnson's House. The parade always ended with the sound of *'The Last Post'* soaring above the school grounds. This was fitting because in the military tradition, *'The Last Post'* is the bugle call that signifies the end of the day's activities. I can recall 'Femi Suleiman sounding notes on it in his younger days as a cadet and he was certainly a sight to behold.

The unit was also a favourite feature at Queen's College, Yaba's Inter-house Athletics Competitions, usually held at University of Lagos Sports Centre in Akoka. The unit was by tradition always invited to provide security patrols and maintain law and order and you always saw many of the Queen's College girls surrounding and lavishing their gaze dipped in awe on them. The bearing of the full uniform of a cadet certainly trumped the 'magic' of adorning a King's College blazer. It was faded Khaki green material, with brass on the buckle of the belts. The ankle of their black boots was wrapped around with brown cloth of some cotton texture with a red sash reserved for ceremonial occasions. Most of the ranks ranged from Private to RSM; however, on the ceremonial occasion the Commandant wore the rank of a junior commissioned officer.

The unit was also required to provide the ceremonial guard of honour during the *'Annual Speech and Prize Giving Day'*. During one occasion in 1981, they provided a guard for His Excellency, Alhaji Sheu Usman Aliyu Shagari, the President of Nigeria. I believe this glamour was one of the reasons why there was a huge stampede from many boys to the join the unit. But it was not all pomp and pageantry; it was also hard work and graft. The boys were expected to be a near perfect specimen of fitness and had to endure a grueling regime of training, including running around the grounds with rifles held up high. I personally preferred the more subdued atmosphere of the Boy's Scout Troop, which I joined and later rose to become a Patrol Leader and the Secretary of the Troop under the leadership of Babajide Keshinro and later Joel Ugborogho.

In 1983, Nigeria's democratic experiment was truncated and the military took over the government through a coup. It was as if in many ways the school's Cadet Unit pre-empted this as it had its own fair share of intrigues and a power struggle. In 1981, Telema Princewill aka 'Printe...Alacrity', who was the Secretary of the Students' Council and was the Vice-School Captain, became the Cadet Unit Commandant succeeding 'Folayan Osekita who had completed his Fifth Form.

'Folayan Osekita aka 'Osay' was quite an enigma; to the junior boys his origins at the time lay shrouded in mystery but this was less about our innocence and more about the character of the school. It is only much later we discovered his origins lay in Ekiti, the southwest part of Nigeria. During the Speech Day of 1978 when he was in command of the Cadet Unit, he over polished his boots; I suspected he was always up for much fun replenished with a variety of dramas. On that occasion, he wanted to spice things up a little. He was invited to the stage by the guest of honour to collect some prizes, and the next thing we saw was the great 'Osay' propelled high up into the atmosphere, landing, but stubbornly refusing to fall on his back! He had slipped but there was to be no 'yakata' experience. To prove it was no fluke it occurred a second time. Instantly the hall, which was graced with a 1960's installed air-conditioning system, fluttering away in the background, working fitfully, was dominated with applause from students and parents with voices chorusing of *'Osayyyyy'* renting the atmosphere. One could however, observe that this unplanned addition to the programme invoked incredulity from the PKC! But that was the great 'Osay' who above all was a man of principle and a defender of the weak. I believe these attributes may account for the lack of any coups during his tenure as Commandant.

In the Cadet Unit 'Printe' had many lieutenants including Prefect Osita Ike, a tall and suave character with a combination of Igbo and Yoruba blood passing through his veins. The two had both contested for the post of Secretary to the Students' Council. The powerhouse of the unit rested within the armoury, whoever controlled it was likely to have full reins of the unit. The armoury was where all the rifles, pistols and military equipment were stored. It was at the far end of the school near the squash court towards Igbosere area.

It is suggested that with time 'Printe' alienated himself from the troops and became rather 'imperial'. At one of the Wednesday parades, some of the troops took over the armoury and disarmed the Commandant. They installed Prefect Ike aka 'Ozidi' as the new Commandant. 'Ozidi' further cemented his power base by announcing the coup in the dinning hall! 'Printe' was left with little option but to invite the intervention of the PKC. On the next day the PKC an ex-Cadet Unit member himself, took the unprecedented step of suspending the unit in order to forestall a *'breakdown of law and order'*. However, by the time, the unit was reinstated in the next term 'Printe' had been retired and 'Ozidi' took full control of the reins. I also believe that at some point, the rifles were withdrawn but I am not sure it was connected with the coup. I believe this coup was the first of its kind in the history of the school but I believe it simply mirrored what was to happen in the larger society in 1984.

'PLAYING UP AND STRIVING'

It is on the fading green and dust filled fields of King's College that my younger brother Adebowale found his mastery. Whilst I was content to engage in fitful romances with 'power', he excelled by playing at the highest levels for the school team. He was a defender of no mean feat and with the advantage that his height of over 6 feet 3 inches conferred; the dominance in the air followed. His athleticism also allowed him to marshal the central defence effortlessly. He always revealed early footballing promise as a child, and I was known to kick him in the shin betraying my frustrations at the praise he constantly received and the fact that my own talent was concealed in awkwardness.

It was not until he joined me at KC I grudgingly accepted that he was a more talented and better player than myself. What I lacked in footballing skills, however, I think I compensated for on the tracks. My claim to sporting fame was being part of the Panes' House 400 relay team in 1983 and 1984. I also managed a respectable 45th position during the 'Ikoyi Run' in my Second Form. The 'Ikoyi Run' was a mini marathon of over five miles, which took us from Lagos through Victoria Island, Obalende, Ikoyi and then back to the school. In our early youth, it was the ultimate test of physical endurance. The victors could look forward to bottles of fizzy drinks as their prize and my own reward was two bottles of very chilled Coca-Cola.

The talented sportsmen in the school were usually discovered during various inter-house sporting competitions. King's College had four houses, Panes, Harmans, Hyde Johnsons and McKwee-Wrights all named after former PKCs. The competition among them was always fierce and everyone extolled or lavished praises on his house but never disparaged other houses. Talents were abound around the school such as Tarvan, Kayoma aka 'Zaaaaaaaaaaaaaaaaaapiiiiiiig', arguably the best school goalkeeper of his generation and there was Dwari Amesimaka, brother of Adokie who was part of the National football team, the Green Eagles. Dawari was a midfield player per excellence and captained the team. Who could forget Adeniyi aka 'Eba' and his prolific rate of goal scoring? 'Gboyega Adebajo, Uche Chibututu came to dominate the goal posts. Chibututu appeared to have the ability at the sight of a football to lift up like a rocket and dive into the air as if his life depended on it. Later on Udom, Simon Faga,

'Emeka Okoro, 'Niran Ade-Onojobi, Garegea, Chima Oleru, Adebowale Ojedokun and many others dominated the footballing scene.

King's College Lions was the name of the school team, however, at the time I was admitted into KC there was no roar left in them. It had come to feed and dwell upon the past glories of 1976. In that year, it lost in the finals of the Principal Cup to CMS Grammar School 'Bariga Bombers' and every year thereafter we tried without success to avenge that defeat. From 1977, onwards we faced a prolonged drought of trophies but we gained laurels for being the best cheerleaders in Lagos State. The debutante boys in our team faced men in schoolboy teams, many who played semi-professional football. Our boys therefore never stood a chance. You could imagine them attempting to play football against those men in schoolboy teams who were intent on smashing the legs of our boys on the football field in preference to securing the ball!

The raison d'etre of their defenders was to smash the shins of the opposition and ignore the football altogether. I certainly knew of Peter Okoloba who I encountered during my brief stay at CMS Grammar School, he was the team goalkeeper. He was registered as a student in the school but he attended no classes and played for a football league club! I believe it is because of these sharp practices that year after year we suffered defeat upon defeat and even the indignity of one or two massacres. All the '*Shakaboo ki bo saa*' in our chants and songs could not rescue us from the yearly ritual of our certain fate.

The KC prowess at cheerleading did not come effortlessly but rather through many late night rehearsals in the dinning hall, where cheerleaders taught us songs and drilled us in its etiquette. There was never a match that our hoarse voices did not filter through the din of the noise on the playing fields. Our cheers always increased in intensity the more we were losing, hoping that we might gain an improbable victory.

In sports such as Hockey, 'Folayan Osekita, 'Tolani Opaneye the Vice-School Captain, Kweku Tandoh, and Edache aka 'Timber!' reigned majestically on the school scene. There was also Oyediran and Omidiora who participated nationally in athletics. However, it was in cricket that we eventually excelled, winning the National Secondary School Championship in 1984. In 1977 when I started out in KC, St. Gregory's College always bested us at cricket but by my departure in 1984, we were the masters of all we surveyed. It was on the cricket fields of various secondary schools that Anthony Ovie-Whiskey, 'Seyi Akinyede aka 'Sobers', Oluyinka Olutoye, Ani, Gbenusola, Musa aka Otosio, Akinwimiju, Frank Inok, Offigo, Sagoe, Longe, Sam Asielue, Aseru aka 'Cambodia' and many others distinguished themselves and played up and strove with all of them doing their best.

I am compelled as I end this chapter, to pay tribute to Terrance Onyewuenyi, the School Captain of the 1978/79 academic session.   He was the ultimate all rounder! He was an athlete of the highest calibre, who featured in cricket, hockey, the sprints and other sports and yet left the school with the best of grades, allowing him to study Medicine at University of Lagos. It was for boys like this that school colours were invented, the honours given to those with exceptional achievement in the field of sports.   He led on the field and in every part of his life, he lost his life in Takwa Bay, Lagos while trying to save another from drowning, and this was the hallmark of School Captain Terrance Onyewuenyi, a man of blessed memory.

'MY RETURN TO KING'S COLLEGE'

Fresh out of King's College, awaiting resumption at University of Ife I was invited back to the school as a guest speaker. It was the occasion of the Students' Council Week and I was honoured to speak about my experiences as a student. I was now holding sway with a captive audience of boys in the Assembly Hall and I hope I was able to say something inspirational and impact a generation of boys. In the words of Brett and Kate McKay, I have realised that while I may never summon troops into battle or debate a Congressional bill, I believe every man or woman can strive to be a great orator. Whether it is giving the best man speech, arguing against a policy at a city council, making a proposal at work, or giving a eulogy, you will be asked to publicly speak at least a few times in your life. Do not be a man or woman that shakes and shudders at that thought. Be a man or woman who welcomes, and relishes the opportunity to move and inspire people with the power of his or her words. When a speaking opportunity arises, be the person everyone thinks of first.

I attended the event with my good friend Olumide Ashley-Dejo the elder brother of 'Rotimi aka 'AD99'. This was a precursor to my later involvement with the old school. My heart was never distant from King's College all through my years at university I had a yearning to return to the old school to contribute my quota, to give something back. The school had bestowed so much upon me and I knew that it was payback time. I was a fresh law graduate and had enrolled at the Nigerian Law School. I enjoyed some 'exclusive' accommodation courtesy of a family friend, Justice Mahmud Babatunde Belgore, the Chief Judge of the Federal High Court, in the choice area of Ikoyi, a beautifully well laid out area with immaculately kept lawns. The area was formerly a British Government Reservation Area with smatterings of wealth hidden amongst the houses.

Whilst at school, from a respectable distance I always admired the Old Boys who came to visit either during the regular meetings of the King's College Old Boys Association or when celebrations occurred. Many had achieved great heights but we had one or two who were eccentrics. Some would regale us with the history of the school or the antics they got up to. Tradition was what they were strong on, but I also noticed they were a close and select club.

My time at Obafemi Awolowo University (formerly University of Ife), Ile-Ife had been very tumultuous I had attained the near heights of political office but there had also been rustication following a politically inspired jailbreak in which I featured with some dubious prominence. In the end, I re-discovered my Christian faith and started to share with everybody who would care to listen about the joy of salvation. So, it was with some relief that I found myself transported away from *'aluta politics'* to the serene but *'bourgeois'* environs of Ikoyi. Justice Belgore my host had kindly allowed Pedro Okoro my best mate from Obafemi Awolowo University, Ile-Ife to share the accommodation with me in his boys' quarters during the Law School year. The Judge generously ensured that I had all my evening meals in his home and I treated his home like my second home.

In 1988, I attended my first Annual General Meeting of the King's College Old Boys Association (KCOBA) in the school hall, it had been widely advertised and I was excited to be present. I was determined to observe and learn from others who had gone before me. I made a few pointed interventions during the meeting and afterwards Otunba Adeniran Ogunsanya was re-elected unopposed. His re-election had become a formality over two decades and this year was certainly no exception. However, to my surprise Mr. Jani Ibrahim, the Assistant General Secretary nominated me and I was elected to replace Mr. Johnson my old PE teacher as Liaison Officer and a member of the Executive.

I was ecstatic to join such distinguished company of men like Adeniran Ogunsanya, P.C. Asiodu, A.A. Ayida, Vincent Maduka, 'Femi Adegoke, Lateef Olufemi Okunnu, A.A. Ibegbulam, Jani Ibrahim, etc. I was now serving with 'Bingo' on the same Executive Committee and it seemed we would become close friends. I later had some opportunity to visit him at his Ikoyi home and enjoyed his hospitality. I was able to explore some issues with him, such as would he have appointed me a prefect if I had returned for 'A' Levels? I am glad he confirmed in the affirmative and went on to drop hints that I might have been an *'effective'* School Captain. It may well be part of my fertile imagination but that is how I remember it. He has now departed the shores of this earth but he will never be forgotten for the marks so indelible he left on us.

What struck me most about the King's College Old Boys Association is the brotherhood, the mutual support offered and the desire to lift each other up. The unbridled ambition they had was for the school alone. I did not sense any fierce rivalry or unseemingly competition for office. We simply trusted each other. I could visit Otunba Adeniran Ogunsanya's home and dine with him while I provided him some update on some Association business. The genuine affection showed to me by the Otunba was also evident in my interaction with other Old boys. As far as they were concerned, I was an equal and they treated me so. I recall on one hot afternoon, I visited Chief Ogunsanya's Pius Okibo home in Suru-Lere to brief him on some arrangements I had been delegated to make for the 70th anniversary celebrations of the school. He received me warmly and asked the steward to serve both of us plates of Jollof rice garnished with chicken and prettied with peas. Here was I, in 1989, barely out of university at age 22 seated, fraternising with one of Nigeria's foremost nationalist, it seemed so surreal. The added bonus was I could walk into the offices of several KCOBs simply because I served on the executive.

The slow disintegration of King's College mirrors that of our country and in 1988; it was already evident from my regular visits to the school as Liaison Officer. My engagements with the PKC, Mr. Agun yielded little but apathy, he was simply unable to understand my point. Discipline in the school was not what it used to be, shirts untucked, badges missing and unruliness had become a constant feature of the school life. To my horror, the Students' Council had been in abeyance for a while and in response to my entreaties the PKC made it clear that he certainly did not appreciate schoolboys could be entrusted with such responsibilities. I brought this to the attention of the Association's Executive but there was so little we were able to do. I knew my work would be cut out in my new role but was taken aback by the extent of the rot presented.

I admit that my role as a member of the executive brought some *'status'* but my former classmates simply could not understand what I was doing with the Association at that stage of my life. Through that role I was able to meet many men, men steeped in the history of our nation, Nigeria, Dr. 'Koye Majekodunmi, Dr. Lateef Adegbite, Otunba T.O.S, Benson, Sir Ademola Adetokunbo, Chief Remi Fani-Kayode, Dr. Alex Ekwueme etc. Incidentally Ken Ekwueme, the son of the Nigerian Vice-President during the Alhaji

Sheu Shagari's administration became my school son. The term school son, was a term of endearment for a junior boy whom you were closest to and took a mentoring interest. Due to the nature of the relationship between Queen's College and King's College, it was not unusual too for KC boys to have school daughters in QC and vice versa and in fact, Mopelola Folashade Olawoye (Obatunsin) was my school daughter. The extent of my friendship with Ken extended to my visiting the official residence of the Vice President where I stumbled across his father and enjoyed close proximity to power. It seemed that with these connections and encounters with history, that my future was now gilded in gold and I could walk in the same path as my father trod before me.

Chief 'Remi Fani-Kayode aka 'Fani Power' impressed me most out of the figures I met, despite his previous notoriety, his sophistication and his calm and considered demeanour was miles away from his fame of the chaos in the 1960s rigging that he was associated with during the elections of the Western region. He was in vigorous health even at age 70 or so and I was surprised that less than five years afterward he had succumbed to an illness and later passed away. Otunba T.O.S. Benson whom we visited in his Falomo residence still displayed a degree of rascality; he never sat at the back when chauffeur driven and chose to sit with the driver in the front seat in order to monitor his activities. He said clearly he was not prepared to allow any chauffeur to run him into an early grave. He was a practical joker and very jovial. Dr. Majekodunmi, the previous Administrator of the Western Region and proprietor of St Nicholas Hospital, Lagos, who lived in a very secluded part of Ikoyi was the most reserved of them all and said very little in my presence.

In the case of Otunba Shobomi Balogun now late, his wealth and opulence were very evident from my encounter with him. In the only meeting I had with him in the presence of Otunba Ogunsanya, I excused myself to use the gentlemen's in his office and was astonished with the décor and beauty that the suite of toilets presented, tiles laced with gold and a beautiful aroma pervaded the space so you could do the business with the uttermost of comfort. I really thought I had seen it all. After learning the ropes from the masters, I soon learnt to visit many other well-connected old boys without the appendage of the more famous ones. It was simply enough to introduce myself as an executive of the King's College Old Boys' Association and the doors swung open.

The next stage of this book focuses on my time of struggle at Obafemi Awolowo University Ile-Ife, the intrigue, betrayal, rustication and triumph of good over evil.

'THERE IS ONLY ONE UNIVERSITY'

In the early 1980s whilst my nascent Christian faith was not a barrier to the increasing bond of friendship that was developing amongst Ayowale Ogunye, Oladele Olawoye and I, slowly but surely our paths diverged. The divergence occurred on account of the progress with their studies and the stalemate with mine. I was marking time at King's College, Lagos while they progressed to University of Ife and Repton College, Derby in the United Kingdom respectively. This was a huge but inevitable wrench but we maintained regular contact. It is interesting to note that through 'Dele, his younger sister Mopelola, a dark petite, pretty and very astute girl became 'my school daughter' and the bond with the family remains strong. I would spend many Fridays visiting her at their campus home and offering any encouragement I could give. Naturally, it evinced some suspicion on the part of her mother thinking I might be nursing some romantic inclinations towards her daughter but that was always further from the truth.

The University of Lagos, Akoka campus staff quarters where they lived was nicely laid out with each of the Professor's houses crowed around with low hedges of the bougainvillea variety and gardens surrounding it and of course a garage and two roomed boys' quarters to complement it. Other staff quarters came in flats but were all decently apportioned with lots of space and boys quarters allocated to each flat. Inside the houses, the sitting areas were nicely set out with spacious rooms, a dinning and a study on the ground floor. The master bedroom on the upper floor was usually en-suite and the other two rooms were of reasonable sizes. The roads were smooth, consisting of two lanes and made of concrete in contrast to those of Abule-Oja where we lived. Those who lived in the quarters were cushioned from the harsh realities of life outside.

'Dele, Ayo and I had formed a close bond from our attendance at the summer school held during the long vacation at the University of Lagos Faculty of Education. Here we reunited with many old Staff School mates and made new acquaintances from other schools. I was known to preach to a couple of the students and was listened to but many just found the whole thing bizarre and hilarious. Once while visiting 'Dele's home in the staff quarters with others, which included 'Damola Adeyeye and I led a number of us in a lunch prayer session in the sitting room. However, in the middle of the session, Dele's father, the law Professor, Mr. C.O. Olawoye arrived, interrupted us in dramatic fashion, and proceeded to lecture us on the dangers of religious extremism!

I remember that every holiday, back from Ile-Ife, Ayo who also lived at the University of Lagos staff quarters with his father a Professor of Chemical Engineering, his mother, his siblings, 'Yinka, 'Tayo, 'Bukola and 'Deji, would, on my visits, entertain me with tales about life in Ife, of its glory, its beauty and the new vista of opportunities it opened up. He would entertain me with *'gist'* about the Elite Club and its intrigues. At home, I also received some interesting accounts from my twin sister, Folashade, through letters or when she ventured home on holidays. I always suspected that there might be some slight exaggerations but I was proved wrong. I was full of envy but was torn between going to Ife or settling into University of Lagos near where we lived. It would have been very advantageous to be in close proximity to Panaf Olajide Olakanmi who now worked at the University so that I could effortlessly resume my career in student politics.

However, there were two hurdles to cross, that of the Joint Admissions and Matriculations Board (JAMB) and the School Certificate Examinations. There was a mix up which caused some confusion with my JAMB registration, which was only resolved thanks to the efforts of Dr. E. A. Akinluyi, the Director of Planning at University of Lagos. I had consistently scored highly in my Fifth Form examinations except in the subject of Mathematics. This was a disappointment to my mother because despite all the investments she made in providing me various Mathematics tutors I simply could not hack it. I acquired a reputation with a few classmates of scampering out through the classroom windows on the arrival of the Math's teacher, I simply dreaded the subject and I was no longer interested in giving it the benefit of doubt.

Eventually I received my School Certificate results and I was sorely disappointed, not because I was unsuccessful. However, I was unable to obtain the highest distinctions in all my seven subjects only managing distinctions in five of them. Of course, I knew there was no hope for me with Mathematics where I managed a pass but Biology? I thought I deserved more that a credit and Oral English, a pass? I thought after my debating experience I could speak English with effortless diction only to be proved wrong. In any case, my results were excellent enough for me to be admitted into university.

Now I had to await the JAMB results to see if I would be admitted into the Ife Law Faculty. The cut off mark for Law was very high, you needed to score over 300 out of 400 to be in with a chance. In my case, I fell short, I only scored 278, it seemed my mother's dream of me studying law would not be realised for the moment. The study of History, my second choice, beckoned me like my father before or I could take up the option of a return to King's College for 'A' Levels so I could retake JAMB, this was the dilemma I faced.

Taking cue from the path my father took I settled for History at Ife but obfuscated when telling my friends what I was studying. I felt rather inferior to those studying a professional course. In the past I had long arguments with Ayo Ogunye when I suggested to him I wanted to study Political Science, he always looked at me puzzled, wondering what for? When I pointed him to the example of my father, he simply responded by suggesting times had changed. I had the opportunity during the long vacation of spending some time in Ile-Ife with Professor 'Kayode Adetugbo. On my first visit I was blown off my feet by its majestic beauty, the immaculately kept lawns, the variety of flowers and the vitality it embodied.

The entrance into the university concealed the full extent of its beauty but as you left the gates behind you and approached, venturing deeper into its grounds much more awaited you. You were slowly but deliberately seduced into the bosom of its environs as it emerged like a tantalising painting from an arts gallery, the beauty of the campus was revealed before you, its magnificence enticed you and its architecture enraptured you, rendering you speechless! There was indeed only one university in the world and any hankering for the University of Lagos simply faded into oblivion. Professor 'Kayode Adetugbo with whom I stayed with was a union activist in the University and he regularly played host to many political activists on the campus and it is from him I received my first introduction in the political life at Ife.

On the university's resumption day, the 2nd of December 1984 my twin sister and I with my mother driving travelled to Ile-Ife in our crammed blue Nissan estate car, which appeared to be anchored down with so much of my sister's luggage. After driving ponderously for four hours, we arrived at *'Great Ife'*. I entered Ife armed with lots of cash, some acquired from my mother but most of it through the generosity of my uncle Dr. Benjamin Abimbola Adigun who was always kind to me. Dr. Adigun, my father's second cousin was a director of AGIP OIL, tall, very regal in bearing, and very wise, a man of great means who spoke Italian effortlessly.

I embarked on a spending spree, eating lavishly, sampling a variety of soft drinks and visiting the Oduduwa Hall to watch the movies. Less than three weeks later in 1985 my spending spree came to an abrupt end when my wallet containing all my cash of over a thousand naira was stolen during a film show at Oduduwa Hall.

While my twin was guaranteed some accommodation in Mozambique Hall, there was no chance I would get one on account of late receipt of my admission letter. However, my uncle, Professor 'Kayode Adetugbo agreed to harbour me temporarily in his staff quarters whilst I settled down. However, that was very far from my mind, I was already plotting on how I would seize the political scene in Ife by storm. Academics was also very remote from my mind; I reasoned that if I could succeed in my acquisition of power at King's College, Lagos there was no reason why at University of Ife it could not be my oyster but here I was to receive a rude awakening.

'ANGOLA HALL'

I had barely spent two weeks on the campus of University of Ife when 'Segun Aderemi and 'Lanre Arogundade, members of the University of Ife Students' Socialist Group approached me with suggestions that I become an ally. They had a claim to being principled and stout defenders of students' rights, they were fearless and 'Lanre Arogundade the National President of National Association of Nigerian Students (NANS) was the immediate past General Secretary of the Students Union. They must have read my articles placed on strategic notice boards on the campus, *'In Defence of Panafism'* which suggested rather flatteringly I possessed great potential. I was quick to retort that I was no Socialist but a *'Panafist'* with allegiance to Panaf Olajide Olakanmi. They listened with bemusement and then assured me we could still work together. The truth was at the time I was in awe of them and would have done much to gain proximity to them.

The Socialist Group was closely knit, highly disciplined and functioned like another family. They had regular Sunday meetings at 3pm prompt in Fajuyi Hall Annexe, one of the large spaces on the landings opposite the staircase that ran through to two floors of rooms where various Marxist texts were explored, critiqued and considered. I attended these meetings and participated in their discussions. I was well placed to contribute to the discussions having learnt a thing or two from my uncle Professor 'Kayode Adetugbo who described himself as a *'Marxian'*. However, the real power in the group lay with the *'Central Committee'*, it actually made the decisions and directed political strategy. It made decisions on whom to offer support at Students' Union elections and whether to sponsor or offer support to any candidate.

In time, I was approached and it was suggested I run for the office of Angola Hall Chairman and Tesslim Adewuyi one of the loyal cadre stand for General Secretary. Angola Hall was traditionally a hall of residence for first year students and it consisted of many sprawling bungalows sub divided into ten rooms each, set out in a dormitory style with four double bunks. It was bounded by another hall of residence, Obafemi Awolowo on one side and the forest on the other side. A few metres from it was Mozambique Hall where the ladies, a significant proportion of whom were new students resided and it was always heaving with human and vehicular traffic at night.

150

In 1975, Angola and Mozambique Halls were built and designed as temporary accommodation with a maximum of 1,320 legal occupants each but the population had increased by a third through squatting and then the halls assumed permanent status. Initially it was named Emergency Hostel 1 while Mozambique was named Emergency Hostel 2 and was the furthest away from the academic centre of the campus.

However, I faced a difficulty contesting because I was a 'squatter' and not a legal resident of the hall. The Socialist boys assured me that they would take care of things and that it should be the least of my worries. I had been unable to secure student accommodation in the hall so I joined the ranks of squatters in Angola Hall. There was an acute shortage of accommodation so many had to sleep on any available space in the rooms. After I moved from room to room in search of a space, 'Emeka Okolo, an old classmate from King's College, Lagos extended his heart of kindness towards me and invited me to be his *'squatter'* in Room D10, but he was sworn to secrecy. To my friends and acquaintances who visited me in the room, they assumed I was the landlord. Emeka Okolo was a Chemistry student with a quiet demeanor, light complexioned, broad chest and legs that formed a slight bow. He had a wicked sense of humour and kindness oozed from him.

The campaign for Angola Hall Chairman commenced but it was miles away from the King's College's *'Marquess of Queensberry'* rules. The campaign was full of dirty tricks. It was while I was campaigning from room to room, that I met Kolawole Onifade aka 'Mazini', a Part Two History/Political Science undergraduate who had previously contested under similar circumstances. He was very sympathetic to me and we struck a cord. Mazini was one of the most generous students I knew, he contained a physique, ample in bulk and a vivacious personality, he was very articulate but also full of mischief and bombast. Mazini was much younger than he looked and claimed but *'his can'* do attitude masked his relative youth.

He joined forces with me and on the Speech Night, he went around the uneven terrains of the hall grounds mobilising for me. I had set up no campaign committee because I had assumed the Socialist boys would take care of things, but in reality, I was left to my own devices. At the Speech Night venue, in the Angola Hall's common room I was disrupted and prevented from speaking, confusion ensued, the whole election descended into utter chaos. In the aftermath, my opponent 'Ozidi' claimed victory and was declared *'the winner'*! This was a huge disappointment for I had promised much and seen little in the results. I had assumed that with my political pedigree, I would walk the election but the rules had changed and I could not expect everyone to play by my own idealistic rules. After a protest in form of a petition lodged at the Students' Union Judicial Council the Angola Hall Executive elections were nullified. The Executive Committee of the hall was left in abeyance for several weeks. I used the hiatus to build up myself, learnt a few lessons and was determined to come back stronger. At this stage, I had completely relegated my Christian life to the background.

The new election date was set in 1985 and I entered the fray once more but was now better prepared. Mazini was on hand to offer strategic and political advice. Using the skills developed at King's College I covered the length and breadth of the hall of residence, the common room, visited every room, shook every hand, and looked the residents in the eye. I espoused Panafism, and a welfarist manifesto; there was no hint that the Socialist boys were *'sponsoring'* me. My posters were everywhere and many where enthused by what I was offering.

At the Speech Night, I wore the same trademark black fess cap and silky white *'Danshiki'* with a pair of black trousers. I summoned all my powers of oratory and my voice soared across the common room:

> *"Gentlemen, fellow compatriots, I Panaf Olu Ojedokun hereby*
> *declare that through the making use of all the resources at my*
> *disposal, supported with facts and figures I will achieve your goals*
> *and will use other means should they become inevitable…."*

The response from the audience in the common room was ecstatic, the whole place went ballistic and my soaring rhetoric had put me ahead for now. 'Ozidi' spoke but only a few paid rapt attention because I had *'bewitched'* them with my speech. At the end of the night, I was declared elected, the new Chairman of Angola Hall while Tess became the General Secretary. The amiable but more mature 'Kolapo Ganiyu aka

152

'Baba Kolly', who had tribal marks decorating his face, became the Financial Secretary whilst Dayo assumed responsibility for Socials and Aladejobi for Sports.

On reflection, I tend to agree with the words of Brett and Kate McKay that there is:

> *"The great myth perpetuated about public speaking is that talent in this area is inherent and inborn and cannot be learned. But our manly forbearers knew better. The great orators of the world from Cicero to Rockne practiced the art of oratory with resolute single-mindedness. Demosthenes exemplified this drive particularly well. As he was a child he was weak and awkward in both body and speech."*

In my new role as Hall Chairman, I automatically became a member of the Students' Representative Council and I was duly sworn in at the next meeting. Soon I became a popular face around the campus. At night, Mozambique Hall was my regular destination, to get replenished in my twin, Folashade's room or to visit my cousin Kikelomo Ojedele. I became famous around the campus due to my distinct form of dressing, which I wore like a uniform. No one except my roommates every caught a glimpse of the top of my head, it was always covered with a black beret or fez cap. I must have been the first chairman in the history of the hall who was a squatter.

On a few occasions when I ventured out without my trademark attire, I was completely incognito. We were, however, hard at work, with Tess at my side, we ensured new fridges were purchased, a successful *'Angola Week'* was organised courtesy of sponsorship from the Angolan Embassy, the common room was refurbished, refrigerators purchased, cleanliness became a priority for the hall authorities and we facilitated the supply of essential commodities. In less than six months we transformed the hopes and dreams of the residents from their past reality and they were well pleased.

'THE STUDENTS' UNION'

The spectre of my father's memory was never remote from me even at the campus of Ile-Ife. Everywhere I went I came across his old colleagues. One of the first acts of my aunt, Mrs. 'Bisi Adejumo was to take me along to visit to the University Vice-Chancellor, Professor 'Wande Abimbola. He had been a colleague and friend of my father whilst at the University of Lagos. He was reputed to have *'mystical'* powers always dressed in the Yoruba traditional gown, *'agbada'* he had the traditional title of *'Awise'* and always bestrode the campus with a horsewhip.

He was very knowledgeable in the history of *'Ifa'*, his area of specialisation. On reflection I now agree with Professor Wole Soyinka's suggestion that *'his face usually betrayed a facial immobility that wavered between bewilderment and cunning watchfulness.'* My aunty reckoned getting to know the VC would make it easier for me to transfer to the Law Faculty later in my second year. His official residence, deep in the campus staff quarters creatively nestled upon a hill, was palatial, beautifully spread out on modulating surfaces, and he lived like a chief of state. Professor 'Kola Folayan an Historian and the Dean Faculty of Arts was another of my father's old classmate who I saw on an occasional basis and there was the mercurial Professor Olajide Aluko of the Department of International Relations.

Professor Aluko had been on the same Ph.D. programme with my father at the London School of Economics sharing Emeritus Professor James Mayall as their supervisor. I met James Mayall in 1991 when I was thinking of pursuing a Masters' degree at the London School of Economics, he was very kind and complimentary about my father and confirmed what I already suspected, that my father had a reflective personality.

With the introductions, out of the way I settled into a life of politics. My first year as a History student was very relaxed because my lectures started on Monday mornings and ended on Wednesday nights. This left me with lots of time on my hands and travelling becoming one of my occupations. It was not unusual for me to travel to Ibadan on Wednesday night and return on Sunday night. After a relatively successful first year in the History Department under the tutelage of Prof Olufemi Omosini and a cream of first-rate lecturers, I left the department transferring to the Faculty of Law.

This occurred with the kind assistance of Professor 'Kola Folayan and Professor Jonathan Fabunmi, the Dean of the Law Faculty.

I felt immense joy and pride and thought I was finally on my way to achieve great things. Above everything else I was now finally reunited with my twin in the same Faculty on the same campus. I was following in her footsteps taking the same path she had trod two years before. She was now in her third year and had moved to Moremi Hall, the hall for ladies in their penultimate and final years. The hall was located a few meters from the Faculty of Science Building and was named after an ancient heroine, Princess Moremi, who was once a ruler in Yorubaland. It was built between 1973 and 1974 with a capacity of about 1,228 students.

There was my regular haunt, the Students' Union Building which was a complex of offices, rooms and shops near the University Sports Centre. It was the secretariat of the Students' Union government where all the elected officers were based. In front of it, was a statute of students in their academic gowns and fists clenched and raised up reminiscent of the black power salute. I recently discovered that it had undergone a revamp and now looks spanking and attractive. The building was opposite Oduduwa Hall, the main University auditorium and venue of many social events, University convocation, and matriculation ceremonies and film shows. The breathtaking architecture of Oduduwa was also very functional for it was split into a covered section and an open section, which was like a modern day coliseum. I had my own office in Angola Hall beside the buttery but I often visited the choice restaurants that lay underneath the building or went to see the Union President. During my first year tumultuous events occurred in the Union. The President, 'Wale Lawal was impeached; the Union's official Peugeot estate car was burnt down and Kola Onifade aka 'Mazini' was maliciously accused of this act by some of the Socialist boys.

This was a strategic error on their part for these events led to the demystification of the NANS National President who prior to that was considered heroic and beyond reproach and dented the Socialist Group's credibility. The Socialist had *'blacklisted'* 'Mazini' but he would triumph over them and later be exonerated. Afterwards 'Mazini' contested and was duly elected to the Students' Representative Council representing the Arts Faculty. He was furious and hurt with the treatment he received and decided to take on the Socialist boys, I thought he must be raving mad!

The Socialists had a long-standing alliance with some of those in the Liberal Grouping, A.T.P. Alao, 'Wole Iyamu (SAN), Ibrahim Pam, 'Kembi Adejare and Jerry. They were ex-Union officials better known for their longevity on campus and were pragmatists. They were not as organised as the Socialists but they were a political force of some sort. The Socialists always treated them with a degree of suspicion but entered into an alliance of convenience with them. I joined the magazine of the Liberal Group as a correspondent and in doing so incurred the wrath of the Socialists early in my Part One. The charge was that I was moving too close to the Liberal's boys. Olubunmi Oyewole, now a Nigerian Federal Appeal's Court Judge, had the task of calling me to order and educating me on the need to keep a respectful distance from the Liberals. Then you had the 'SUs', the *'Born-Again'* Christians mostly belonging to the Evangelical Christian Union and affiliate of NIFES, Brother Joe Tarkon was prominent among them. Their chances of winning elections were always limited by their uncommon fidelity to the truth. I was always sympathetic to them but due to my lust for 'power', I saw them as politically irrelevant. It was later in time that 'Mazini', 'Garibaldi' and others constituted themselves into another counterweight group.

In the meantime I had joined the campaign team of 'Bimbo Bamidele who was campaigning to be the next Union President. She was my opposite number in Mozambique Hall as Chairperson; she was bright, articulate and beautiful and a Law student. She was not the typical 'aluta' student that you would imagine; she was cosmopolitan and her voice drowned in sophistication. With the backing of the Socialist boys, she became the first female President of the Students' Union. Prior to that, ladies were content with the office of Vice President. Due to my role on her campaign team, I became part of her close circle and acted as her envoy to a number of universities including the University of Benin. I also joined her on the team that travelled to visit the *Ewi of Ado-Ekiti*, the paramount ruler in Ekiti land to resolve the intractable Student Union crises at the University then named Obafemi Awolowo University. By the end of my first year, I had become a regular feature on the Student's Union scene. Many speculated that my ambitions lay in the Presidency of the Student Union but for now, I kept my counsel.

156

I was now a Law student and a little application to my studies was required, I could not afford to fail. Later on my twin and her friend Abiola Ijalaye, the daughter of Professor David Ijalaye, a Law Professor, had to repeat their third part of the Law programme after they were unable to pass a re-sit examination. I later discovered this happened only because she would not succumb to the seductions of a particular lecturer. Ironically both of them, 'Biola and 'Shade succumbed early to the ravages of cancer, united as friends even in the transition to heaven!

Anyway chastened by this I assumed the second year would be politically quiet for me while I consolidated my studies. I was no longer a squatter and moved into an accommodation *'befitting'* my role as the Angola Hall Chairman. However, as the election season resumed in 1985 the Socialist boys had other plans for me, they suggested I run for the Office of Assistant Secretary, however, after some political calculations made on the assessment of my success as Angola Hall Chairman, they conceded I run for the post of Welfare Officer. I felt at home with this and Mazini was delighted for me. Whatever suspicions Mazini had about my alliance with the Socialist boys he never betrayed it to me. I constituted a campaign team and we began to plot how to take the campus by storm.

This was no easy road, there were about 20,000 students eligible to vote, dispersed over a campus the size of 20 kilometres by 53 kilometres. In the course of the campaign, my voice went hoarse, my legs ached and studies were relegated to the background. I ensured it was Panafism *'everywhere'*. The charismatic *'La Pre'*, a Part Two History undergraduate was my main rival for office. He was a resident of Obafemi Awolowo Hall and had a large and loyal following mostly ex-students of Oyo State College of Arts and Science (OSCAS) on whom he could rely on. With words, industry and application I was able to peel off some of his support. I laid out an ideal and I prodded them to purchase it. All Union Offices were being contested and the main protagonists were Ajayi Owoseni, a Part Three Law Student who had previously been a teacher in Ijero-Ekiti and 'Deji Balogun an ex-journalist and reputed to be the leader of the *'He dey happen boys'*, the name used to describe the middle class socialites. However, Owoseni was odds on favourite to become the next President.

I rehearsed my speech again and again and I was advised by my handlers that the speech had to come from memory. I realised that in order to appeal to the noblest and finest sentiments within the audience of Great Ife I had to fill it with allusions to the greatest characters, events, and artistic expressions of history. My speech therefore embroidered with all of these.

I had acquired a white flowing gown, an *'agbada'*, to be worn on top of my *'Danshiki'* and a new black fez cap to provide me with a fresh look. The Speech Night was held at the University Sports Centre. When it came to my turn to speak, you could hear a pin drop, silence so essential to me was secured. With my voice ringing with rhythm, I started out:

> *"Ladies and Gentlemen, fellow compatriots, boys and girls, we face times of great uncertainties, that is why I Panaf Olu Ojedokun I am contesting to be your new Welfare Officer.... The past is a story told, the future may be written in gold..."*

The more rhythm evinced, the more enraptured the crowd became. At the end of my speech the result was not in doubt. We retired to Angola Hall in the confidence that we would win an unassailable victory. I was as expected declared the Welfare Officer-elect and Ajayi Owoseni became President-elect, 'Joke Akinlade, Vice-President-elect, Taiye Taiwo as Director of Socials-elect while 'Segun Adeyemo aka 'US' succeeded me as the Angola Hall Chairman and Segun Carew aka 'J O Jasper' became the Hall Financial Secretary.

But that was only the beginning of the political drama. We still had to contend with the elections into the leadership of the legislative arm and the potential fallout I was to experience. In the meantime I had invited 'Mazini' to join me in my new official room at Obafemi Awolowo Hall, together with 'Kehinde Bamgbetan who was elected the Public Relations Officer, we shared the room located on the second floor and we had Medical Students as neighbours. The hall had been built in 1970 and was very similar in style to Adekunle Fajuyi Hall. Mazini was becoming much feared by many, he had the habit of wearing flowing gowns of the faded *'Ankara'* variety late into the night and early in the morning to preserve his modesty. He enjoyed issuing elaborate threats to his perceived opponents, especially those of the Socialist Group. Some rumoured that he had *'mystical powers'* and disguised some hidden charms under his flowing gown but in reality it was all youthful bombast and his claim to mysticism lay in the land of fertile imaginations.

At the first meeting of the newly constituted Students' Representative Council elections were held for its principal officers. Olaitan Akinwunmi aka 'Santana' from the Socialist Group who contested against Olurotimi 'Shadow' (of beloved memory) a close ally of the Student Union President won the post of Speakership because they were easily the most organised. Olaitan Akinwunmi aka 'Santana' settled into the traditional room of the Speaker in Adekunle Fajuyi Hall and had began to lay out plans for the next parliamentary session when something extra-ordinary happened.

By custom and convention, only members of the House were allowed to contest for the post of Speaker. However, the constitution was ambiguous about the exact eligibility requirements. A classmate of mine, Lucky Omo Takpor in the Law Faculty who was not a member of the Student Representative Council had been disqualified from contesting became disgruntled. He proceeded to the Judicial Council to challenge his disqualification. Many suspected the allies of Olurotimi aka 'Shadow' put him up to this. After a bit of horse-trading and high wire politics the Judicial Council voting seven votes to six votes nullified the election of 'Santana' as Speaker. This was a shock to the Socialists and those of us who had supported him. The Students' Representative Council was reconvened in Moremi Hall Common Room for new elections to be held. The moon was out and shining brightly that night, the air was fresh and many were determined to smoke out the *'closet'* Socialists and their supporters. It seemed there would be no hiding place even in bosoms of Moremi Hall.

Therefore, against all convention it was agreed that the election would be by show of hands. This presented a huge dilemma for me for I could not betray the Socialists boys because they had been good to me, supported me and not sought to control me. I was determined to support them at risk to my popularity. 'Mazini' and Gbolahan aka 'Garibaldi' were at the forefront of the opposition to the Socialist Group and had begun to suspect my fidelity to them. Tension began to suffocate the space in our room as my roommate began to sense that I was on the other side. The elections were held and with little hesitation, I raised my hands up to indicate support for 'Santana'. He lost this time to Olurotimi 'Shadow' and there was jubilation by 'Mazini' and his group. Many were aghast that Panaf was in *'league'* with the Socialists and 'Mazini' threatened me at the scene with brimstone and fire! We all retreated to the Socialist Group's headquarters in Adekunle Fajuyi Hall to lick our wounds.

When I returned to our room in Awolowo Hall, 'Mazini' fully expecting to be turfed out invited me to do my worst. I really did not see the point in making any enemies at this stage so calmly and coolly I responded to 'Mazini', assuring him that I was not going to throw him out and even though we disagreed on principle, he will always remain my friend. He accepted my entreaties and remained my roommate. However, from then under relentless pressure my alliance with the Socialist boys cooled.

As the Welfare Officer, I had responsibility for all Students' Union tenants and made it a point of duty to pay an introductory visit them to introduce myself and get to know them. My visit to the proprietor of the main restaurant produced a shock! He had welcomed me into his office and then I tucked myself comfortably into the chair opposite him when he offered me an envelope padded and full of crisp notes! In a daze, I asked him what he thought he was doing, he assured me he meant no harm it was simply something to defray my election expenses. I erupted in disgust and told him in certain terms he had attempted to bribe the wrong man. I also suggested I was minded to revoke his tenancy. He pleaded with me and I left cautioning him that he was on borrowed time. I am afraid that even in 1986 he was not the only one who attempted to bribe me, but because he was so casual with it, I suspect other office holders before me may have indulged. The man, however, was inscrutable; he instructed his staff to give me extra special service and extra fried rice and assorted pieces of fish, my favourite dish. In response, I issued advice to all his staff that they could only provide me such extra special service provided they did so to all students. I was not surprised that afterwards normal service was resumed and all the silliness ceased.

As the months wore on my academic work began to take the strain, I hardly had any time to attend lectures but made sure I attended all tutorials and borrowed notes from my colleagues. In those tutorials, I have fond memories of Professor Odunmosu,

Dr. Boparai an Indian gentleman and Mr. Barnes a Black American. Amazingly, I scored the highest in a mock test held for the Law of Contract course. It was as if like my father I was treading the same path. He had participated in students' demonstrations in Lagos against the Anglo-Defence Pact, ignoring entreaties from his cousin, Uncle 'Dejo Ojedele, I was intentionally strolling along the same path. However, this path seemed even thornier and more precarious.

'THE VICE-CHANCELLOR'

Only a selected few knew of my relationship with Professor 'Wande Abimbola (In later years he ventured into politics and became the Senate Majority Leader) and they assumed because he was my *'guardian'* I might let him off lightly. However, they were proved wrong. Whilst I had become more circumspect in pursuit of power, I was still capable of verbally trampling on anyone who stood in the way. We had many thorny issues to resolve with the University authorities and the Vice-Chancellor called several meetings. Typically, the University's Principal Officers and Students' Union Executives attended these meetings. At the meetings, I was always quick to speak and was rather hard on the Vice-Chancellor, who never quite understood why I never learnt the virtue of restraint with him. It was as if my picking on him allowed me to demonstrate virility. I think for me it was simply business and no hard feelings as I felt the needs of students were paramount. Mr. Seasan Dipeolu, the bald and dark complexioned man, whose legs had a pronounced bow was the University Librarian and was usually the one that brought wise counsel to proceedings when we reached a stalemate. There was Dr. Ezekiel Oyelami Adetunji, the Ibadan man whose face was patterned with decorative tribal marks, the willy University Registrar who was always impatient with our antics.

I also attended some statutory University committees as a Union official. During one of those meetings I struck a very close relationship with Professor 'Wale Omole, an alumnus of the University and a Professor of Agricultural Economics who later became the Vice-Chancellor of the University. He was open, very friendly and always dressed in a smart cream coloured French suit. He chaired the New Bukateria Complex Committee, a complex of mini restaurants the University had built and let out to private caterers. Prior to this, the government had subsidised all student meals and provided them through the caterers employed by the University. The Students' Union was granted one of the units in the Bukateria to run and the Welfare Committee, which, I chaired, was responsible for its management. 'Gbenga Ojo was secretary to the Welfare Committee and the Buka Manager, he gave up so much of his time to run it and I trusted him implicitly. I am afraid that despite all the hard work, we never made any money and it was simply a drain on the Union resources. It was at this point that I began to question my views on natioinalisation of industry. Good intentions were

162

never good enough to run a business. At the Buka, we employed staff, went to wholesale markets and ensured that all students paid for their meals and yet made no profit. I was careful never to eat free meals at the Buka in order to avoid any potential conflict of interest.

The Bukateria was the place to eat if you were awash with cash, with rows of open restaurants, you had a wide variety of choice and you could adapt your finances to suit your preferences. There was Mama 'Funke's Buka, *'the fried rice o!'* Fried rice laced or garnished with slices of dodo (fried plantain), crowned and decorated with a choice selection of meat and fish. You could then decide to cleanse your palate with water or a selection of soft drinks. There was always a long lingering queue there as people rushed there to be fed in sumptuous style. These were the kind of competitors we faced at the Buka even our lower prices did not dissuade the students from visiting Mama 'Funke. However, for those hard up with little cash, up on one of the hills of the campus lay the 'Old Buka', a collection of shanties made from corrugated iron sheets where you could indulge in some *'Lafu and eran hu hu.'* *'Hu hu'* was the phrase coined for those who eat their morsels from a variety of pounded yam and cassava with no meat and it was popularised by 'Jasper'. This was never out of choice but rather a function of lack of financial means. On a few occasions I would visit the Old Buka with 'Segun Carew Oladimeji aka 'Jasper' who had introduced me to this money saving alternative. You could have a dish for about Thirty Kobo (a few pence) provided you were prepared to forgo the delicacies of meat or fish.

In any case, I have arrived at the conclusion that whilst I am not for *'unregulated markets'*, governments simply should have no business running some utilities. Yes there might be one or two strategic utilities governments needs to run but we must explore other means of ownership that is for the common good and ensures profit is reinvested accordingly.

1986 was a time of great crises in Nigeria there was the introduction of the much-derided Structural Adjustment Plan (SAP), the IMF loan, and the Austerity Measures etc. In response to all these measures, Ife Students' Union was in the vanguard of opposition. This meant we were always in the eye of the storm and addressed regular 'World' Press Conferences. In reality, these were local press conferences at NUJ

Headquarters at Iyanganku, Ibadan. I can still picture 'Shadow', Olurotimi, the Student's Union Representative Council Speaker, in his navy blue academic gown and mortarboard on his head, the traditional garb for his office seated beside the Union President as we addressed the Press.

However, the incident that shook me the most was when one of our students was killed in the Ile-Ife Township, his head was almost severed from machete cuts. I received a call to go to the Teaching Hospital to identify some remains, which, the hospital authorities thought might be our student. Sunday, the Union driver drove me over to the hospital and as soon as I entered the cold and freezing morgue, the transience of life hit me in the face, seeing the row of corpses I gasped at the inexorable lowliness of mortality, which is usually obscured by the vibrancy of life. Instantly I recognised the student, he was one of us I had dealings with him in the past! Immediately I felt shivers running down my spine. It was a beheading gone wrong; the head clung on to the body but it was almost severed off. This brought memories flooding back of 'Bukola Arogundade who was beheaded a decade earlier. I suspected ritualists were at work and we were determined to seek justice.

When the news filtered out to the students, they urged us to invade the town, but taking lessons from history, we knew it would be unwise. We met with the University authorities who counseled restraint. We summoned a *'Supreme Congress'*, a gathering of all students and gave emotional speeches, however, the students wanted action and only that would assuage them.

> *"Greaaaaaaaaaaat Ife, Greeeaaaaaaaaaaaaaaaaaat! In the nameeeeeee of every student martyr, in the nameeeeeee of 'Bukola Arogundade, in the nameeeeee of Akintunde Ojo, in the name of Wemimo Akinbolu… I counsel your attention…."*

These were my emotive-laden words to a very charged audience of students in the Obafemi Awolowo Hall Cafeteria. In the end, our tactic of making speeches upon speeches had worked this time and calm was restored. Then as a cabinet, we took the decision to travel to Ibadan to visit the then Oyo State Military Governor, His Excellency, Colonel Adetunji Olurin of blessed memory (retired as a General) and present him with a list of demands. After a few days, we were invited to the Government Secretariat in Ibadan. The Governor dressed in his green military uniform received us, listened to our demands and then responded. He counseled restraint and promised his government would take action.

It was my responsibility as the Welfare Officer to liaise with the family in respect to the burial arrangements. I had the sad and painful task of accompanying the brother to the mortuary to identify the student's remains. We made arrangements to transport the remains in our union Volkswagen Kombi bus to Ibadan, but when the coffin arrived, it was too small. We had asked the family whether they wanted us to arrange the coffin, but the family insisted they had the arrangements in hand. The wooden coffin they managed to purchase was unfortunately not the right size. Through the journey to Ibadan, the student's remains kept on popping out of the coffin because its lid would not shut. However, despite that mishap we were able to give him a befitting burial. This time we had managed to contain a potentially explosive situation but that would not last long.

However, it would only be a partial impression to suggest we were only dealing with tragedies during our time. We organised some events that made University of Ife the envy of many. I recall the 'Fela Anikulapo-Kuti extravaganza that we organised and the *'Miss Culture'* event put on by Taiye Taiwo, the Director of Socials and compered by the irrepressible 'Deji Balogun who had previously contested for the Presidency of the Union. The event that remains etched in my memory, however, is the *'Major Kaduna Nzeogwu Day'* we organised. We invited the retired Major 'Wale Ademoyega to deliver a lecture to mark the event. I was his compere so I had the responsibility for organising his accommodation and transport arrangements and thanks to Mrs. Kuku the Chief Catering Officer and wife of Mr. Femi Kuku a former President of the Student Union he received first class treatment. The Vice-Chancellor was scheduled to meet with the Major but at the last minute he pulled out pleading prior engagements.

The Major who had been part of the original five majors who took part in Nigeria's first coup was a dark, tall, brooding and a contemplative character. He did not speak much and it was obvious that the events leading to the assassination of the Prime

Minister Alhaji Abubakar Tafawa Balewa and the Finance Minister Okotie Eboh still haunted him. When we settled into his suite at the University guesthouse with some reluctance he described to me in stark and gruesome terms the last moments before they were killed.   Whilst the Prime Minister only requested to say his last prayers before he was shot, the Finance Minister was pleading and promising all manner of cash gifts if he was spared. I was with him through the duration of his stay in the guesthouse and accompanied him in the University official car, a Peugeot 504 to return him to his home in Lagos after the event. This was an encounter with a slice of history and brought home to me the opportunities we have wasted, opportunities to transform our lot as a country.

All through this time my mother heard rumours about my antics and was very concerned, I was getting increasingly militant. I rarely visited home during holidays but chose to stay in Ibadan with my cousins, the Odeniyis and the Ojedeles; it was closer to Ile-Ife and which meant easier access. I also enjoyed my time with cousins Oyinkan, Eyitayo, Temitope, Eniola, Mobola, Olaolu, 'Leye and 'Jibola, Kike, Moji, 'Ranti, Ope and Babatunde.   There was never a dull moment with them and my Aunty, Mrs. Odeniyi was one of the kindest I knew.

My faith was not much to write home about, I had visited the campus based Evangelical Christian Fellowship once or twice at the Faculty of Agriculture where its general meeting held and my attendance at Church held in the same venue hardly registered. I was unable to muster any courage to resort to any wild immoral activities as I was constantly focused during my free time on political plotting. The 'Almighty June' examination was approaching, because at the time the Law Faculty was not modular, so there was only one examination in June each year. I realised that it really was going to be difficult to pass the examinations. The Law of torts, Land Law and Nigerian Legal System I could cope with, but Law of Contract?

'ANGO MUST GO!'

'Oro nla le daa a ooo oro nla le da, eyin tee pa omo eku te e joo dagba ooro nla le daa.'

This was the solemn lament sung again and again, in Yoruba language, more like a dirge that emerged from the lips of the masses of students bemoaning the loss of such young lives during the annual commemoration of the brutal murder of 'Bukola Arogundade in the Ife Township. In 1982 'Bukola a student of University of Ife had been beheaded in circumstances which bore suspicions of ritual murder in the town. The students had responded by demonstrating in town near the palace of the Ooni of Ife, 'the spiritual head' of the Yorubas and the police response of teargassing them caused a predictable stampede in town leading to more deaths of students. The song had been etched into my memory from my days as a critical observer at the University of Lagos under the tutelage of Panaf Olajide Olakanmi. It was not only 'Bukola we commemorated but also Akintunde Ojo, a student of University of Lagos tragically killed by police bullets during the 'Ali Must Go' riots of 1978.

The lament had a mesmerising and hypnotic hold on students and most marches of commemoration ended up in violence because it pitched the legion of emotions against a brutal vavolent 'police force' always determined to prevent such outward displays. It was under similar circumstances that the killings of students occurred in a far away University town.

Reports reaching us confirmed the police had killed a number of students in Ahmadu Bello University (ABU) during a raid on the campus. Ahmadu Bello University in Zaria was over 526 Kilometres from us and had been a hotbed of radicalism in Northern Nigeria. Our immediate reaction was to call for a boycott of lectures until Professor Ango Abdullai the ABU Vice-Chancellor was removed. Unrest spread across many Nigerian Universities and higher institutions and there was chaos all over. The military government of the then Major-General Ibrahim Badamasi Babangida was not ready to budge. After a few days of boycotting lectures the students began to agitate for more action, they wanted us to go into the Ile-Ife Township.

It is important to understand the context here, the University of Ife Students' Union had an illustrious history of providing leadership in times of confrontation with the government. It took the principled stand, that an offence against one Nigerian student was one against every student. It therefore saw its role as mobilising other universities and also the general populace. Some within the Union went further to argue that the Union should be in the vanguard of overthrowing the old order and ushering a new socialist and democratic one. Whilst others posited the Union should simply concern itself with basic welfare issues on the campus and the general condition of students. Anyone in leadership at that time had to straddle these extremely diametrically opposed tendencies.

We were able to control events for a while then suddenly a number of students without our prior knowledge ransacked the Police Station near the campus gate and burnt it down to ashes. While this was happening the NTA Ibadan News Television crew invited me to be interviewed in front of the burning embers of what was once the Police Station. In those days, my lust for power was laced with a craving for publicity and I gobbled up the bait. I proceeded to issue a stark warning with my eyes starring intently into the rolling television cameras as I choose my words intentionally, the warning I conveyed to the government was spoken with chilling precision:

> *"This is just the beginning of our struggle we will continue until the government responds to our demands and we are prepared to explore other means if necessary."*

The interview was relayed all over the NTA network news for all to watch and it would seem that one brief moment of impetuousness transformed me into a marked man. At the roadblocks set up by students outside the University I met a visibly concerned Assistant Commissioner of Police and assured him that our students had no grouse with them and we would remain peaceful. The roadblocks consisted of burning tyres and debris and the air was thick with acrid smoke, hardly, indicating a peaceful intent. The situation was becoming desperate and the police unleashed volleys of teargas in a bid to disperse our students.

In his attempt to manage the unfolding crises Professor 'Wande Abimbola, the Vice-Chancellor had followed the throng of students to the gates of the campus at the Ife/Ibadan Expressway junction the previous day. He was futile in his attempts to persuade them to remove the blockade from the road. In a style reminiscent of the man with students in tow, he walked back the entire length of Road One, the University's main artery. Many students trailed him dancing to the melody and discordant tones of 'solidarity songs'; some of which were less complimentary of him. It is suggested that irrespective of his lapses, he was one Vice-Chancellor who strove to understand students and was willing to match their rhetoric word for word. It took a lot of courage to do what he did that day while many of his fellow professors followed, keeping a safe distance from the students.

The next day the 27th of May 1986 was 'Children' Day', a designated Public Holiday, with rallies held by school children all over the country. What we had failed to appreciate was that student protest was like a kaleidoscope, constantly, shifting, and the morning's foe may well be the afternoon's friend. Without any prior consultation, the students decided to go on a solidarity visit to the local stadium where the rallies were held. We decided to follow them in order to maintain control of the rapidly unfolding situation.

I followed in the Students' Union's Volkswagen Kombi bus to monitor the situation. However, by the time we got there all hell had broken loose, our students had overwhelmed and then overpowered the guards at the nearby prisons with 'shock and awe' tactics and then set all the prisoners free! They were intent on forcing through a revolution! We arrived into what was effectively a war zone and I was now on foot with many others. All of sudden from no where we were surrounded and the anti-riot policemen began a game of cat and mouse with us. In my mind, panic had taken over and I thought we had actually bitten off much more than we could chew. This was now big time and no longer amateurish secondary school stuff.

Through the 'fog of war' with the firing of tear gas by the police in the air suffocating us, I managed to locate the Students' Union's Volkswagen Kombi bus and filled it up with as many students as I could find, packed tightly as sardines. I could smell the sweat and fear in the air as I hung out clinging to the back of the bus we drove away to safety at full speed! As we sped back to the campus alarmingly through the roads of Ife I could feel the cold gush of wind bristling across my face and the trees and building disappearing before my eyes. In the meantime, the liberated prisoners were running all over Ife town expressing full gratitude to us for their release. The anti-riot policemen labeled *'Kill and Go'* for their record of mindless brutality gave us the chase, I was weighing down the vehicle and there was adrenaline in free flow through my small frame, in a split second I signaled to Sunday, the Union driver to slow down so I could jump off.

The next moment I found myself laid flat *'yakata'*, on the road, expecting to be scooped up by the chasing police. For a few seconds I lay paralysed with fear but the marauding police simply ignored me and passed me by. I believe that day there was the hand of God upon me. I think they were after the ultimate prize of seizing the instigators in the bus blissfully unaware that one of the Union leaders lay prostrate before them. The bus continued at full speed, managed to navigate the various roadblocks, and escaped to the University campus. In the entire melee, the Union President was missing and it was rumoured that he was under arrest. I observed chaos interwoven with excitement everywhere as I emerged from the back gates of the University, a bit shaken, bruised and walking with a limp. I had heard of the existence of those gates where the junior staff resided but had never had any cause to use it. This time with succour and assistance from local residents, I was able to navigate my way successfully to the centre of the campus.

I was now presented with the urgent task of securing the release of the Student Union President at the urgings of some students I proceeded to the Vice-Chancellor's Lodge with a few. Once there I was the only one let in, there was an emergency Senate meeting in progress, they had heard about the jailbreak facilitated by Ife students and was aghast at the implications. With tension soaking the atmosphere, pretending to be oblivious to their concerns I demanded the Vice-Chancellor use his office to secure the release of our President. Many of other professors at the meeting asked for a situation report and indicated the release of the President was the least of their worries.

I departed from the presence of the Vice-Chancellor and the Senate to return to the halls of residence, then the ground in front of me caved in as I was confronted with the intrusion of my mother and twin sister who were outside waiting for me, they had been searching for me. My mother's face convulsed with worry, it was a look I had seen a few times when I would resist her encouragement to resort to the use of drugs to combat the onset of malaria because I had absolute confidence in divine healing. My mother was very concerned and was shocked about the extent of the trouble I had allegedly caused. In the meantime, the Federal Military Government had announced the indefinite closure of the University and the immediate suspension of the Students' Union. It took a lot of persuasion from my twin sister to accompany her and my mother to Ekiti. By this time rumours were abound that the Secret Security Service (SSS) were searching for all the Union officials including me. The rugged terrain and lowlands of Usi-Ekiti, my mother's hometown was an ideal place to hide away and cool off while things settled down.

We travelled through the thickness of the night, emerging through the rugged hills separated by rivers and arrived at my grand uncle's home. Mr. Agboola was my mother's uncle and a retired civil servant. There my aches and pains were tended to while we rested. I was insistent that I needed to return to Ile-Ife, but my mother was not persuaded. The compromise reached over breakfast was that I would proceed to and stay in Ibadan from where I could monitor the state of affairs at Ife.

I stayed at my uncle, Chief Odeniyi's home; he was not pleased with me and ceased the discussion of all political matters with me for a while. But rather than settle into a period of penitence I approached another uncle who lived in Ibadan on the excuse that I needed to borrow his official car to collect some belongings on the campus at Ife, an hour away. The uncle was a senior government official and he had been generous in the past, providing my twin and I with car lifts to and from the University. However, this time my designs were more clandestine and sinister, once in possession of the car, a Peugeot 504 saloon and the driver I collected some propaganda material from some of the Socialist boys at Ife and drove under the protection of the government registered vehicle to NTA Ibadan and other news outlets to distribute the press release indicating that Ife students were not about to surrender and the struggle would continue in other ways and other means would be deployed if necessary. I returned my uncle's official car back to him and he remained in ignorant bliss that he had aided and abetted 'the struggle'. The Peugeot 504 was the vehicle of choice of the government during that period, it was a car introduced by the then Head of State General Obasanjo in his low profile crusade meant to shun the excess and extravagance of government. The car, a family vehicle was manufactured by the French automaker with permission granted to a plant in Kaduna to assembly it. It was a four door equipped saloon with a carbureted 1,796 cc four-cylinder petrol engine 97 72 kW; 98 PS) with optional fuel injection and 82 bhp (61 kW; 83 PS) in carbureted form. A column-mounted four-speed manual transmission was standard; a three-speed ZF 3HP22 automatic available as an upgrade. It was also the car of choice for many taxi owners in Nigeria.

My uncle Chief Odeniyi was a classmate of Lt. General Alani Akinrinade, a minister in the federal government, so my mother suggested he put in a word for her son to moderate the anticipated wrath of the government. At some stage my mother, Chief Odeniyi and Mr. Ojedele visited the Vice-Chancellor of the University of Ife to plead my case. The Vice-Chancellor let them know in certain terms that we were in trouble and the government was minded to be ruthless with us.

I was invited to a University internal enquiry into the events leading to its closure. At the hearing the tape of my interview with the NTA Ibadan, where I had claimed the struggle had just started, was played endlessly. Dr. Doyinsola Ojutiku (later on the University Registrar), a member of the panel interrogated me repeatedly, for me it seemed they had the smoking gun that would nail me to the mast. The government also set up a public enquiry led by Justice Mustapha Akanbi to probe the crises. In the midst of all these, the University remained closed and all entreaties to re-open it fell on deaf ears.

In the meantime all other universities closed at the aftermath of the crises had re-opened on 14th July 1986 while Ife and Kaduna Polytechnic remained closed due to *'intolerable lawlessness'* the government claimed we had caused. I returned to Lagos for a while and spent some of my time in the University of Lagos where my mother ran a buttery. Once she noticed me trying to mobilise students in Jaja Hall for action and she lost any semblance of coolness instructing me to be quiet and not seek to disrupt the campus. I protested that I was simply conscientising the students but the hard reality is that my mother's income was always severely affected when there was a closure of the campus so she did not need me stirring things up.

In October 1986 whilst on my way back from the University of Lagos staff quarter's I noticed my mother waving me down from her blue Nissan car. She had bad news for me, apparently, the University of Ife had been re-opened but I had been rusticated! The circumstances surrounding this and how I was delivered from it is the sequel to the next chapter.

'JUSTICE AKANBI JUDICAL PANEL OF ENQUIRY'

In August 1986, certain events conspired to ensure my rustication by the Military Government of General Ibrahim Babangida. The government was livid and had set up a Judicial Panel of Enquiry into the 'Ango Must Go' crises, an Investigation of Remote and immediate causes of student crisis in the Nigerian Universities and other Tertiary institutions. The government was determined to get its own pound of flesh from University of Ife. However, the Judge had a reputation of being one of the most fair-minded and independent on the bench. The question was would he bend to the iron will of the regime and be used to deliver their goal? The panel convened for its first session of sittings at the Conference Centre of the University of Ife and I was one of the dramatis personae at the time. Justice Mustapha Akanbi then a Judge of the Federal Court of Appeal chaired the enquiry and Prince Orji Nwafor-Orizu, the son of the ex-Senate President and acting President of Nigeria was one of the members.

The transcript of the University's own enquiry had been published and I had sought the counsel from Professor 'Kayode Adetugbo and a Mr. Ojukwu (Prof.) then a law lecturer on the best approach to take. I was urged to be pragmatic and not speak too much. By then, I was feeling a sense of remorse and was determined to protect my own interests. The Socialist Group had hired Mr. 'Femi Falana (now Senior Advocate of Nigeria) of Alao Aka Bashorun's Law Firm to defend their own interests. During the hearings, I was questioned on my membership of the Socialist Group but in all the questioning, I was not prepared to acknowledge membership. I stated that as far as I was aware there was never any membership list.

My role during the crises was probed in some depth. I was not proud of my display at the enquiry! During one of my interrogations I over heard Professor T. O. Odetola complain about how bad my pronunciation was, he referred to the word *'thing'* which I pronounced *'ting'*. I blame it on our sojourn in Abule-Oja, before then we spoke with an English affectation and clearer diction, but in order to fit into the area we had to adapt fast and our spoken English was the first casualty. I resolved from then on that I would re-master the art of speaking English Language correctly to avoid a similar faux paux. I have always wondered why the East and South Africans speak and pronounce words in English language much better than we do in Nigeria and I suspect the answer lies in their longer and deeper associations they had with the British during colonialism.

The panel re-convened in Lagos at the National Assembly Complex, it was while this was proceeding that the rustication of the following students was announced: Owoseni Ajayi, the Union President, 'Kehinde Bamgbetan, the Public Relations Officer, Olu Ojedokun, the Welfare Officer, (myself) by the Federal Military Government. My twin had returned to Ile-Ife and upon hearing the news broke down in tears, she thought that was the end of my academic studies. The truth was that I was not particularly sad; I simply thought my fantasies of relocating to England would be realised if the government made it impossible for me.

The evening my mother received the news we went to see Professor Clifford Odunayo Olawoye of the Law Faculty of University of Lagos, my friend and school daughter's father, to explore the possibility of a transfer to University of Lagos. After initially suggesting it, he advised against it but was happy to link me up to Alao Aka Bashorun a lawyer in the renowned firm of Barristers and Solicitors. It was at this time that I re-discovered my Christian faith and decided that I had experienced enough of hiking around the mountains. The stakes were high I had been rusticated and the examinations that would promote my classmates to Part Three would be held in a week! Miraculously my rustication was rescinded a day before examinations were due to start. I was not given much hope by many of passing the examinations at short notice. The examinations were the toughest I had ever sat but could not afford to fall at this hurdle!

Thank God, after weeks of tension and worry I discovered that I managed to pass all my papers by securing a *'D'* in every one of them, I had amazingly survived! Now with the Student's Union in abeyance I could face my academics. However, the re-dedication of my faith became a vivid reality, with careful mentoring from my lecturer Mr. Wale Ajai (now a Professor at the Lagos Business School). Now I began to openly profess my Christian faith, took to the regular attendance at Evangelical Christian Union fellowship meetings and joined the discipleship class. Mr. Ajai was kind enough to give the keynote message at my 21st year birthday party, held at the Student's Union

175

Building.   My goal now was to commence lecture room-to-lecture room evangelism and it would seem my affair with power had come to a shuddering stop!

'EVANGELICAL CHRISTIAN UNION'

I was determined to seek the path of righteousness and atone for the past few years of disguising my faith under a political bushel. There would no longer be the subordination of my Christian faith to the pursuit of power. I was determined to humble myself and join my brothers and sisters in fellowship and to use my facility of the speech to the glory of God. I started attending the Evangelical Christian Union (ECU) meetings on a regular basis, met with Brothers Joe Tarkon and Peter Olonade, the President of ECU and immediate past President respectively. The fellowship meetings were held on Sundays at the University's All Souls Chapel, a large auditorium that was largely uncompleted at the time, it usually started at 3pm and dragged on into the evening. It sat deep in the forest so we had to navigate a path through the recently cleared bushes and shrubs in order to get there. The ECU was one of the few fellowships at the time in the days before the proliferation of campus fellowships. It was also affiliated to Nigerian Fellowship of Evangelical Students (NIFES).

I joined the ECU Follow-Up School so that I could undergo the teaching and discipleship in rudiments of the Christian faith. There was to be no short cuts, I was prepared to thread the road that every 'baby' Christian had trod before me. I needed to know I could now humble myself as a servant of the Lord and that I would place myself under submission to the brethren. A classmate of mine Pedro Okoro, unassuming, but a man of great faith who was the Principal of the ECU Follow Up School, became a very close friend of mine and eventually my best man at my wedding in February 1993.

'Mazini' now in his final year and continued to be my roommate and close friend but my other roommate, Kehinde Bamgbetan had moved out to be replaced by Ogidi, the ex-Clerk of the Students' Representative Council and newly crowned 'World Chief of the Palm wine Drinkers Club'. Unfortunately, for me, he and his squatter Mike had a voracious appetite for the ladies, which was at odds with my re-discovered faith. I had the misfortunate of waking up once to the moans of the intimate variety occurring at the other side of our room in which Mike was the culprit and I was not well pleased! After eight weeks, I graduated from the Follow-Up School and joined the Drama subgroup of the fellowship. It was here I built on the little performance art I learnt while at King's College's Afro Culture Society with Rotimi Ojo (now a Consultant psychiatrist) as one of my accomplice but this was performance art with a difference this was spiritual warfare, which required regular fasting and prayer. I came to respect Brother Francis Unegbu, Sisters Ebele Ogboli, Adeoti Adewale, Isede, Brother 'Gbenga Daramola, the Olugbodi brothers and of course the well respected Brother Akin Davies who showed me much love. At some stage a delightful Sister 'Foluke Babasanya and my friend Brother Pedro Okoro also joined the group. We went on many outreaches as far as Ilorin and many other cities and saw the manifestation of God's power. At my first fellowship after re-dedication, I was asked to introduce myself, and I being always the 'showman' would respond:

> *"My parents christened me Olu Ojedokun but my political contemporaries named me Panaf."*

People were constantly amazed that I was now part of the Christian community; many had thought I was an unyielding non-conformist and quite irredeemable unbeliever. I joined CLASFON, the Christian Lawyers Students' Fellowship of Nigeria, which, had Brother Olufemi Ayandokun as President and was succeeded by Christian Wogu another class mate. There I became close to 'Titi Fawehinimi, Ayo Alao, 'Jumoke Oketiri and many others. 'Busola Emuleomo was a friend I spent so much time encouraging and as she grew in faith we became quite close to the chagrin of one or two, a closeness that endures till today and was instrumental to my commencement of ministry at Lead City University, Ibadan in 2013.

During my sojourn as a member of the fellowship, the ECU and other Christian ministries on the campus collaborated to invite Archbishop Benson Idahosa, a charismatic Pentecostal preacher of the Church of God Mission based in Benin City to a weeklong crusade. The man was reputed to be the first Pentecostal Archbishop in Nigeria and he was robust in stature, in faith and in words. The crusade was held at the University Sports Centre's main bowl and drew students in their numbers. What I remember about the crusade was the emphasis on giving to God so that one would receive prosperity in double and multiple portions. A colleague of mine 'Yinka Odumakin (of blessed memory) attended one of the crusades and willingly obeyed the call from the Archbishop to the gathered students to take out all the money in their pockets and raise it up to towards the heavens for blessings. However, that was where 'Yinka's obedience extended, after he finished praying rather than drop the cash into the nylon carrier bag being passed around by vigilant ushers, 'Yinka's account was that he simply placed the ten naira note he presented for blessings back in his pocket, left the crusade and proceeded to the Bukateria to indulge his insatiable palate in a sumptuous meal. As far as he was concerned he was not willing to part with any naira notes on the whims of anybody.

In 1987, my lust for power now seemed like a distant memory, there was much ground to cover, many people to share the goodness of God with and I was determined to leave no stone unturned. Later in the year, Chief Obafemi Awolowo lost his life and the change of name of the University of Ife to that of the sage's caused some uproar but that soon fizzled out. We mobilised ourselves to visit Ikenne to pay our respects to his family. With 'Sanmi Obasa one of my allies we set up a magazine called *'Gong'* to speak to many issues on campus, I could at least indulge in my love of writing.

I became close to 'Segun Carew aka 'JO Jasper' a jester of no mean feat and my class mate in the Law Faculty. You never knew whether to take him seriously. He delivered a menu of jokes and the delivery was always perfectly executed in a deadpan manner. Jasper's joviality masked his exceptional brilliance and seriousness of purpose. He also had a repertoire of *'isms'* and could usually be found about my room holding court and dispensing his uncommon wisdom to all who would listen. He also walked with a funny bounce, many considered him an eccentric, but as far as I knew it was all an elaborate act. He could usually be heard on occasions hailing me in his peculiar fashion, calling me *'Baba Panafooooooooooooo!'* when he sighted me approaching. He remains one of the finest minds of our generation one, which his opponents underestimate at their constant peril. In later years, 1988 to be precise I was able to link 'J O Jasper' and 'Dele Oloke to Chief Agboola Akomolafe, the Obanla of Ido-Ekiti and a Legal Practitioner so that they could continue their compulsory articleship required by the law school.

With better attention paid to my studies, I was able to secure better grades at the end of the third year. I was also able to bid Mazini farewell on completion of his final year. The relationship with Pedro had become much stronger and as an ex-Union Official, I was able to secure a choice a room in Adekunle Fajuyi Hall in my final year. I came to an arrangement with Taiye Taiwo who was my official roommate so that I could share the room with Pedro. With Pedro as my roommate, we could turn our room into a *'hotbed'* of prayer! We purchased some wallpaper and set about decorating the room in our own image. It was a second floor room with its own front and back veranda and we were the envy of many brethren. I had arrived and felt at home with my Christian brothers and sisters but unaware at the time that I was to pay a huge political price. But in all these memories from my father continued to urge me on to be the best that I could be.

'A LAST DALLIANCE WITH POWER?'

I honestly thought as far as the craving for political office was concerned I had partaken in my fair share and it was simply was not my priority. I was on a borderline between a Third and Second Class Lower and it would take a herculean task to avoid a Third Class Degree. It was quite obvious that much application and dedication was now required. The Students' Union was reinstated in 1988 in my final year and it was not the custom for final year students to contest. But many were convinced that I should put my name forward, my response was always the same, and I had to seek God's face. I actually did pray very hard for I was determined not to fall into the trap of the past years.

Kekemeke D. Isaacs Esq., a classmate of mine pleaded with me passionately to enter the race for President of the Students' Union but I was non-committal. Kekemeke, was an interesting man, he always spotted an Afro, was Ijaw from Ondo State and was uncompromisingly anti-Socialist. Whatever his politics I felt he sought the greater good of Ife students. At the 21st birthday dinner party held in honour of Oluyinka Olutoye in January 1988 and attended by his father the retired Major-General Olufemi Olutoye, the second graduate to become an officer in the Nigerian Army, I managed to give a rousing toast to 'Yinka. In response 'Yinka said that I would have been the next President of the Students' Union if I had not been in my final year. It now appeared my political fate was settled. As the days wore on my resistance to contesting was waning but I was still in prayer. In the meantime many of my natural supporters had identified an alternative candidate from the Faculty of Education, the stakes were now very high. Sisters Ebele Ogboli, Adetola Ajayi, a close friend and a medical student and her sister Omolara encouraged me to be certain I heard God's voice before making any move.

I consulted with Brother Joe Tarkon, he was very encouraging but reminded me that my Christian faith would be an issue. After more days of prayer and contemplation I made my decision, I was sure God wanted me to contest. Hillary Okoronkwo approached me to run and we agreed he should manage my campaign, many Christian brethren like Sean Akinrele, a Law Student rallied behind me, the scene was set. There was a setback as Kekemeke apologised to me, that he had given his word to another candidate, 'Yemi Adegbite so he could no longer support me. I assured him that since he took the decision in good faith I would not hold it against him. 'Sanmi Obasa my erstwhile ally was not prepared to support me on account that I left him in the lurch to run the '*Gong*' magazine.

I had thought that the Socialist Group identified 'Segun Adeyemo aka 'US' who succeeded me as Angola Hall Chairman as their candidate because he was closely allied to them, however, I now realise they fully backed the eventual winner from Faculty of Education. This was a very interesting alliance in view of Kekemeke's consistent opposition to them. The Socialists were against my candidacy and mobilised against me. The truth was that once I rededicated my life as a Christian I became very uncomplimentary towards them and I was no longer prepared to be intimidated. I went about telling the younger members of the Socialist Group about how '*I wined and dined*' with 'Lanre Arogundade and they were not well pleased. The Christians on campus were overwhelmingly supportive of my candidacy. This campaign was going to be harder, the hardest I had ever fought and I was determined not to subordinate my beliefs for political expediency.

With Hillary Okoronkwo, we covered every ground that we could, spoke to those who would listen. However, so much disinformation was out there which we did not respond to them with adequacy. I was labeled '*Jesus of Ife*', with claims by 'Cobra' magazine, a University tabloid that I would impose a fundamental version of Christianity on the campus. For some it was pay back time and for the first time I actually lost my voice, it became hoarse. I had much confidence that with my voice, I could sway many doubters, that with soaring rhetoric, my past record and the logic of my position I could still win. Many were simply not convinced that a final year student should become President; they thought I should simply be thinking about my grades rather than politics. To some I was a backstabber and power monger, pure and simple.

The climax of the elections was the Speech Night held at the Sports Centre, rumours had spread that Panaf had great oratorical powers and that he must be stopped from speaking at all costs. I spent a lot of time in contemplative prayer, rested my voice and I was quite confident that if I spoke many would be swayed to my side. In my speech I prepared to deliver, I responded to the counter arguments of my critics and deftly addressed and defused them. I had already begun to imagine myself as President but I knew this election was going to be close. At the Speech Night held on a Sunday the crowd were more rumbustious than ever before, excitement and tension filled the warmth of the night. There was a sense that there would be trouble. I rested in Hillary's room a few rooms away from mine in Adekunle Fajuyi Hall. He prepped me for my speech and assured me that all was well. I wore my customary attire and was ready to go. However, before I went on 'US' Adeyemo had been booed off with chants in Yoruba language stating that he did not understand English. This was a portent to the treatment I would receive.

When it was my time to speak, the crowd responded with a mixture of booing and adulation, I had never experienced anything like it before. I rose with a sense of purpose and got on to the stage, commencing my speech, with my voice more sonorous that usual. I started:

> *"Ladies and gentlemen, fellow compatriots, if in the course*
> *of my service I have offended you then I offer wholehearted*
> *apologies……….."*

And then all bedlam was let loose, bricks, stones and all manner of debris were thrown in my direction, my speech was disrupted initially with chorusing of '*All we are saying give us Panaf*' and then suddenly crowds rushed towards me, some crushing against me and then carried up and then attacked by what seemed to be a bristling, snarling pack of hunting hounds. It appeared I was at their mercy as I felt hands grabbing and teasing my private parts, I was shivering violently and then in the split of a second, Hillary, 'Tunde Olupona and a few of my Christian brothers lifted me up and spirited me away with a few of the violent mob in hot pursuit as we ran the gauntlet of their viciousness. I felt a palpable sense of terror all around me as we raced towards Adekunle Fajuyi Hall. I was kept in the safety of Brother Joe Tarkon's room for the next few hours while things subsided.

As I lay in Joe Tarkon's bed reflecting, I never doubted that God had cleared me to run for office this time but I felt congealed with anger that the spirit of freedom of speech was violated and I was disrupted and prevented from speaking. Afterwards a few Socialist boys were known to boast around the campus that they engineered it all. It seemed to me that to the Socialist boys all means was fair in order to achieve their objective. It was going to be a very long forty-eight hours and it would be a very close election indeed! I was proud that at last I was true to my beliefs and it did not matter now whether I won or lost, what mattered was God's will had been accomplished.

My mind drifted across into the distant centuries, thinking about what it must have been for my ancestors as they roamed around from town to town in display of their acts, sometimes to applause and acclamation and other times to boos of disapproval. Why did they give up their act as performing masquerades and settle down as subsistence farmers in a strange land? What was it like for them to be outsiders? It is remarkable that in less than a century they became fully acculturated and became foundation members of St Peter's Anglican Church, which laid the foundation for my father and his cousin.

My mind also raced to the fact that all my fathers' siblings and cousins had their faces scarred with tribal marks of varied intensity but my father having benefited from the foundation laid by the church ensured that his youngest brother, Dr. Ayoku Ojedokun never experienced such trauma! It is suggested that tribal marks came into being in Nigeria during the colonial era when the colonial masters were capturing people and taking them to foreign countries for slavery, people started giving their family members marks to locate them if ever they were captured and to recognise them when they are freed. These tribal marks were usually permanent scars, patterned on the face of the bearer. It is a way of identification passed down from family to family, members of the same village, identification of royal lineage and people from the same lineage. But different sets of people have similar tribal marks that differentiate them from people from a different lineage or village. Since tribal marks are used mainly to differentiate or even brand ethnic groups, they varied from place to place.

The next morning was Election Day and voting was brisk, it was essential that you voted for your candidates in their University registered names or else the votes cast would be nullified. Most knew me as 'Panaf' and it was to be a mammoth task to get them to identify me as Olu Ojedokun on the voting slip. Quite a few simply put down 'Panaf' and it was to cost me very dearly. At night the polling stopped and under the chairmanship of my friend and classmate 'Dele Oloke the counting commenced. Olupona, a Law undergraduate and classmate of mine was my electoral agent. The reports reaching me as I waited patiently for the results were that it was very close but I was in the lead.

I was also told that there was a great concern that many of my votes were coming in as *'Panaf'* and were being voided. After midnight the results were settled after several recounts, I had lost to 'Yemi Adegbite by about 21 votes! I was informed that more than 40 of my votes were voided because of the use of the name *'Panaf'*, but the truth was I gave in the towel and felt I had lost fairly. I reflected and drifted off to sleep as I resolved to return to my Father's business. Initially I was lost in thoughts and bereft of power and panoply, succumbing to common fatigue and sank into a tantalising solace but then I snapped out of it and became sanguine and relieved that it was all over and that my long romance with power might now be placed firmly in the box. Hillary and others were very gutted and I consoled them. Many brethren were kind to me and offered empathy and I duly appreciated all of them.

The truth was I had identified my role, played it as best as I could and made many mistakes along the way but I was still standing, still standing for the Lord as Deaconess 'Toyin Adesola my primary school classmate would say and used in the title of her classic book.

My father's dream was for me to become an engineer, an innovator but in a short space of time detailed in this book, I believe with the teams I worked, progress was achieved, lives were transformed and we made a difference. I became an engineer of social transformation rather than a civil or mechanical one. My mother was very pleased that my election loss spared her the daily anxiety of wondering what I might get up to.

'FAREWELL TO GREAT IFE'

Over the next few months in 1988, I devoted my attention to my budding *'legal practice'* on the campus. The Obafemi Awolowo Student's Union allowed law students to set up chambers and law offices. It is through these that many students were represented when they had matters before the Students' Union Judicial Council. Practising final Year law students were addressed as *'Senior Advocates of the Campus'* (SAC). Pedro Okoro, my friend was elected the *'Lord Chancellor'* and sat with other elected judges who adjudicated over various cases. As a result of my practice, I became the Legal Adviser to the Medical Students' Association and was involved in providing them some strategic political advice during their national convention. I took on a number of cases, spending a significant amount of time before the Judicial Council. I remember representing 'Tunde Olupona (now a notable Ibadan lawyer and lawyer in the Chancery of the Anglican Diocese of Ibadan), my friend and classmate who had been dismissed as an Editor of the Bang magazine. Through grit, application and determination we won the case and he was reinstated.

It was with some regret that I narrowly missed obtaining a Second Class Lower degree and I had to settle for Third Class honours. It was International Law that appeared to bring down my cumulative grade point average and even though I was rebuked by one of my lecturers for the choice of course I do not regret choosing it. Many of my friends were not surprised feeling it was a reflection of the limited time I devoted to my studies. I place things in perspective and believe it was a joy to graduate, for someone who was rusticated just before promotion examinations; I am at least very thankful to God. The pain of a Third Class degree was later erased when I obtained a Masters with distinction and acquired a Doctorate degree in the United Kingdom at The Nottingham Trent University and latterly a Master of Laws.

It was onwards to Victoria Island, Lagos to attend the Nigerian Law School and qualify as a Barrister and Solicitor. Once I got there, in search of my father's identity and achievements, I spent a lot of time visiting the Nigerian Institute of International Affairs (NIIA) on the Victoria Island and I became an Associate member. I felt at home and dwelt on pleasant memories of my father and was able to meet with his friend Mr. 'Gboyega Banjo, the Director of Library and Documentation Services at the Institute.

Mr. Banjo had been one of the librarians at the University of Lagos while my father worked there and they had struck up a close friendship. I have kept close contact with him over the years and I appreciate the time he has always given me.

The Institute's buildings were completed in 1965 but its architecture had been designed far ahead of its time. It had the main building, an imposing two floors, surrounding with verandas and flats at the top; the ground floor housed the open plan library. The lecture theatre was attached to it like a complex and was regularly hired out to members of the public because of the sedate atmosphere it projected. There was the octagon shaped council chambers used for roundtable conferences and other seminars. It was in here all the portraits of past Directors-General including my father's adorned the walls. Later on and extension of a two story building was added but it struggled to conform to the earlier classical architecture. It was there the offices of the Directors of the Institute was relocated.

At the NIIA, in the lecture theatre, I became reacquainted with General Olusegun Obasanjo who was then the former military Head of State of Nigeria. He had been invited to deliver a lecture and his invitation was solely because of the stature and the added credence he gave to the event.

In 1985 through the courtesy of my Uncle Chief Adeagbo Odeniyi, I had visited him on his farm at Otta. My uncle a budding farmer was intent on expansion and thought the General could offer a way forward. We were ushered into the presence of Obasanjo who was bedecked in a simple danshiki and was seated on a table. He looked older and his frame less rotund but he had maintained his wicked sense of humour. I had looked forward to sumptuous meal to satisfy the cravings of my palate, however, all he was able to offer was a visit to the worker's canteen, which I politely declined. However, this was not my only close proximity to the General, his son Olusegun was close to me at King's College where I was his senior and then we later became classmates. The General impressed me as someone who had the good of the country at heart but was too self-opinionated to accept mistakes when he made them.

At the same NIIA lecture theatre, I also had the privilege of listening to baritone voice of Alhaji Adamu Ciroma, an ex-minister under President Sheu Shagari, who later became the Finance Minister under Obasanjo. He had come to deliver a lecture at the Institute. He shared an anecdote about two ministers, a Nigerian and an Argentinian in an attempt to describe the extent of the prevailing corruption. The Nigerian minister had visited the Argentinian minster in Buenos Aires and was astonished by the extent of his wealth and the opulence he displayed. The inquisitive Nigerian minister asked the Argentina about the source of his wealth. In response, the minister took him to a newly constructed bridge, pointed to it and I said:

'You see that bridge, ten percent of it was mine.'

The Nigerian minister shook his head assimilated the information and returned to Nigeria. A year later, there was an exchange visit by his Argentinean counterpart. The minister was befuddled and confounded by the extent and extravagance displayed by the Nigerian minister. He wondered aloud to the Nigeria about the newly acquired wealth. The Nigerian took him on a tour of a derelict site, a site so extensive and then pointed to it and told the minister:

'You see that uncompleted project out there? Hundred percent of it was mine.'

After completing Law School I found myself following my twin's footpath, she had undertaken her one-year compulsory National Youth Service in Ogun State and now I discovered I was posted to the same state of the Nigerian Federation. I arrived early in the morning at Onikolobo, Abeokuta the Youth Corpers' camp, a derelict school, with classrooms set up in dormitory style. I remain grateful to the then Treasurer of the KCOBA who ensured I had adequate pocket money at the time. The washing facilities where make shift and we had to make do with dug up pits in the ground. Abeokuta, a Yoruba town with some very recent illustrious history behind it, got is name because of its hilly terrain and it means a town under the rock. Most of its indigenes were refugees from the ravages of the 19th century Yoruba Civil War.

I assumed that I would settle for a quiet life in Ogun State but when I saw Kekemeke D. Isaacs, 'Yinka Odumakin, Adeniyi Adewunmi and Adeniran at the camp I knew that it would be far from quiet. I was elected the Chairman of the Food Committee of the camp and this meant I avoided most of the strenuous activities other Youth Corp members were expected to engage in. The whole catering operation in the camp was a hotbed of corruption and Adeniran and I spent most of the time thwarting attempts by staff to pilfer the food. On a few occasions the staff attempted to bribe us with choice cuts of prime beef, but Adeniran and myself took a principled stand and rejected any such attempts. I made it a point of duty to accompany the staff to the wholesale markets to establish none of the purchasing processes were inflated. It was at the camp I became close to a reserved but beautiful lady, Olajumoke Olubunmi Akinkuolie who later agreed to become my wife. My attempts at foiling corruption once brought the wrath of one of the caterers who proceeded to give me a trouncing. It was the quick thinking of Adeniran and other Camp staff's intervention that saved me from a utter and complete mauling.

At the end of the six weeks camp, to my utter surprise I was elected into the Executive of the Christian Corpers' Fellowship as Abeokuta Zonal coordinator. This ensured that my time of service was occupied with spiritual exploits, which I mixed with my new life as a State Prosecutor. I would hold court in Oke-Ijeun a nicely proportioned bungalow which Dr. Olufemi Ashley-Dejo the father of my friend 'AD99' had allowed me to use for the year. You could hear many in the locality hailing me *'Lawyer, Lawyer.'* It would seem that from now on I would restrict myself simply to matters, which seemed spiritual.

However, whilst Nigeria continues to stumble around for lack of leadership I cannot remain silent nor on the sidelines and the next chapter will begin to explore the way forward for our nation. I repeat the words of Dr. Martin Luther King that:

> *"Our lives begin to end the day we become silent about things that matter."*

It would seem that my history, my father's memories have prepared me for such a time as this.

'THE TROUBLE WITH NIGERIA'

In my later years at King's College I developed a fascination for Ikoyi and Lagos Island and I spent a few of my holidays at the home of my uncle Dr. Benjamin Abimbola Adigun on Saka Jojo Street, Victoria Island. It is from there I would link up with 'Bayo Oyesanya and other school mates. It was here that we heard about a senior ranking officer in the Army, Ibrahim Badamasi Babangida. We had heard of the myth built around his foiling of the Buka Suka Dimka coup, his identification with the left and his radical tendencies. However, this never seemed to marry with the array of cars that littered his compound at the time. He seemed to be very wealthy and I could not square this up with the image I cultivated of a clean living army officer.

Once while at Ikoyi, visiting a Falomo barbing saloon with my friend and school mate Ogenof, Babangida, a newly promoted Major General walked in and began exchanging greetings in Yoruba with all those in sight. He was very much at ease, accessible and confounded me with his easy style. As suddenly as he emerged he disappeared into the shadows as we sought him out. This intensified my love affair with the myth surrounding his image. It was this man that became the Army Chief after the military truncated the civilian administration of President Sheu Shagari. I secretly harboured the desire that Babangida now a Major General would one day take over the reins of power. My wish was granted when in August 1985 he overthrew his colleague Muhammadu Buhari and became the 'President', the title an omen to his ambitions to transform into a civilian ruler. Later on when he was Nigerian President during my Law School year I caught a glimpse of him as he casually drove around Lady Oyinkan Abayomi Road in a Santana Volkswagen car.

I now believe that Nigeria made an error of monumental proportions by allowing the man called 'IBB' to take over the reins of power. I believe the beginning of his administration began the irretrievable spiral downwards. A regime that was meant to be corrective became destructive of all of the basic Nigerian values. Corruption became a byword and a fundamental objective of state policy. The blur became public funds and personal funds assumed a new dimension.

According to 'Tolu Ogunlesi by 1985, Nigeria's foreign debt had ballooned to $18 billion, up from $3.4 billion in 1980 (it would rise beyond $30 billion by the end of the 80s), and external reserves had dwindled to less than $2 billion[6]. Oil prices had been in free fall for three years running, and in January 1986, they finally fell to less than $20 per barrel, a record low since the start of the decade. It is suggested that to his credit Babangida made all the right noises about revamping the economy. In his Independence Day 1985 speech, barely two months old in office, he declared a state of economic emergency for the next 15 months. That speech went on to lay down a comprehensive plan for economic reconstruction. The plan included a moratorium on new foreign debt, promotion of agriculture and industrial development, restriction of importation to essential commodities, financial sector reform and privatisation.

IBB appeared to be a master of the populist move and led an activist government, dancing from left to right and never sitting still - ambitious government programmes targeted at tackling poverty, and empowering rural dwellers. His government churned out program after program, in a bid to actualize his promises to run an inclusive, people-facing government. In 1986, Babangida launched the Mass Mobilization for Self Reliance, Social Justice, and Economic Recovery (MAMSER).

In 1987, the Directorate of Food and Rural Infrastructure (DFFRI) was launched to promote agriculture and transform Nigeria's rural landscape by providing modern infrastructure. Other Babangida creations include the National Directorate of Employment (NDE), National Economic Reconstruction Fund (NERFUND), Peoples Bank of Nigeria (PBN), National Board for Community Banks (NBCB), Nigerian Deposit Insurance Corporation (NDIC), Nigeria Export-Import Bank (NEXIM), National Planning Commission (NPC), and the Urban Development Bank.

No other Nigerian government presided over such substantial expansion of government bureaucracy as the Babangida administration. In time, the fiscal prudence that Babangida espoused vanished: billions of naira were sunk into an endless transition programme, and in the early 90s, 12 billion dollars worth of windfall crude oil revenue (courtesy of the rise in the oil prices due to the Gulf War) could not be accounted

---

[6] Ogunlesi, Tolu (2010) The Babangida Years, 17th April 2010. Accessed from [http://www.nairaland.com/522441/babangida-years-facts-may-want]

for General Babangida also came to perfect the art of dispensing patronage through political appointments (mostly targeted at leading members of the opposition) and a far-from-transparent allocation of lucrative oil blocks.

He devised a maddeningly convoluted transition programme, whose terminal date soon became a mirage, with no ending in sight - first 1990, then 1992, and then 1993 - is one of the most significant things Babangida will be remembered for. Early on in his administration, Mr. Babangida inaugurated a Political Bureau to kick off, as it were, the national debate on a viable future political ethos and structure for our dear country. The political bureau was soon followed by a Constituent Assembly, which in 1989 fashioned a new constitution for the country.

Also, in 1989, he created, by presidential fiat, two political parties, the Social Democratic Party and the National Republican Convention. Then in 1991, he released a controversial list of prominent politicians whom he said were banned from participating in the transition programme.

In October 1992, he cancelled the results of the parties' presidential primaries, causing new primaries to be held in March 1993. And then in June 1993-he annulled the results of the presidential elections, which was presumed to have been won by the billionaire businessman MKO Abiola. By this time, Nigerians had finally had enough of his shenanigans, and violent protests forced him to step aside on August 27, 1993:

"My colleagues and I are determined to change the course of history."

General Babangida told Nigerians in his maiden speech as Head of State, on August 27, 1985. By the time he reluctantly relinquished power exactly eight years later, he had achieved that goal, far more successfully than he, or anyone else, could ever have imagined.

By the time the general left office unceremoniously, he had bequeathed the collapse of the Nigerian economy and the mass exodus of Nigerian professionals: It is suggested that the confounding corruption, failed policies and the eventual collapse of Nigeria's economy profoundly diminished people's living standards. He inherited a fairly strong economy that was on the path of recovery. The Naira was basically at par with the United States dollar but by the time he left, the Naira had plunged to an all-time low, exchanging for 44 Naira to the dollar. This nearly 50-fold (or nearly 5000%) drop eroded the purchasing power of Nigerians. A Nigerian worker who made 50 Naira per day before Babangida's era could purchase a 250-dollar refrigerator with a week's wage. If the same worker made 4 times that amount (i.e. 200 Naira per day) during Babangida's era, his daily wage would be 4.5 dollars per day, or 22.7 dollars per week. This worker required 12 weeks wage to purchase the same refrigerator. That was a 1200% fall in living standards of living. By the time Babangida left office, the economy had completely collapsed like a pack of cards.

Here is a man to whom much hope was given and invested and proceeded to squander it playing games, indulging in trickery and unleashing corrupt machinations. It is suggested that by the time he left office is name had become synonymous with corruption. The irony is that IBB might have become a synonym, the present crop of rulers have become corruption itself, surpassing him in all facets and confounding all. How else do you situate the decision of a sitting President to grant pardon to a well-established kleptomaniac who is still being pursued the world all over? What message does that send?

'THE QUESTION THAT IS NIGERIA'

In 1960 whilst at the Nigerian College of Arts, Science and Technology my father Olasupo Aremu Ojedokun rebuffed the counsel of his cousin Mathew Oladejo Alamu Ojedele who pleaded with him:

"Ema loo Eko, ani ema lo ekoo."

He joined other students to demonstrate against the Anglo-Nigerian Defence Pact. The response they received from the police encountered on their way to Lagos was unexpected brutality, it manifested itself in stifling fumes from the teargas they fired.

It seems I had picked up the mantle of my father and carried it with me through secondary school into my university experience, living in the shadow of anti-authority struggles. This also mirrors my spiritual life, where I have experienced the lows of the valleys and the heights of mountains. I have collapsed into the depths of despondency so many times but God has been faithful on each and every occasion, making a pathway of escape for me and I have come out more formidable.   There was a time when no one gave me a life chance of success and here I am today defying that expectation all because of what the Lord has done. I am therefore reminded of the Christian chorus:

"My lifetime. I will give God my lifetime.
And if I give God my lifetime,
He will take care of me.
He will never, never let me down,
If I give God my lifetime."

I solemnly believe my narrative does not differ from that of Nigeria where there is no doubt that many men and women of integrity have vacated the scene of governance and left it to all shades of characters. The space of our governance has been left to those who are after their bellies to plunder at will with no shame at all. But more fundamentally, the voice of the Church for the most part remains eerily silent causing the absence of a prophetic voice that speaks to the nation in times of despair. In very many cases the Church, which I am part of has been relegated into a messy and unseemly compromise with power. The reality is that many in the Church are content to focus on greed, increasing materialism, personality worship and the trappings of power.

The Church in Nigeria is in danger of being consigned into a multinational business with branches in the world's major cities. And yet, there are many rays of hope, where Nigerian Churches are prepared to fund, partner and sacrificially give to worthwhile projects in the United Kingdom. Today I throw down a challenge to the church that is in Nigeria and will be glad for them to prove me wrong.

I contrast this with South Africa during the heydays of Apartheid when the Church spoke *'Truth to Power'* as evidenced by, Desmond Tutu's words before the Eloff Commission set up to investigate the South African Council of Churches on 20th November 1981, stated:

> *"I want to say that there is nothing the government can do to me that will stop me from being involved in what I believe is what God wants me to do. I do not do it because I like doing it. ……………… I cannot help it when I see injustice. I cannot keep quiet. I will not keep quiet, for as Jeremiah says, when I try to keep quiet God's word burns like a fire in my breast. But what is it that they can ultimately do? The most awful thing that they can do is to kill me, and death is not the worst thing that can happen to a Christian."[7]*

The current climate in Nigeria presents a 'Kairos' moment for the Church; however, many Christians appear to be smeared with dubious activities. If stories constantly circulating in the Nigerian press are to be believed then it appears that the hallmark of many *'Christians'* today does not in fact manifest itself and consist of being salt and light in/of respective communities.

---

7 Du Boulay, Shirley (1988)., Op. Cit., pp. 174-5.

Yet the scripture they are meant to hold with reverence and believe to be inerrant states:

"If any man be in Christ he is a new creature".

It is also sad that some of the traits described above are not limited to Nigeria but have assumed a global dimension.

However, it will be a wrong and a gross misrepresentation of the many Nigerian Christians who manifest the grace and love of Christ to take the above as the common narrative that dominates the landscape. For every Christian that betrays their profession, there are many who by the power of God live exemplary and sacrificial lives attempting to bring, truth and grace into many situations they face and encounter. There are many acting as the salt and light of their communities and therefore any brush that sweeps away born again(s) or characterises them together as charlatans would be misleading and unfortunate.

The difficulty we face is that the Church has been slow to recognise that beyond the *'propagation'* of the gospel there is the need for Churches to realise their role in initiating social action is part of the same propagation. We must look beyond the rhythm of periodic feeding of the hungry and destitute, the seasonal visits to orphanages or the periodic missions into parts of the hinterland. What I have in mind is integral mission in Nigeria one that allows the Church to assume its prophetic role and to *'Speak Truth to Power'*. Simply put, I draw from Justin Thacker, formerly of the Evangelical Alliance UK's, quotation to illustrate my point:

> *'Integral Mission: Jesus Style does not deny that evangelism and social action are distinct activities – on occasions, they may be – but it does say that the nature of the integration does not reside in the fact that we enact the two alongside each other, or that we find appropriate connections between them. Rather, it argues that the integration that is relevant is that we respond as whole people to the whole person or person before us.'*

The scripture used by Justin in the illustration of the above point states:

> *"So he came to a town in Samaria called Sychar, near the plot of ground Jacob had given to his son Joseph. Jacob's well was there, and Jesus, tired as he was from the journey, sat down by the well. It was about the sixth hour. When a Samaritan woman came to draw water, Jesus said to her, "Will you give me a drink?" (His disciples had gone into the town to buy food.) The Samaritan woman said to him, "You are a Jew and I am a Samaritan woman. How can you ask me or a drink?" Jesus answered her "If you knew the gift of God and who it is that asks you for a drink, you would have asked him and he would have given you living water." (John 4:5-10)*

The question I venture to ask is when Jesus voluntarily engaged a social outcast like the Samaritan woman in face-to-face conversation, was he performing a *'political action'* in challenging the political taboos of his society?[8] It has been advanced that Jesus responded not as simply the evangelist, nor the social reformer, but as Jesus the Christ, or the Integral Missionary. We see in that text, the whole of Jesus responding in love to the whole of this woman's needs, and we see him doing it in word and in deed. This woman clearly had social, emotional and psychological needs, but Jesus met them by openly talking with her. She also had spiritual needs, to know him as a saviour, and Jesus clearly communicates both her need and his ability to meet it. He neither neglects any aspect of who she is, nor any aspect of his responsibility towards her. By his words and his actions he communicates God's love into the whole of her life and both evangelism and social reform are communicated together.

I suggest that the Nigerian Church must fully appreciate the aspect of integral mission that brings the vastness of its resources, both material and spiritual to deliver wholeness to the soul and is capable of reforming and transforming society. The

---

[8] Ramachandra, Vinoth, *What is Integral Mission?* Available at:
http://www.micahnetwork.org/library/integral-mission/what-integral-mission-vinoth-ramachandrahttp://en.micahnetwork.org/integral_mission/resources/what_is_integral_mission_by_vinoth-ramachandra

continued inability of the Church to fully grasp and understand its integral mission in Nigeria could have the following implication, as Ramachandra argues:

"Integral mission flows out of an integral gospel and integrated people. There is a great danger that we transform the mission of the church into a set of special 'project' and 'program', whether we call them 'evangelism' or 'socio-political action', and then look for ways to integrate these methodologically. Rather, the mission of the church is located in the adequacy of faithfulness of its witness to Christ. Our core-business is neither the take-over of the world's systems nor the maximising of church membership. Moreover, we need to remember that the primary way the church acts upon the world is through the actions of its members in their daily work and their daily relationship with people of other faiths. A congregation with huge social welfare projects or many 'church planting' teams may be far less effective in secular society than congregations which have none of these things but train their members to obey Christ in the different areas of civic life which they are called."

The missing link in Nigeria remains the Church for whilst the Church has a mandate to prepare people for eternity and is driven by proclamation evangelism, church planting and personal discipleship it must also balance it with passion for the vision *to:*

"….feed the hungry, clothe the naked, provide shelter for the refugees, and loose the chains of injustice."

Today Nigeria presents a distorted but legalised distribution of power brought about by a warped social system, backed by strong-willed and corrupt political class. Yet, we stand at a moment of great challenge and opportunity. All around Nigeria and its diaspora are voices being reclaimed, breaking out in rhythms, chorusing in high decibels with one sound, that of change. Nigerian people want simple things: An economy that serves the efforts of those who work hard, a national security policy that addresses the threat of Boko Haram and makes our cities, towns and villages safer, a politics that is centered on bringing people together across the various divides to work for our common good. This is the minimum we demand, the basic request we make for it is the change that the Nigerian people are entitled to.

The reality, however, is that our nation is at war with a confounding enemy whose name is corruption, our economy is in turmoil from the excesses of the recurrent expenditure and the abuses prevalent in our governance.   The healthcare system is broken and only accessible to those who can travel abroad. On healthcare I am struck by how almost all our elected and 'selected' leaders fly abroad every year for treatment. Government schools fail to provide opportunities to many of our children. Across the land, families are paying record prices to fill up their shopping baskets and many Nigerians worry whether they will be able to raise their offspring in safety and security.

But these challenges were not bound to happen, they are the consequence of flawed policies and failing leadership. As the world has transformed, the thinking of our leaders has remained ossified in time with the absence of new thinking. The first few years of this new century should have been our moment, the time when our leaders turned adversity into opportunity, launching us to the next phrase of our development. This should have been the time when bold and visionary thinking challenged conventional wisdom and took us down a pathway of development and innovation.

Instead, our history is cluttered with white elephants and corruption on a monumental scale. I imagine what Nigeria could have achieved if we were united and worked together.   The last half-century of our independence has been a failure of our leadership rather than that of Nigerian people. I believe that we can change course and that we must, and I project into the future an optimism that seems foolhardy but comes from the hope that after darkness emerges light – *'Post tenebras spero lucem'*. This is certainly not the first time our nation has faced grave crises of confidence but each time, our people have found the strength to call out together and address our challenges. This moment cannot be different, and this time demands more urgency. Working together we can restore some sanity to our body politic, we can perfect our federation and work towards a more worthwhile union by asking unthinkable questions of ourselves. But to bring about profound change we must be prepared to countenance some of the ideas I am expounding in the chapters to come.

To develop my narrative further I proceed into some background of the Nigerian chaotic economic planning and a series of questions using anecdotes to prise them open. I am aware that the implementation of medium-term *"development plan"* has been the major framework, which Nigeria has relied upon to restructure the economy since independence. Four national development plans were launched between 1962 and 1985. The First National Development Plan, 1962 - 1968 sought to put the economy on a fast growth path, by giving priority to agricultural and industrial development, as well as the training of high level and intermediate manpower. The Second National Development Plan, 1970-1974, was launched after the civil war, primarily to undertake reconstruction and rehabilitation of the infrastructure damaged during the war.

The Third National Development Plan, 1975-1980, was designed under a more favourable financial condition of huge oil revenues, which accrued to the nation from the mid-1970s. It emphasised diversification, balanced development and indigenisation of the economy. However, a significant portion of the plan was not executed because of unanticipated financial and executive capacity constraints. Thus, many key projects were carried over into the Fourth National Development Plan, 1981-1985. The execution of the fourth plan was also adversely affected by the unexpected collapse of the international oil prices soon after its inception. Thus, the volatility of the oil sector largely determined economic policy direction as well as the financial capacity to execute public investment programmes.

The adoption of the Structural Adjustment Programme (SAP), initially for two years (July 1986-June 1988), was the major response to the dwindling oil resources, macroeconomic policy distortions and the increasing need to diversify the productive base of the economy. The economy witnessed a number of policy reversals between 1988 and 1989 in an attempt to cushion the adverse effects of the belt-tightening measures implemented in 1986 and 1987. Consequently, some of the gains of economic adjustment in those two years were gradually eroded. From the start of the 1990s, the government shifted the instrument of economic transformation from the five-year plans to the three-year rolling plans, as they were more flexible and amenable to periodic reviews. However, there was no appreciable improvement in the performance of the economy since the commencement of the rolling plans thus necessitating further economic reengineering for sustained growth.

In the early 2000s, a comprehensive economic reform programme was initiated to fast- track economic growth. Central to the reforms was the Medium-Term Expenditure Framework (MTEF), 2003 – 2005, which provide a macroeconomic framework to strengthen fiscal management and improve the planning and budgeting of public expenditure to curtail abuse and mis- allocation of resources[9]. What became apparent was during the Babangida and Abacha regimes all pretentions of following a development plan were abandoned.

The powerful and narrow sectional interests have been the bane of Nigeria. I understand that when the initial plans for Nigeria's principal container port, the Tin Can Island Port which handles about 5.75 million tons of cargo each year was laid, it included rail lines, however, by the time the port was completed the rail lines had been expunged! What modern nation builds a seaport without and rail links? The other port at Port Harcourt, a transshipment port located 66 kilometres from the Gulf of Guinea along the Bonny River in the Niger Delta, handles about 815,000 tons of cargo each year and has a railway connection but it is not the commercial nerve centre. Thankfully Major General Buhari's administration was able to connect the port rail to the Lagos Ibadan rail, an error now addressed.

When the old Western Region built 24-storey Cocoa House at one time tropical Africa's tallest building, all the materials and cement used to build, it came via rail links because the road network could never have coped. Yet, when we built the Federal Capital Territory Abuja with a land area of 713 kilometres square we relied entirely on road links from Lagos to Abuja to transport all the materials needed, the limited road network was never going to be able to cope with the multiplier effects of so much traffic. Today we wonder why we do not have any good roads. The limited rail infrastructure we have, we have allowed it to be degraded through years of neglect of both the rolling stock and allowed the right-of-way to seriously reduced the capacity and utility of the system.

---

[9] Mordi, Carles N O et al (2011) The Changing Structure of the Nigerian Economy, Central Bank of Nigeria

Nigeria with the largest road network in West Africa and the second largest south of the Sahara, roughly 108,000 km of surfaced roads in 1990 has had a history of poor maintenance. In 2004, Nigeria's Federal Roads Maintenance Agency (FERMA) began to patch the 32,000-kilometre federal roads network, and in 2005, FERMA initiated a more substantial rehabilitation. However, this has not kept pace with over use by the powerful interests who we allowed to lay siege to the Nigerian economy. What of electricity? Have you wondered why most of the funds invested in the sector make no difference? It is the powerful interests that benefit from lucrative generator sales that conspire to make nothing work. The stark analysis of the sector reveals Nigeria had 5,900 MW of installed generating capacity, however, the country was only able to generate 1,600 MW because most facilities have been poorly maintained. The country has proven gas reserves and around 8,000 MW of hydro development has been planned.

The same extends to the scandal of the refineries where most of the refineries are not working or under utilised because of sabotage by powerful interests. It simply pays the few entrenched interest that Nigeria does not work, they thrive and get rich on the misery of the many.

Whilst Chief Asiodu's own central thesis of the problem with Nigeria traces it to the Murtala/Obasanjo purge of the Civil Service in 1975.He suggests that before purge, from after the civil war Nigeria grew at 11.5 percent per annum.[10] That if we had sustained 10 percent per annum for 20 more years, today the per capital income of Nigeria would not be less than 20,000 dollars. He makes a comparison with Malaysia that is reputed to have borrowed palm oil technology from Nigeria and is now so far ahead of us. He claims that many countries overtook us because, we destroyed the civil service; we abandoned the plan of 75 years which was the emphasizing of capital and intermediate products, agro-allied industry, petrochemical, which would have given us a very serious developmental pyramid.

---

[10] Asiodu, Philip (2011): Op. Cit.

I suggest we need a government that makes it its fundamental objective to govern in the interest of the many and not the privileged and powerful few. This would mean challenging and taking on the powerful interests that have ground our nation to a halt. But we need a process that compels our government to take on these interests. It would require an active imagination, which allows us to think outside the box and contemplate the unthinkable. I propose a process, which allows the powerful interests to render a full and honest account of their crimes and receive amnesty on the basis that a degree of restitution is made. The next chapter grapples with the details of such a process one that needs to be free of government manipulation and interference.

Whilst this book presents this as a choice, a way forward, the reality is the Nigerian situation is unsustainable it cannot go on as before and time is fast running out for the present crop of leaders. I have carefully considered the option of a truth and reconciliation process because I want my nation to avoid a schism that would make that of Ghana a kindergarten play, the process I offer remains the last hope for a peaceful resolution of the peculiar mess we find ourselves in, the risk is to ignore it and the peril that may follow.

'TRUTH AND RECONCILIATION PROCESS'

To achieve this end I am suggesting that Nigeria needs to adopt the template of a Truth and Reconciliation Commission to clear its decks before it can move forward. I am aware that the administration of President Olusegun Obasanjo set up a panel in Nigeria but its powers and roles were far too limited.[11] The Commission he appointed on June 4, 1999, was restricted to the investigation of human rights abuses committed from December 31, 1983 until taking office on May 29, 1999. However, the Commission had serious shortcomings. It assumed Nigeria's problems started in 1983, it had no powers of subpoena and it was subject to the jurisdiction of the courts.

The new Nigerian Truth and Reconciliation Commission I propose will be free of government control and have a remit that allows it to go back to 1914 Amalgamation of Nigeria up to the present time and examine the legitimacy of the transaction which led to the purchase of the area called Niger area from the Royal Niger Company (now Unilever) for £800,650. It suggested that most countries are birthed from shared ideals; however, Nigeria seemed to have been created to fulfil a business requirement. The question is how do me move from a transactional relationship to build a nation of shared ideals? Is it still possible? Therefore main remit of any such Truth Commission will be to explore:

> *"The establishment of national shared ideals, unity and reconciliation in a spirit of understanding which transcends the conflicts and divisions of the past"*, the Commission's objectives will be to:

(1) establish the legitimacy of the transactional relationship that led to the establishment of Nigeria; (2) establish as complete a picture as possible of gross human rights violations and corrupt practices perpetrated between 1914-2012 by conducting investigations and hearings; (3) facilitate granting of amnesty in exchange for full disclosure of truth for acts with a political objective within guidelines of the Act and

---

11 United States Institute of Peace., Op. Cit., Sources: Post Express 07/25/1999 and 06/16/1999. http://www.postexpresswired.com/; The Electronic Telegraph, 08/22/1999. http://www.telegraph.co.uk:80/; Washington Post 06/08/1999.

on condition in the cases of corruption that appropriate restitution is made to their respective local government areas; (4) make known the fate of victims and restore their human and civil dignity, and allow them to give accounts and recommend reparations; (5) make a report of findings and recommendations to prevent future human rights violations. (6) make provision to exclude all those who have admitted to gross human rights violations and corrupted practices from any future political dispensation in return for their amnesty and on condition that appropriate restitution is made. It will report to convocation of the Nigerian people freely chosen through a democratic process.

These should mean that traumatic events, like the Nigerian Civil War and the various coups will be covered, ancient myths unravelled, hidden truths exposed. It will also question the legitimacy of the amalgamation of North and South and the creation of States. The setting up of such a Commission will be seen as a testament to the power of truth in the face of denial, the resilience of the human spirit in the face of despair, the triumph of the Nigerian people over the kleptocrats, the 100 percenters, mismanagers and crooks who's only ambition is the murder of their dreams and a reminder to all peoples, that atrocities and injustice against the Nigerian masses must and will never stand. It will also give voice to the words of Franz Fanon who said:

> *'The future would have no pity for those men [and women] who, possessing the exceptional privilege to speak words of truth to their oppressors, have taken refuge in an attitude of passivity, of mute indifference, and sometimes of cold complicity'*

The setting up of the Commission will be part of a process that allows us to convene a sovereign conference of the people, which re-examines the question that is Nigeria, and determine future constitutional relationship of its constituent parts. It must be a process that allows Nigerian people to reclaim their voice. A process which brings out the courtesy of the Hausas, the principled positions of the Tivs, the flamboyance of the Yorubas, the determination of the Igbos and the very positive aspects the other tribes offer us.

I am aware that some might argue that we would be letting criminals go free in order to aid political expediency. I will draw them to the quote from Kadar Asmal who argued that:

> *"I therefore say to those who wear legalistic blinkers, who argue that immunity would be an affront to justice, that they simply do not understand the nature of the negotiated revolution that we have lived through, we must deliberately sacrifice the formal trappings of justice, the courts and trials, for an even greater good: Truth. We sacrifice justice for truth so as to consolidate democracy, to close the Chapter of the past and to avoid confrontation."*[12]

If we are to stand any chance of moving forward as a nation we must construct a process which allows its peoples to reclaim their voice and *'Speak Truth to Power'*, but also that allows power a negotiated way out into retirement. Power must be presented with two alternatives negotiate or become oblivion itself.

A valid question about this process, is does a Truth and Reconciliation process not re-open old wounds and create more bitterness? However, this is premised on a suggestion that the wounds were closed or healed in the first instance. What remains abundantly clear is that the wounds of old remain like an open sore, untreated and festering as evidenced by Chinua Achebe's recent book *'There was a Country'*. I suggest that only a process that allow people to tell their own stories, to reclaim their voice will lead us to the kind of progressive nation we crave.   We need to embrace the belief that:

> *"A lie cannot use truth to sustain itself' and because of the importance of people being able to tell their stories, because their identity was linked so inseparably with their stories."*[13]

---

12 Asmal, Kadar (1995)., Hansard 1995: pp. 1382 –3 Act No.34 of 1995: Promotion of National Unity and Reconciliation Act 1995.

13 Du Boulay, Shirley (1988)., Tutu, Voice of The Voiceless., London: Hodder & Stoughton., p.264

I also think the proposal of a truth and reconciliation process is not an abstraction limited to academic research but one that can help uncover pervading myths. Judge Albie Sachs, the intellectual force behind the South African Truth and Commission who I was privileged to meet during my fieldwork for my doctorate argues that:

> *"So I think the reasons for a truth commission close to the event is to prevent future generations from highjacking memories and manipulating them. Once could see the examples of Yugoslavia how ancient stories began to be used at dehumanising the opposition."*

This argument is supported by a speech made by Adv. de Lange during the President's tabling of the recommendations relating to South African TRC, where he stated:[14]

> *"Inner unity requires reconciliation and this in turn requires the public recognition of the historical truth. Those who are meant to forgive must know what they are forgiving. It is therefore insufficient to establish the historical truth in merely an abstract manner. Instead, the violence of the past and its causes must be named, the suffering of the victims concretely established. Truth has precedence over punishment, but also over amnesty. Acknowledgment legitimises amnesty silence excludes it. Punishment can to a certain extent, be negotiated. The truth cannot. This is South Africa's message to societies in transition. There is no reconciliation without truth."*

There still too many myths in Nigeria; there is the story of how the first Prime Minister, Sir Abubakar Tafawa Balewa consumed forty-two cups of tea at conference in London because he was unaware of protocol. Yet, when you saw him from old videotapes on You Tube, bestriding the globe after Nigeria's independence you saw the confidence of a man certain of his destiny. When you heard him speak, his diction was that of a well-educated and enlightened man, in fact was eloquence had a silky feel, he was indeed golden in his voice.

---

14 De Lange, ADV Speech during the President's tabling of recommendations relating to the TRC 15 April 2003.

http://www.anc.org.za/ancdocs/speeches/2003/sp0515b.html [Accessed on 13th April 2005].

In the myths also surrounding the persona of the Rt. Hon. Dr. Nnamdi Azikiwe,

Phillip Emeagwali explains:

> *"For many of those who lived in colonial Nigeria, Nnamdi Azikiwe was a super-man sent especially to free them from alien rule. Unable to understand Zik's persona, fables were woven around him. A story has it that as a child, Zik saw an old woman carrying a heavy load. Moved with pity, he offered to help her. On reaching her home in the forest, the old woman who was in fact a spirit, asked Zik what she could do for him. Zik requested for wisdom and power. The woman obliged. She cut Zik into bits and boiled the flesh in a big pot. Later, she magically brought him back to life. On her request, Zik killed the woman to prevent her from performing the same feat for others. That explains his legendary source of wisdom and power over his fellow man.*

> *Another has it that with the magical gift from the old woman of the forest, Zik managed to extricate Nigeria out of a deadly situation. Ages ago, the Atlantic Ocean was inhabited by a wicked mermaid who caused the water to overflow its banks perennially to drown thousands of Nigerians. For a long time, the people of Lagos prayed for a redeemer. None came. When Zik learnt of their predicament, he went into the ocean and challenged the wicked mermaid to a contest. First, Zik changed into a spirit, entered a bottle and then came out. Then he dared the mermaid to do the same. The mermaid quickly changed into a spirit and entered the bottle. But before it could come out, Zik corked the bottle and took it away. Since then the Bar Beach has been given less trouble. The moral of the fable was that if Nigerians annoyed the politician too frequently, he could release the mermaid to torment Lagosians again. Could if be that he had actually released the mermaid to cause the recent flooding of parts of Victoria Island?"*

In the same way, myths have been built up over the Nigerian Civil War, coups and the pre-independence period. Only an open process independent of the Nigerian

Government can open up a space where people's voices can be heard and the truth established.

Finally, I believe the adoption of such a truth and reconciliation process represents the only opportunity to prevent a messy and uncontrolled schism with its devastating consequences. It represents the last chance saloon for the current crop of our ruling class to relinquish power and the fruits of their corruption peacefully. It is a compromise solution but one that might guarantee we move forward beyond the present malaise. What is certain is that Nigeria cannot go on as before, business as usual.

In drawing from my research into the South African truth and reconciliation process I am certain that while many countries emerge from a totalitarian or corrupt system through a state of collapse rather than military victory, South Africa emerged through negotiation, and therefore had to deal with the messy business of compromise. It is a lesson that Nigerian can learn. I know that many will be concerned that I advocate for a process where truth might be compromised but Judge Albie Sachs who I have spent some time with does not agree that truth itself was compromised in the South African context, he concedes depending on the definition of Justice, however, justice may have been partially compromised.[15]

In Nigeria like in the South African context, we will have to grapple with the question of whether a moral basis exists for compromise. I suggest that the Nigerian process

---

15 Sachs, Albie (2003) **Interview with Olu Ojedokun held on 9th March 2003** at King's College, London, he says: *"If people say that justice was compromised…....but I don't think any truth was compromised whatever your standards. If justice is understood strictly in terms of accountability and punishment, by deprivation, then one might say it was affected. But to my mind justice is a much richer concept than that, accountability yes, there was accountability in the sense of having to publicly acknowledge what you have done and that was accepting responsibility. Accountability to shame, imagine a person goes home and Daddy did you do that its on television? It is not an easy thing, its not getting away scot free, it is not the same as impunity. The fact that it was individualised personalised created a direct link with individual responsibility, which is at the heart of accountability. There were pragmatic reasons as well, we just did not have the evidence, we would have had cases dragging on for years, placing burdens on the already overburdened law courts.*

Albie Sachs agued that from a purely functional point of view, they could not get the evidence and it could have been arbitrary in its impact that many people who had done terrible things would get off because there was no evidence and others more smaller agents of wrong doing would be sent to jail. That a new sense of injustice will emerge.

must have an irreducible minimum and that is a commitment to truth. As Roberto Canas of El Salvador puts it:

> *"Unless a society exposes itself to the truth it can harbour no possibility of reconciliation, reunification and trust. For a peace settlement to be solid and durable it must be based on truth."*[16]

The plea for a proper truth and reconciliation process was first made in 2014 when were on the cusp of a new government, 8 years after Major General Muhammadu Buhari's administration, the call remains even more relevant and clarion.

---

16 Boraine, Alex (1996) "Justice in Cataclysm: Criminal Tribunals in the wake of mass violence: alternatives and adjuncts to criminal prosecutions" http://www.truth.org.za/reading/speech01.htm [Accessed 23rd October 2005]

'RETURN TO ENGLAND'

I guess a return to the land of my birth was always on the agenda and almost inevitable you might say. I had dreamt for so many years of what it would be like to savour and saunter down the fabled paved streets of London. But I never once believed the myth that it had paving made of gold and opportunities which were littered all through along the paths. Months of correspondence with my cousin had made me more circumspect about the reality. I was impatient to complete the Youth Service Corp programme in Abeokuta, a mandatory service year all Nigerian graduates had to be enrolled on and they were posted to various work establishments.

During my law school years after much toil, much going back and forwards I had obtained a black coloured British passport, to ensure I was allowed entry into the shores of the United Kingdom without a visa. Yes I had enjoyed my time work as a prosecutor at the State Ministry of Justice, I appreciated serving God as an executive of the Christian Corpers' Fellowship but above all I was seriously in love with Olajumoke, the beautiful, dark enameled lady with elegantly sculptured body and perfectly shaped almond eyes, who was to become my wife. None of these, however, were enough to mitigate the draw of England at the time.

However, a few obstacles stood in the way of my ambition, the finances needed to acquire an air ticket, accommodation on arrival, the imminent possibility of my twin sister's wedding and the thought of leaving my fiancé on her own whilst I returned to England. I had approached my uncle, Dr. Adigun for a soft loan to buy a ticket, and he agreed. My terms were simple I would pay him back within a year once I got to England. However, my uncle reconsidered his promise and decided rather than offer a loan he would advance me a significant gift. The gift, however, still left me significantly short, my mother then decided to part with her savings and pay the difference for the cost of my ticket. She had been saving for the raining day and my travel back to UK was considered such.

In 1990, I attended my twin's introduction held at my uncle, Mr. Oladejo Ojedele's Ibadan home, but no dates were fixed for the wedding. Introduction was customary in Nigeria where the families of prospective bride and groom got to know each other over the informality of food and drinks. I had sketched out plans with 'Jumoke deciding that I would go ahead and settle down to a job in England and then return to marry her once it was feasible. With her agreement secured and with financial support from Dr. Adigun and my mother I booked a Nigerian Airways one-way ticket to Heathrow Airport in London.

I made arrangements with 'Ranti Oguntokun (as she then was) nee Lawunmi my cousin to arrive and stay in their home whilst I sorted myself out. I enjoyed the last moments of my time with Olajumoke, who prepared a delicacy of coconut rice, said my goodbyes to friends and relatives and then on an Harmattan filled evening in October 1990 made my way through the cluttered roads of Lagos and I flew out from Murtala Mohammed Airport Ikeja on a Nigerian Airways DC 10 flight. On the way through the mist of traffic, I saw the legendary Akintunde Asalu, the President of the Shareholder's Solidarity Association he had abandoned his car because it had broken down. I waved him goodbye, reminiscing about his unremitting kindness to me in times past. I thought my return to the United Kingdom would only be for a few years but remained in England for more than two decades.

My arrival at Heathrow Airport early on Saturday morning was shaken by the sudden cold blast of autumn air that rushed through from outside, my jacket and coat, *'a pass me down'* from Uncle Ayo Akinsonmi, offered little in the place of warmth, I was shivering to the marrow. I was armed with forty pounds and expended half of it on my taxi fare to Ponyders Court in South Clapham. I returned to the exact area where in 1966 we were born as twins. 'Ranti and 'Yinka welcomed me by establishing a few ground rules, it was clear my stay there would be very temporary for my cousin was now heavily pregnant with her first son. She navigated me through the cultural issues of my new country, took me to my first church Bonneville Christian Centre where I met Pastor Les Ball and she ensured I went to the Department of Social Security office to sign on for dole, the government's handout to the unemployed. In no time through Threshold Housing, I acquired accommodation on 26 Montrose Gardens, Mitcham, Surrey in a small box room, big enough to contain a wardrobe and a chest of drawers but it suited my finances.

My first night in the room was intolerable, it seemed the cold sneaked up on me, I came with a blanket and wore thick clothing to bed, but these were no match for the unrelenting and unremitting cold that seeped through the crevices and gaps into my tiny room. I lay shivering in bed, wondering why I had decided to leave the warm shores of Lagos to subject myself to torture of this kind.

Ian, a young Caribbean boy became my closest mate in the house, introduced me to all the cheap shops, and gave me a crash course on life in the UK. I settled down, savoured my new reality and began to think about securing a job. Macdonald Restaurant came calling in the meantime, but after only three days, I gave it up. I reckoned that losing my entitlement to unemployment benefits and housing benefits for a low paid job was not my best option. I needed to devote my time to securing a well-paid job and being unemployed offered me the space and time to do that. I linked up with 'Dele Olawoye and 'Deji Adeogun my old friends and over a weekend we reminisced over our past. With time, it became apparent that my search for a job would be much harder and more frustrating than imagined. I joined the Job Club at Bonneville Christian Centre in Clapham South, where I was put through my paces in the search for a job and where I had the opportunity to volunteer.

I became re-acquainted with Morounke Jacobs, a niece of Professor Wole Soyinka. We became like brother and sister quite inseparable; my name for her was *'Aburo'*, which meant younger sibling. She had returned to England to study for her Master of Arts in International Relations at University of Leeds. It was because of her that I ventured up to Leeds and the City of York. Through her I was introduced to her uncle, Pastor 'Kayode Soyinka to whom my wife and I became very close. I was privileged to travel with her to attend her wedding to Mr. Akin Somorin in Lagos, Nigeria in 1994 and by mere coincidence we were on the same flight with her uncle, the Nobel Laureate Professor 'Wole Soyinka.

In the end after two hundred and seventy applications, visits as far as Liverpool and eighteen months of uncertainty I received the offer of three jobs, Administrative Officer at the Home Office, Prison Officer and Executive Officer at the Inland Revenue. The Prison Officer job was a very well paid position and the security checks took over 12 months to complete, but with an eye on the Nigerian scene I could not see any transferability of skills. After much careful consideration, I settled for the Inland Revenue job in Thames Ditton, Surrey, a position that would later take me to

Nottingham in the Midlands. It was at the Revenue I was reunited with Sheyi Oriade for a period and met 'Banjo Aromolaran an Ijesha Prince and Brother 'Tunde Jayeibo a minister of the gospel.

'SOME THOUGHTS'

After my father's death, impaled by grief and immobilised by circumstances the odds were stacked against me. My progress, my development and my chances of a break-through in life were greatly diminished. I faced a Harmattan period, with heavy fog filling the sky above and the Saharan dust choking out any hint of hope. But in my darkest hours, something kept the flame of hope burning and I refused to give up. My own history challenges me that walls can be torn down but the task is never easy. True progress requires constant work and sustained sacrifice. I project my story on to Nigeria's, its problems, its frustrations and its tragedy with an unstinting belief that it can overcome. In the last twenty-three years, I have lived abroad, but not too far from the scene of Nigeria's devastating stagnation and pervading cynicism. My relatives and friends have ensured that I have maintained a watching brief through my regular visits.

To Nigeria, I sound a clarion call, to those who are dissatisfied with the current status quo I conclude with a series of posers. If there is anybody out there who still disbelieves that my life is an example of someone who demonstrates the art of the impossible becoming possible; who still wonders about the legacies that my ancestors left me; who still questions whether a small diminutive boy with little academic potential can rise to great heights; then this book is your answer. Is there is anyone that doubts the potential of the question called 'Nigeria', this book is my response. If there is anyone who asserts that our country will only end in sorrow and tears and blood, this book challenges that assertion.

In 2010, I lost my beloved twin Folashade Feyisara and I was convulsed and imprisoned by grief, it was even more traumatic than the loss of my father and it took me so long to recover from it. My life was in shambles and it took prayers and counselling to arrest my slow descent into depression and to set me free from its shackles. My work and ministry were affected and it appeared there was no way forward, as I stumbled around blindly in the wall of darkness. Today I still continue to feel the effects of her absence, the power of the present silence of her voice, one so complete and assuredly speaking to us from the past. My country Nigeria which has faced so many traumas, so many false dawns and is in a slow decent into anarchy can draw a leaf from my present circumstance as a source of improbable hope in dire situations.

I realise that I would not be writing this book without the unflinching support of my earthly rock and the love of my life, Olajumoke and that of my family. However, above all the ownership of this book really belongs to the long suffering Nigerian people, those who are subjected to the daily scandal of mis-governance, to those who deserve better healthcare, to the child who has a right to decent education and also the family who simply want to live in security.

This book and its words continues to grow from the strength of my friends, Kolawole Onifade, Hillary Okoronkwo, Ismaila Zakari, Victor Amokeodo, Muhtar Bakare, Anyante Ephraim, Oba 'Dokun Thompson, 'Femi Suleiman, Olumide Adisa, 'Sheyi Oriade, The Revd. Gideon Para-Mallam, 'Folayan Osekita and 'Dayo Oleolo. These are people who reject the myth of their generation's apathy; they have challenged me to take on the orthodoxy of current thinking and to ask the hard questions. You have challenged me because you understand the gravity of our task, which lies ahead and the futility of doing nothing. I hope I have been able to resist being imprisoned in a polemic that obscures the import of my story telling.

The pathway ahead remains hard, our ascent steep, and we may not get there with one book, but I am filled with more hope now than ever before that we will get there and we will reclaim our voice. I do not in a thousand years suggest that a book conceived in the depths of my anguish should end in the hype of a book launch. I am certain that this book is not the change others and I seek; but it creates a space for us to make that change. This is our chance to reclaim our voice to answer the call for this is our moment and this is our time. By default, we have had bad governments in Nigeria because we have allowed the past and present rulers to operate on the unending margins of despair and apathy. They acquired power not because they had a genius about them but because we were asleep in deep slumber and the coalition of progressives was fractured.

In the past, I have made reference to the template of President Obama, the improbability of a black man becoming the President of the United States. I have written about the near impossibility that was overcome when the first man was sent to the moon. The obstacle that Apartheid presented and the dismantling of it without a bloodbath, the impregnability of the Berlin Wall which came tumbling down! I therefore lay down a challenge to the cynics who claim that Nigeria is an impossible case and that without our abject surrender to corruption and its accompanying violence we simply do not have a chance at mounting a challenge to the status quo.

I ask what do we have to lose by trying? I suggest we lose more in not trying at all. I go further to state today that by helping the people find their voice across the diaspora in Nigeria from Sokoto to Lagos, Kwara to Taraba, Borno to Imo, Cross River to Kano, we will be able to proclaim with all certainty and voices soaring above the skies of Nigeria that our time has come!

My dream is of a Nigeria governed by policies based upon welfarism, premised on programmes, decisions and/or rules evaluated on the basis of their consequences on the governed. Welfarism based on the view that the actions of the rulers have significant consequences that impact on the human beings they serve. Welfarism, which, produces ideas that stem from having a human face. Our Welfarism must personify every structure of government. These structures must be treated with dignity and care because failure on any part will have dire consequences on others and have fatal effect on the governed.

I visualise a quality of leadership whose style is outstanding. Leadership that influences others through inspiration, generated by a passion and ignited by a genuine and sincere purpose. Not a leader who lords it over the governed and is only after personal aggrandizement and avarice. The vision is of a new crop of leadership, which demonstrates the passion and willingness to serve and serve responsibly.

I suggest that the principle of good governance is acknowledged as essential for the success of any Nation. Leaders at the helm of our affairs should play a vital role in serving their causes and communities through committed passion as well as skills and experience to the instruments of governance and the governed. The principle of good governance enhances the provision of long-term vision and protects the reputation and values of a Nation. To make a difference our politicians need to have proper procedures and policies in place. The principle of good governance will ensure the delivery of welfarist promises made through a team that is accountable, sincere and astute.

For me my search has come to an end, 'I have found my voice'. My fervent hope is that you discover what you seek as you tread your own path, read my story and as you follow the end of the journey presented in this book.

'OH ENGLAND!'

In the 14th century Richard Whittington, a wealthy merchant and later the Lord Mayor of London had captured the imagination which prevails up today amongst outsiders of a London with streets in paving of gold. This proved to be ironic since Dick Whittington found when he went to London that the streets were in fact grimy and poverty stricken. The second irony was that with persistence, belief, and luck, Whittington was able to become successful. The phrase also appears in The Universal Songster (1826) — "The tykes no more can now be told / That London streets are paved with gold; / For, wishing their tales e'en to trespan, / He knocks gold from the stones does the highway."

My earlier acquainting with the enigmatic Akin Odulate, the endearing 'Dele Olawoye, and the beautiful Abiola Akinsete had led to my fantasies about England. A constant feature of my adolescence was a profound longing and panting to return to London, the land of my birth. The regular summer holidays of my friends, spent on the shores of England painted a very evocative and desirable picture and of course I was drawn into the illusions that it was a land laden in abundance with nestled in unending flows of wealth. A few discerning acquaintances tried to dampen my expectations, but I was not having it. My twin, Folashade to my dismay did not share or hearken back to a London with paving of gold but was focused on settling into marital bliss and developing a legal career as a main preoccupation.

There is, however, a speculation in around the 1580s, the fools gold brought back from the New World was salvaged for use in road metalling – which is basically road aggregate used to provide a solid road surface. At the time, there were few roads in London of any significant quality, so the use of the "fools gold" in the roads would have been fairly notable in London society, especially considering how many people had lost money on his adventures.

By the time I landed in London in my oversized coat, ill-fitting trousers and breathable and worn black baileys, I was to discover that the wooden blocks that were the features of the 18th century had been gradually replaced with asphalt and tar and there was certainly no gold in sight. I was to learn that it is only in Turkmenistan, the secretive Asian dictatorship that is stricter than North Korea may you find streets with gold pavements.

My new reality settling into London in the 90's also met another shuddering shock, arriving in the middle of a recession I had thought through qualifications, charisma and power of my oratory I would waltz into the choice jobs in England, I had imagined that the world was my oyster, however, I was met with rejection upon rejection, futile applications and months on the dole! I was holed up in Mitcham, Surrey in a box sized room in a shared accommodation with the largely unemployable, existing on a predictable routine of hope, dashed and then renewed hope. My cousin 'Ranti Lawunmi tried to rouse me, my fiancé in Nigeria, Olajumoke tried to pep me up with regular letters and my twin tried to connect me with opportunities but to no avail. Few solaces were on offer at the Bonville Christian Centre, Clapham, its Sunday services and the Job Club it ran. I also was able to link up with my blossom friend 'Dele Olawoye, his cousin 'Dumbu', an Oyewunmi and 'Deji Adeogun-Phillps (a former prosecutor at the International Criminal Court) in North London. The weekends I spent there were laced with light merries, jollies, fun and games and an escape from my immediate troubles.

On some level I met a London, bustling, vibrant, multicultural, and cosmopolitan. A London littered with gigantic, lush parks, financial districts, and cosmopolitan vibes, it could be called a traditional, evolving, and vibrant city. In my forays into the City, I was held in awe of the city's elegance for it was much more refined than anywhere I had ever been.

'MY JOB INTERVIEW'

A blend of the frenetic, frantic, frozen and frazzle is the feeling I felt as I approached the Solicitor's office, I had been informed about the opening, a vacancy for a clerical position in the big time London City firm at the Job Club I attended. It suited me perfectly, allowing me time to figure out what I wanted to do. The information about the vacancy came through a connection, an inside link. I had assumed that all I had to do was slither through the office of the firm, present myself and I would be shooed into the job. I adorned myself with a cotton white lawyer's shirt with a vintage cufflink inherited from my father to hold the sleeves together, slightly oversized grey cotton, classic single buttoned suit, the pair of trousers had been adjusted to hold it up at my waist, it was a hand it down from my Uncle Ayobami Akinsonmi and I topped it off with a King's College, Lagos tie to provide the contrast.

At the interview held in a top floor boardroom with a layout consisting of one large table that everyone sat around, the table was made of oak and its surface had the face of ancients about it, and the lines on it were his well-earned wrinkles, as if it was recording accounts of so much that occurred in the last century. It was a setting that captured the history behind the firm and the walls were with portraits of its founders carefully placed so as to peer down into the room and offer a reminder of 'untarnished' past. I was now sat gingerly on the seat offered me betraying nervousness from my surroundings, nothing could dampen it down. The closest I had experienced to this in Nigeria was the oak paneled chambers of Alhaji 'Femi Okunnu, SAN, but it was pale in its imitation.

All the faces were white, smartly dressed men, decking business suits which were loose-fitting sack suit that was used by conservative businessmen, the fabric sturdier and of more quality, their ties were silk and hung like a lash around their neck and draping down their chest. I was offered the opportunity to sell myself and I simply froze, all I could hear myself saying was 'mortgages', droning on and on with no adequate context and nothing to evince their interest. It was a short and uninspired interview, but I had prayed hard for divine favour and was confident his grace will suffice at this time.

I wonder why I was immobilized at the time? I ponder on whether it was the weight of expectations, the improbability of my own story or simply sheer over lack of confidence that had come from quite a few rejections?

I still felt I might swing it or even wing it, soaring, but I did not get the job, and the feedback through the inside channel was I was rather stilted and unimpressive. It was a huge disappointment; I had thought connections to the Holy Spirit might swing it and failing that his emissary might be the backup. For now there was to be no job situated within a suite of swanky offices, it was back to the drawing board to renew my hope and start again.

'MY EDUCATIONAL ODYSSEY!'

My deep impression of my father, Olasupo Aremu Ojedokun was that he had the title 'Doctor' about his name. Any time I referred to him as a 'doctor' it caused a barrage of confusion around my fellow cousins because they always wondered how come he had the title when he had no clue of medicine. I was fascinated and even after his death I dreamt of attaining a doctorate and felt the singular achievement would draw me closer to the identity of his identity. My twin Folashade was always befuddled and wondered what all the fuss of doctorate was all about, my brother Adebowale being the more practical one simply was never interested. I had observed how my father in the short space of his existence had transformed from a shoeless and rustic village boy to an urbane, sophisticated, polished, cultured, refined *man*.

I had imagined that the acquiring of a Ph.D. was the sole reason, so I placed it on my bucket list at the age of 7. At age 10, I attempted and failed spectacularly to devour the contents of his London School of Economics PhD thesis titled '*The Anglo-Nigerian entente and its demise, 1960–1962*'. All my notebooks and every available scrap of paper was filled with sketches of me and with a range of degrees after my name. I made sure that etched on my desks at secondary school were craving of such drawings with my imaginary degree following in tow.

However, I faced several obstacles in pursuing this goal, for my initial odyssey in secondary school was far from satisfactory. My entrance into King's College, Lagos masked an unfortunate flaw, that I was a late starter whose progress had been stymied by long and unremitting grief at the loss of his father. I kept on toppling at many hurdles presented to me. My second and third secondary school years were marked with failures in most subjects, even my penchant for the subject of History and Fine Art were I always scored 'A' did not rescue me for I had to repeat these classes. Even my nascent Christian faith did not appear to help me, prayers did not hack it, I lost all confidence, was drenched in hopelessness and thought my dream might never be realised. Whilst my twin and classmates were proceeding ahead with a flourish, I laid there immobile, under a canopy of trauma and at loss at to what to do. My mother, visibly worried never gave up. It said that with time I mellowed and began to flourish and left King's College, Lagos with very decent grades. I thought I had stemmed the tide of failure and I was on the march. I could now trod along the path of success as I gained admission into University of Ife.

At Great Ife my engagement with 'Panafism', my fitful romance with the struggle, my desire for the emancipation of our lot and my penchant for the struggle soon got entangled with my academics, my earlier promise of excellence became subsumed. I made painstakingly slow progress as I hardly had the opportunity to attend lectures. The Students' Union Buildings of the campuses of the South western Universities became my regular haunt. I preferred Aluta to most meaningful engagements in class and at the end of my studies my Bachelor of laws degree was below par. In all this my ambition to match my father's achievement remained undimmed.

I had come to the realization that the sturdy inflexibility of the Nigerian University system would put paid to my ambitions, but I was simply propelled by my father's memory and was not prepared to sentence my lot to unfulfilled desires. I discovered that it was not a prerequisite for a doctoral student to have obtained a Masters in United Kingdom and the USA, yet to this moment, every Nigeria University under central dicta that insists a Masters is a sine quo non to moving forward. I stumbled across the fact that a few years of work experience allowed you to use a lesser degree to enroll for a Masters without much qualms, whereas in Nigeria, latterly there was no pathway forward except you re-did your degree or attain a PGDE. I was amazed that medical doctors in the UK could attain an LL.M without an LL.B, yet Nigeria through its regulatory bodies insist in imposing this barrier. I wonder whether all these practices and stipulations has made us more accomplished or any better than the West? This convinced me that my immediate future lay not in Nigeria but back in the land in which I was sired and nurtured.

Whilst exploring my option for further studies I travelled with my adopted 'aburo' Morounke Jacobs (Somorin) to meet my father's erstwhile supervisor Professor James Mayall at the London School of Economics and Political Science. We ventured into his workspace, which appeared cluttered with the detritus of scholarship. There were books piled everywhere, and manila folders on the top of a long mission long mission oak table under the windows. It was a useful time of dredging up memories of my father and of his friend the mercurial Professor Olajide Aluko, the father of my classmate 'Bola. It was also a pivotal moment is resolving the question before me whether to explore further studies in law or make a detour into the study International Relations, where my father made his mark and held centre stage for a period so fleeting. After much ponder, I decided that further studies in International Relations will do and equip me for the future. This led to the acquisition of my first masters but that was not the end but simply the beginning of a journey through academia.

REFERENCES

1. Soyinka, Wole (1994) *'Ibadan; The Penkelemes Years; A Memoir 1946 – 65'*; Methuen Publishing Limited, London

2. Soyinka, Wole (2009) *Conversations with History.* Available at: http://saharareporters.com/art-life/conversations-history-wole-soyinka-uc-berkeley

3. Gulger, Josef and Flanagan, William G (1978)., *"Urbanisation and Social Change in West Africa."* Cambridge University Press: Cambridge

4. Du Boulay, Shirley (1988) *Tutu, Voice of the Voiceless.* London: Hodder & Stoughton

5. Ramachandra, Vinoth; *"What is Integral Mission"?* Available at: http://www.micahnetwork.org/library/integral-mission/what-integral-mission-vinoth-ramachandra

6. United States Institute of Peace, Sources: Post Express 07/25/1999 and 06/16/1999. http//www.postexpresswired.com/; The Electronic Telegraph, 08/22/1999. http://www.telegraph.co.uk 80/; Washington Post 06/08/1999

7. Mordi, Carles N O et al (2011) *The Changing Structure of the Nigerian Economy*, Central Bank of Nigeria

8. Asmal, Kadar (1995) Hansard 1995: 1382 -3 Act No.34 of 1995: Promotion of National Unity and Reconciliation Act 1995

9. De Lange, ADV Speech during the President's tabling of recommendations relating to the TRC 15 April 2003. http://www.anc.org.za/ancdocs/speeches/2003/sp0515b.html [Accessed on 13th April 2005]

10. Sachs, Albie (2003) Interview with Olu Ojedokun held on 9th March 2003 at King's College, London

11. Boraine, Alex (1996) *"Justice in Cataclysm: Criminal Tribunals in the wake of mass violence: alternatives and adjuncts to criminal prosecutions"*, http://www.truth.org.za/reading/speech01.htm [Accessed 23rd October 2005]

12. Ogunlesi, Tolu (2010) *The Babangida Years,* 17th April 2010. Accessed on 2nd March 2013 [http://www.nairaland.com/522441/babangida-years-facts-may-want]

13. Odusote, Oluwakayode (2013): *AWOISM and the AWOIST: The Battles over a Political Philosophy.* [Accessed on 3rd March 2013 from http://actionkay.wordpress.com/2013/02/09/awoism-and-the-awoist-the-battles-over-a-political-philosophy/]

14. Asiodu, Philip (2011) *'Main reason Gowon was toppled, by Philip Asiodu'*; Interview of December 31, 2011 by Bashir Adefaka [Accessed on 10th March 2013 from http://www.vanguardngr.com/2011/12/main-reason-gowon-was-toppled-by-philip-asiodu/]

15. Rijani, Harshada (2012) *'I Found My Voice in a Hopeless Place'* [Accessed on 22nd March 2013 from http://www.huffingtonpost.com/harshada-rajani/i-found-my-voice-in-a-hop_b_2264756.html

NOTES

Printed in Great Britain
by Amazon

35745922R00128